READING SEATTLE

READING SEATTLE

The City in Prose

Edited by

Peter Donahue and John Trombold

UNIVERSITY OF WASHINGTON PRESS

Seattle and London

For Susan

For Brent

University of Washington Press
P.O. Box 50096, Seattle, WA 98145
www.washington.edu/uwpress

Library of Congress Cataloging-in-Publication Data
Reading Seattle : a prose anthology / edited by Peter Donahue
and John Trombold.—1st ed.
p. cm.
Includes bibliographical references and index.
ISBN 0-295-98395-7 (pbk. : alk. paper)
1. Seattle (Wash.)—Literary collections.
2. American prose literature—Washington (State)—Seattle.
3. Seattle (Wash.)—Fiction.
4. Seattle (Wash.)
I. Donahue, Peter.   II. Trombold, John.
PS572.S4R43   2004   818'.508032797772—DC22   2003026883

Contents

Contents

Contents

Contents

Contents

Foreword

CHARLES JOHNSON

IT HAS BEEN MY GREAT PLEASURE and privilege to live in Seattle, this "city of neighborhoods," as it has been called, and beneath that looming epiphany of timelessness called Mount Rainier, for twenty-seven years. In other words, for half my life now. Occasionally this city's contemporary *genius loci* or "spirit of place" (to borrow a phrase from D. H. Lawrence) has found its way into my short fiction since the 1980s— tales like "China," "Menagerie," and "Sweet Dreams"—but, like so many Seattle authors who came here from elsewhere, I have set my novels in the regions that had the first, primal influence on shaping my sense of the world: namely, the Midwest of my childhood, places like Chicago, or the little farm towns, champaigns, and hot cornfields of southern Illinois where I first went to college (or an imagined South Carolina delivered to me in family chronicles). So even after nearly thirty years, and despite the fact that this polysemous city, poised at the edge of the nation's western end, renews my spirit like none other, I'm still obliged to work, as a transplant, at deepening my "reading" of Seattle, not only as a physical location but, even more important, as a landscape rich for the literary imagination.

No prose anthology, in my view, could be more helpful—to immigrants or lifelong residents—in delivering Seattle's relatively recent but startlingly rich history and diverse literary voices than the volume you presently hold in your hands. Its editors, Peter Donahue and John Trombold, have assembled forty-two well-chosen selections that sweep us across more than half a century of Seattle literature, alternating nicely between essays and excerpts from fiction that assay this city's nature. That alone, for readers, is worth the price of admission. Yet *Reading Seattle* offers something more.

Here, we find often cited, de rigueur essays by white interpreters of the city such as Mary McCarthy, Roger Sale, Murray Morgan, Emmett Watson, and Richard Hugo, but we discover as well those frequently marginalized, often elided racial "others" who sang the experience of living in this city from perspectives black, Native American, and Asian. Hearing *these* voices, a reader comes to simultaneously understand what is unique about Seattle, and he sees just how thoroughly American it has been toward people of color, beginning with the "red children whose teeming multitudes once filled this vast continent as stars fill the firmament," according to Archie Binns's account of Chief Seattle (Sealth) in *Northwest Gateway: The Story of the Port of Seattle.* Equally revealing are excerpts from John Okada's powerful classic *No-No Boy* and Horace R. Cayton's *Long Old Road,* which freezes the transitional, fluid moment in the city's history when, as Cayton's father says, it changed from being a race-neutral territory boasting that "a man was as good as his word" to a place where "the South has overtaken us, and freedom is only in name— not a fact.... Your mother and I ... neither of us ever dreamed the insanity of the South could catch up with us out here." Sadly, and soberingly, it was not until the 1950s, as Neil Henry reports in "Pearl's Secret: A Black Man's Search for His White Family," that the Emerald City achieved the civility, latitudinarianism, and "laid back" *geist* for which it is known today.

Reading Seattle, like a cornucopia, overflows with insights into the city, large and small, quotidian and grand, and the best of these are observations that only Seattle's most talented literary artists could achieve—for example, Mary Brinker Post's lovely description of the Old Curiosity Shop on Colman Dock, where showcases contained Alaskan Indian masks carved from driftwood and "the Lord's Prayer etched on the head of a pin" (How does one *do* that?); or Jonathan Raban's first impression of the city, which to him "looked like a free-hand sketch, from memory, of a sawmill-owner's whirlwind vacation in Rome and Florence."

Lovers of both Seattle and literature will treasure this book for years to come, finding in its pages the feelings some of us have difficulty putting into words. For that, we are indebted to the literary artists represented here, those like Raban, an immigrant from England, who, I discovered, captures perfectly my own sense of Seattle, twenty-seven years ago and today, when he writes:

> It was something in the disposition of the landscape, the shifting lights and colours of the city. *Something.* It was hard to nail it, but this something was a mysterious gift that Seattle made to every immigrant who cared to see it. Wherever you came from, Seattle was queerly like home. . . . It was an extraordinarily soft and pliant city. If you went to New York, or to Los Angeles, or even to Guntersville [Alabama], you had to fit yourself to a place whose demands were hard and explicit. You had to learn the school rules. Yet people who came to Seattle could somehow recast it in the image of home, arranging the city around themselves like so many pillows on a bed. One day you'd wake up to find things so snug and familiar that you could easily believe that you'd been born here.

For those unable to live in or visit this ever-surprising city, *Reading Seattle* may just be the next best thing.

Acknowledgments

WE WISH TO THANK THE FOLLOWING people and institutions for their role in making *Reading Seattle* a reality.

We owe a special debt of gratitude to all the writers and their family members, friends, and representatives who generously granted us permission to include their work.

Thanks also to the Seattle Public Library and the Pacific Northwest Collection at the University of Washington for the access they provided to their materials.

Thanks to Mary Braun at Oregon State University Press for her early belief in the project, and to Roger Sale for his author recommendations and guiding comments on early versions of the manuscript.

Thanks to Val Clark for her wise and generous consultations on publishing and to Marcus Gilmer for his work in tracking down author bios and Wilson Web hits for "Seattle."

Thanks to Ruthie Newman for her residential (and moorage) support.

Thanks especially to Michael Duckworth and all the good people at the University of Washington Press who saw the promise of this anthology.

I wish to thank Birmingham-Southern College (BSC) for providing me with invaluable support through summer stipends and year-round staff assistance. The Interlibrary Loan folks at the BSC library brought Seattle to me when I could not get to Seattle. Thanks to Betty Marschall and Brendan Gallagher for discovering Seattle with me way back when. And thank you, of course, to Susan, my dear wife and steady reader, for her unwavering support over the long course of this project.

—P.D.

As an itinerant scholar at Seattle University, Seattle Central Community College, Pacific Lutheran University, the University of California at Santa Barbara, the Lakeside School, and Eastern Oregon University, I have enjoyed a variety of unusual housing arrangements, thanks to the generosity of relatives and friends. I would like to thank Kevin Trombold and Heath Foster, Robert and Sandy Shulman, Ren Dietel and Michael Stout, Mark and Sallie Aldape, Phil and Lisa Ruder, Bob Van Dyk and Nancy Kristoff, Mark Bradley and Amy Bosch, and especially Ruthie Newman for their accommodating natures. Finally, I owe special thanks to Brent Davies for her support and patience.

—J.T.

READING SEATTLE

Introduction

PETER DONAHUE

Seattle lies at the crossroads of the ruling events of my life. I have arrived, left, and returned countless times over the decades. The bearing of my life always draws me back . . . because Seattle has always been where I feel most at home, where I belong.

From my first arrival in 1976 to deliver a drive-away car from New Jersey, where I grew up, I was smitten by the city. I spent my first night in the front seat of the behemoth green Bonneville, underneath the Alaskan Way Viaduct, sipping clam broth and watching ferries dock and depart in the rain. The next morning the sun was out, and when I delivered the car to a family of Hasidic Jews living in a small house in Northgate, they invited me in for blueberry muffins. Later that morning, I found the nearest I-5 on-ramp and began the eight-hundred-mile hitchhike down to San Francisco to rendezvous with my father.

Two years later—with images of snow-capped mountains tracing the horizon, beryl waters lapping barnacled pylons, terra-cotta cornices and carved walrus heads dripping rain, moss-softened sidewalks lining the streets, slicker-clad pedestrians hurrying onto yellow-and-brown buses, and schooner glasses of beer lining the wood bars of spare yet homey taverns—I returned to Seattle. Arriving this time via Amtrak at the King Street Station, I promptly rented a studio apartment in an old brick apartment building in the downtown neighborhood of Denny Regrade—and began calling Seattle home. Eventually I would live in a number of such places, buildings with names like the Windham, Rivoli, Cornelius, and Charlesgate, which remain standing in the Denny Regrade and many of the city's older neighborhoods.

Over the next decade, I rarely traveled beyond the city limits. Running delivery routes for the warehouse where I worked, using (and reusing) my Metro transfers, and riding the old Schwinn bike I bought for $30 from a guy down the hall, I came to know Seattle's streets and alleys as well as a person can. I also found a second home on the campus of the University of Washington, to which I'd been admitted after taking courses at Seattle Central Community College on Capitol Hill. In the Graduate Reading Room of Suzzallo Library and the noisy cafeteria of the HUB, among the azaleas and rhododendrons, cherry and linden trees of the parklike grounds, I studied toward my bachelor's degree. Taking courses with William Irmsher, Nelson Bentley, and Lois Hudson, I eventually earned a B.A. in English. Yet, not long after this, believing a person could become a writer only in New York, I went back East and quickly became miserable. Ten months later, my senses restored, I drove an Astro minivan drive-away over Snoqualmie Pass, down I-90, and back into Seattle.

For better or worse, this arrive-leave-return motif marks my love affair with Seattle. We don't always get to choose where we find work and settle. We fall in love—in my case, luckily, with a Seattle girl—and discover that others have wills of their own and that there can be attachments greater than geography. Nonetheless, we all need a place to call home—a place to which all roads lead, a personal Samarkind—and Seattle is mine.

For this reason, when I could not live in Seattle—ride my bike through Pioneer Square on my way to a Mariners game, fish off the public pier at Myrtle Edwards Park, stroll down Broadway to see a movie at the Egyptian Theater, take the #11 bus to Madison Park for a swim in Lake Washington, or just stare out my apartment window as a whitish gray mist enveloped the city—I would read about Seattle. Except for the handful of classic Seattle works by Murray Morgan, John Okada, Roger Sale, and Tom Robbins, there was not much Seattle literature to be found, at least not in print, until the 1990s. Any short story or novel passage set in Seattle, even from such unlikely sources as Mississippi writer Barry Hannah, whose story "Power and Light" depicts a woman line worker employed by Seattle's power company, thrilled me. I read every work of Seattle fiction and nonfiction that I could lay my hands on, no matter how passing the reference to the city, and even wrote some of my own. (All works referred to in the introduction that pertain to Seattle but are not included in the anthology are cited in the bibliography.)

Then in the late 1990s, after accepting a teaching job at a state university in Texas, I met John Trombold, my future co-editor and a Seattle exile reared there—well, Mercer Island—who was teaching at the same university. Our offices were next to one another, and when John knocked on my door to welcome me, I had just logged onto the University of Washington's web site to glimpse, via the live Red Square cam, the current Seattle weather (and perhaps Mount Rainier), and thereby escape the Texas swelter temporarily. John and I bonded instantly. Recounting Seattle scenes to one another, we entered a kind of Seattle satori that afternoon, and before long colleagues were calling our corner of the building "Little Seattle." It was during this period that the notion of a Seattle anthology came to us as a way to honor and celebrate the city we both loved and called home, though neither of us lived there. It would be a way for others to experience Seattle—to read Seattle—just as we had through the ever-expanding body of Seattle literature.

For John and me, Seattle is so obviously the greatest city in the world. Its relationship to its natural setting, its conscientious and unassuming inhabitants, its fascinating and often radical history, its cultural diversity and vitality, its welcoming neighborhoods, its moist and temperate climate . . . all these elements combine to make Seattle a city without equal. Given this, we wondered if there was or could be such a thing as "a Seattle literature." In our minds, a Seattle literature would be distinguished not only by a descriptive preoccupation with the cityscape but also by a sensibility that reflected the more intangible elements that make the city so great. Eventually, with these criteria, we gathered the fiction and nonfiction about Seattle that we read with such intent and chose the selections for this book.

The fiction and nonfiction in *Reading Seattle* tend to be geographically savvy, smart and subtle, historically informed, diverse in both style and content, and highly readable. Seattle prose literature is also distinguished by its exceptional literary standards. This host of qualities in the works selected for *Reading Seattle* allows us to proclaim that there is a bona fide Seattle literature. In recognizing the breadth and depth of this literature, the anthology offers classics of Seattle writing by beloved, well-known writers (Murray Morgan, Emmett Watson, Tom Robbins, J. A. Jance) as well as fiction and nonfiction by exciting young writers (Paisley Rekdal, Michael Byers, Lydia Minatoya, Mark Lindquist). The anthology includes writers who have garnered national and international reputations (Sherman Alexie, David Guterson, Jonathan Raban) and writers who are well known locally (Barbara Wilson [Barbara Wilson Sjoholm], Peter Bacho, Rebecca Brown). The anthology also reintroduces works by important Seattle writers who may have been overlooked in recent years (Archie Binns, Josephine Herbst, Horace R. Cayton, John Okada).

The fiction here is distinguished by attention to language, concern for character, and a regard for place as integral to narrative. A remarkable richness in the fiction quickly becomes apparent: Tom Robbins's verbal pyrotechnics and metaphoric riffs, Sherman Alexie's dark humor and fabulism, Lynda Barry's cartoon-inspired narrative, Michael Byers's exquisite literary realism, Matt Briggs's Carveresque characterizations, and so on. While certain images and motifs recur throughout Seattle fiction—gray skies and rain, most obviously—the central quality that each novel and short story excerpt in this anthology shares is an understanding of the important role that the city plays within narrative. More than mere backdrop, the city infuses each narrative, helping to shape character and determine situation. As the Mississippi writer Eudora Welty recognized in her essay "Place in Fiction," "Location is the crossroads of circumstance." Place, she added, "has the most delicate control over character, too: by confining character, it defines it."

In the Seattle fiction collected here, the writers allow Seattle to control their characters so that the particulars of the city itself function as a kind of character in their narratives. We begin to see how, as Hana Wirth-Nesher explains in her book *City Codes*, "symbolic worlds shape the perception of physical form itself." Thus, the reader of Seattle fiction becomes, in effect, a reader of the city. A symbolic exchange occurs between writer and reader, imagined city, and physical city. One of the main objectives of *Reading Seattle* is for readers, whether they were born and raised in

Seattle or have never visited, to know and understand Seattle far better than they had before. These literary representations of the city will amplify, augment, and add to each reader's ever-evolving experience of Seattle. Wirth-Nesher summarizes the process in a comment that serves well as the creed for *Reading Seattle:* "The metropolis is rendered legible, then, by multiple acts of imagination; it is constantly invented and reinvented."

The burgeoning of Seattle fiction in recent years may not have been possible, however, without nonfiction writers first authenticating the city as an historical and physical entity. Before a place as complicated as a city can figure epistemologically in narrative fiction (as Eudora Welty seems to say it should), the city must be given a history, be remembered by those who lived there, and be reported on to the rest of the world. In this regard, the nonfiction writers here can be classified into three groups: historians (Archie Binns, Murray Morgan, Roger Sale), memoirists (Monica Sone, Horace R. Cayton, Richard Hugo, Colette Brooks, Walt Crowley, Paisley Rekdal, Natalia Rachel Singer) and journalists (Nancy Wilson Ross, Emmett Watson, Jonathan Raban, Timothy Egan, Emily Baillargeon Russin).

None of these classifications, however, neatly contains any one of the nonfiction writers included here. They're each too good for that. While recounting Seattle's history, Binns, Morgan, and Sale each offer a vision of the city that is uniquely his own. In profiling present-day Seattle, Raban and Russin each reflect upon their personal relationship with the city: Raban as an emigrant to Seattle from England, Russin as a city native returning after an extended sojourn on the East Coast. Meanwhile, among the memoirists, Brooks, Rekdal, and Singer each write about coming of age in Seattle with both the narrative dexterity of fiction writers and the keen sensibilities of poets. And with respect to Seattle poets, there's Richard Hugo, one of Seattle's most accomplished writers, writing about the subtle relationship between memory, place, and poetry in his prose memoir about growing up in White Center.

The writers in *Reading Seattle* cover a wide variety of areas within the city. Indeed, as this anthology attests, Seattle is a city of distinctive neighborhoods and districts. Mary Brinker Post returns us to Seattle's turn-of-the-century waterfront. Betty MacDonald offers lunch in the Pike Place

Market. J. A. Jance drives us over to Fishermen's Terminal. Tom Robbins walks with us down First Avenue (circa the 1970s) into Pioneer Square. Mark Lindquist takes a tour of the Belltown club scene. Barbara Wilson explores the seedy side of the Sea-Tac strip. In all, the writers here range far and wide through Seattle's various neighborhoods and districts: from Capitol Hill, Queen Anne Hill, and Magnolia, to the University District, Central District, and International District; from Green Lake, Eastlake, Montlake, and Lake City, to Ballard, Ravenna, West Seattle, and White Center. And for an excursion to one of city's oldest suburbs, formerly known as East Seattle, John Trombold takes the floating bridge to Mercer Island in the epilogue.

Of course, what makes the city's neighborhoods so special are the people of Seattle. The writers in *Reading Seattle* understand this simple fact well. This becomes apparent in the nonfiction through Archie Binns's version of Chief Sealth, Emmett Watson's remembrance of Rudi Becker ("the quintessential Seattleite"), Jonathan Raban's sketch of the manager of the Josephinum, Charlotte Watson Sherman's depiction of Oya camped on her corner, and Neil Henry's loving account of his mother and father arriving in Seattle. Meanwhile, the fiction writers' appreciation for the eccentric, conscientious, courteous, tolerant, drunken, bizarre, diverse, intelligent, hardworking people of Seattle is evident in the many memorable characters that populate the fiction here.

Such an open recognition of the importance of place and people by the writers in *Reading Seattle* is what, in great part, qualifies their work as Seattle literature. Given the city's long-standing (though now fading) tendency toward self-effacement, this recognition of Seattle's distinctive qualities by its writers is notable. In the past, people living in Seattle tended not to think of themselves as inhabitants of a city, as urban dwellers, making it difficult to conceive of a Seattle literature. Indeed, mid-twentieth-century Seattle residents seemed to prefer to think of themselves as town folk within the greater domain of the Pacific Northwest. Partly because of this self-defining notion, residents and nonresidents alike for most of the past century have viewed Seattle as a remote and inaccessible, albeit pretty, cityburg. Seattle was, as Seattle chronicler Clark Humphrey has noted, "a forgotten corner of the world, stuck out on the west-coast-that-wasn't-California, the region that didn't count for anything." Seattleites both guarded and bemoaned this persistent sense of their hometown's provincialism, even as city boosters vigorously pitched the city to the rest of the nation and the world, from public relations man Erastus Brainerd promoting Seattle as the jumping-off point for the Yukon-Alaska gold rush in the 1890s to businessman Edward Carlson helping to secure the Century 21 World's Fair for the city in 1962.

Yet more than most American cities, and perhaps befitting its introspection-inducing weather, Seattle has never been comfortable with any single rendition of itself. New York boasts of being the Big Apple, New Orleans the Big Easy, Chicago the Windy City, and Los Angeles the City of Angels. Seattle, though, has proudly and quietly resisted such all-engrossing characterizations. Boasts of the famed "Seattle Spirit" at the end of the nineteenth century and fanfare adoption of the nickname "The Emerald City" at the end of the twentieth have been tolerated by Seattleites who generally recognize the catchphrases for what they were: well-intended but simplistic promotional slogans. On the whole, Seattle prefers not to subscribe to such clamorous designations of itself.

Where the slogans fall short in rendering a version of the city acceptable to multifarious Seattleites, popular culture occasionally attempts to fill the void. These versions of the city have tended to be superficial depictions based on some event or trend associated with Seattle being bandied about by the popular media to the rest of the nation—such as the city's pioneer history, its World's Fair, its "grunge" music scene, or its latte craze. Seattle has been represented as a muddy, buck-skinned frontier town in the TV series *Here Come the Brides* (based on Asa Mercer's recruiting of East Coast women to the logging town in the 1860s), a swinging playground for Elvis Presley in the movie *It Happened at the World's Fair*, a mildly edgy yet upwardly mobile playground in Cameron Crowe's movie *Singles*, an haute bourgeois haven in the TV sitcom *Frasier*, a post-apocalyptic battleground in Fox TV's *Dark Angel*, and a splendid yet humorless home base for the short-lived TV drama *Citizen Baines*. While good and interesting films set in Seattle exist (mostly independents, such as *American Heart*, with Jeff Bridges), the movie and TV representations of the city have typically been trite and forgettable—and rarely filmed in Seattle.

For most of the twentieth century, literary representations of Seattle were too scarce to counter these pop culture depictions. Early in the century, there were some prose descriptions of the city, many of them reminiscences of Seattle's pioneer days, such as pioneer daughter Emily Inez Denny's *Blazing the Way* (1909), a volume of stories, songs, and sketches about pioneer life, and Charles T. Conover's *Mirrors of Seattle: Reflecting on Some Aged Men of Fifty* (1923), a volume of humorous sketches of local characters. During this period, most Seattle writers penned works about regions of the country that they had emigrated from and were familiar with, or they wrote about foreign locales that they deemed far more exotic than Seattle, such as Elizabeth W. Champney's historical romances set in imperial Rome, feudal France, and ancient Japan. Despite literary organizations in Seattle such as the Ladies' Literary and Cultural Improvement Society, literary modernism, as it was manifesting in Paris, New York, and Chicago, had not advanced so far west. As Mary McCarthy says in *How I Grew*, her memoir of growing up in Seattle in the 1910s and 1920s, "Our city, despite its artistic reputation (or perhaps because of it), was remote from the vanguard. . . ."

This does not mean that an effort was not being made in the first half of the twentieth century to advance Seattle's literary standing. As early as 1897, Sarah Ritchie Heath's "The Wager: A Seattle Story," about a young woman's sojourn to Seattle on a wager from a gentleman suitor in San Francisco, appeared in the *Overland Monthly*. Sentimental and lesson-ridden, the late-Victorian-era story primarily gives a tourist's purplish view of the city: "Before the end of the week Marion enthusiastically pronounced Seattle the most charming spot on the globe." Yet by the end of the first decade of the twentieth century, several popularly known authors were residing in Seattle. Most prominent among these was Ada Woodruff Anderson, with her best-selling trilogy of novels, including *The Heart of the Red Firs* (1909), which spanned the history of European settlement in the Northwest. The fact that nationally recognized writers such as Ada Woodruff Anderson could occasionally be spotted on Seattle sidewalks in the early part of the century prompted Charles T. Conover to exclaim in *Mirrors of Seattle,* perhaps too eagerly, how "even in literature we [Seattle] have not been without representatives who have won national recognition. I do not mean the mush that passes currently as literature in the 5- and 10-cent periodicals of phenomenal circulation, the sort that appeals to maudlin sentiment and unintelligence, but the real thing."

One writer who was the "real thing" during the sinophobic early years of the twentieth century was Sui Sin Far (English name: Edith Maude Eaton), a Chinese-English woman from Canada who arrived in Seattle in 1899. A journalist and fiction writer, Sui Sin Far published *Mrs. Spring Fragrance* in 1912 (reissued by Amy Ling and Annette White-Parks in 1995), a collection of stories about Chinese immigrants in America, including in Seattle. In a 1912 newspaper piece, Sui Sin Far described her own venturing to Seattle: "To Seattle I sailed, and the blithe greenness of the shores of Puget Sound seemed to give me the blithest of welcomes." According to Annette White-Parks, her biographer, Seattle offered Sui Sin Far her most steady work during the first decade of the century, culminating in 1909 when she published a series of sketches called "The Chinese in America" in *Western,* a monthly published in Earlington, Washington.

Despite the examples of Ada Woodruff Anderson and Sui Sin Far, however, literary activity in Seattle remained limited for the first two decades of the century. The 1920s and 1930s, though, saw more deliberate efforts to foster a literary culture in Seattle. As Ralph Bushnell Potts says in *Seattle Heritage* (1955), this effort stemmed from "the hope fomented into actual belief that there must be a unique and distinguishable Pacific Northwest literature springing up in the Northwest corner of the nation and that the capital of this activity should be Seattle." The person who worked most diligently to turn this "belief" into actuality was Lancaster Pollard, the book page editor of the Sunday *Post-Intelligencer.* Pollard served as promoter and redactor of Northwest writing. In 1925, Pollard founded the Credo Club in Seattle, a group of artists, writers, and critics that in time counted among its members James Stevens, author of the popular collection of tales *Paul Bunyan* (1925), Nard Jones, author of the Seattle-based mystery *The Case of the Hanging Lady* (1938), and Archie Binns, author of half a dozen novels set in the Northwest, including *The Timber Beast* (1944), about a timber baron and his family in Seattle. From 1932 to 1934,

Pollard published *Fortnightly,* a magazine of opinion, cultural reviews, and an occasional short story and poem, every other Friday from the Arcade Building in downtown Seattle. The magazine gave particular attention to Northwest literature through reviews and checklists of Northwest and Seattle authors. Yet even as Pollard gave exposure to regional and local authors, a perennial concern of the magazine's contributing writers remained "Seattle's provincialism." One columnist lamented "the absence of any integrating influence that should be expected to operate here, as it does elsewhere, to bring together men and women of discrimination and taste." To help bring about such an "integrating influence," Pollard, in 1940, compiled and published *A Check List of Washington Authors,* an annual index that has continued to this day under the auspices of the Washington State Library.

While Lancaster Pollard made Seattle the base for his literary mission, his efforts remained focused broadly on Northwest literature. For most of the twentieth century, in fact, the notion of a Seattle literature has been subsumed by efforts to establish a Northwest literature. This accounts for why the now well-recognized canon of Northwest literature is largely comprised of writings about the rugged and rural reaches of Washington, Oregon, Idaho, and Montana—works such as H. L. Davis's *Honey in the Horn* (1935), Ken Kesey's *Sometimes a Great Notion* (1964), and Norman MacLean's *A River Runs through It* (1976). Because of the region's stunning natural beauty and frontier past, the outdoors focus of its literature is understandable. Unfortunately, this focus has too often excluded writings about the Northwest urban experience. Within the canon of Northwest literature, cities seem anathema to the idealization of the region as a land of mountains, forests, lakes, wildlife, loggers, and fishermen, where nary a high-rise, housing project, freeway, back alley, or apartment dweller is seen.

This focus on the Northwest's natural beauty held true for most of the fiction writers living in Seattle in the 1930s and 1940s. Among the numerous novels produced during this period by Seattle writers such as Nard Jones, Archie Binns, Albert Richard Wetjen, Bertrand Collins, Melvin Levy, Alan Hart, Howard M. Brier, and Vaudis Fisher, only a handful have Seattle settings. In two of Alan Hart's novels, *The Undaunted* (1936) and *In the Lives of Men* (1937), the author recasts Seattle, for reasons unclear, as "Seaforth" and "Fairharbor," respectively. In *The Undaunted*, the doctor protagonist takes a ferry from Battenridge Island to get to his work at Safe Harbor Hospital in Seaforth. In *In the Lives of Men*, the narrator proudly declares that "Fairharbor would eventually be the metropolis of the Puget Sound." Melvin Levy's *The Last Pioneers* (1934), about a Jewish immigrant from a Polish village who settles in Seattle prior to the Great Fire of 1889, is one of the more interesting Seattle novels from the pre–World War II period. The novel calls the city "Puget" and offers a rare depiction of Seattle's Jewish community up through the first two decades of the twentieth century.

One of the earliest and most popular literary representations of a Northwest city comes from Guy Gilpatric's and Norman Reilly Raine's "Tugboat Annie" stories, published serially in the *Saturday Evening Post* in the early 1930s as *The Glencannon Tugboat Annie Affair*. Set in Tacoma (although the 1933 film version with Marie Dressler and Wallace Beery is set in Seattle), the Tugboat Annie stories helped popularize, in their corny Damon Runyonesque way, an image of the Northwest that was distinctly urban to a degree that Alan Hart's and Melvin Levy's novels did not achieve. In the Tugboat Annie stories, the Northwest city is a gritty place of hard-working, hard-drinking men and women. This depiction stems from— and often overlooks—the city's history as a labor town with a strong history of unionization, epitomized by the 1919 General Strike.

One of the few fiction writers from this period to address Seattle's labor history was the journalist and novelist Josephine Herbst, who depicts the hopes and fears that the strike stirred in Seattleites in her novels *Pity Is Not Enough* (1933) and *The Executioner Waits* (1934). Nancy Wilson Ross also recognizes the "genuine revolutionary spirit" found in Seattle via the historical role the I.W.W. and old *Union Record* played in the city. She notes in *Farthest Reach* (1941) that "Some of the most dynamic American liberals are still to be found here, quite unfairly pigeon-holed as 'Reds' by the more placid citizens." Nonetheless, Seattle literature has not significantly recognized the city's important labor history. Rather, it has been the city's legendary Skid Road, the namesake for the down-and-out "Skid Row" districts of many American cities and perhaps Seattle's best-known contribution to the nation's lexicon, that far more influenced literary depictions of the city.

Even more than Seattle fiction writers, non-Seattle writers readily picked up on this rough-and-tumble version of the city. In Willa Cather's *My Antonia!* (1918), one of the characters, a young woman named Tiny Soderball, leaves the small prairie settlement of Black Hawk, and, the next she is heard of, is living in Seattle where she has opened a boardinghouse for sailors in an empty building on the waterfront. To people in Black Hawk, this news does not bode well for Tiny: "This, everyone said, would be the end of Tiny. Even if she had begun by running a decent place, she couldn't keep it up; all sailors' boarding-houses were alike." Tiny proves the naysayers wrong, though, by parlaying her connections with Alaska gold miners into her own claim in the gold fields and turning a profit. Tiny is more fortunate than the two out-of-work characters who come to Seattle in John Dos Passos's *The 42nd Parallel* (1930). Flush with cash from working on the Canadian railroad all summer, Mac and Ike take a steamboat from Vancouver to Seattle in search of women since, as Mac says, "I've heard tell there's swell broads in Seattle." (Earlier Ike says, "We'll have swell coffee in Seattle, damned if we won't, Mac.") The next day they meet two women "in front of the totempole on Pioneer Square," buy a quart of whiskey to drink with them, and eventually get tossed in jail for public drunkenness. The following afternoon they drink coffee in a Chinese restaurant, while "Outside it was raining pitchforks," and end up in "a thirtycent flophouse where they spent the night and the bedbugs ate them up."

Nonfiction writing about Seattle in the twentieth century depicted the city as such a destitute place less frequently—especially nonfiction by Seattle writers, who generally advanced a more dignified version of the city to their readership. Notable among the early Seattle nonfiction writers are the city's many historians, including Welford Beaton, Clarence B. Bagley, Roberta Frye Watt, and J. Willis Sayre, all predecessors to Archie Binns, Murray Morgan, and Roger Sale. Although alternating between nostalgic and boosterish in tone and content, the histories by these early writers nonetheless offer an invaluable, often firsthand record of Seattle's first fifty years. However, unlike the Seattle histories published decades later by Morgan and Sale, these early histories are not especially noteworthy for their literary merit. Not until midcentury, beginning with Archie Binns and Nancy Wilson Ross, did more literary-minded nonfiction writers begin to write about the city and its past. In recent years, Seattle's literary historians have given way to literary journalists and creative nonfiction writers such as Jonathan Raban and Paisley Rekdal. Literary personal essays set in Seattle, in fact, now rival in their volume and quality the surge in Seattle fiction over the past decade.

Overall, Seattle writing in the post–World War II period has increased exponentially with each passing decade. The postwar proliferation of Seattle writing has, not surprisingly, paralleled the city's overall rise in the national consciousness, especially in the 1980s and 1990s, when most of the selections here were written. Yet, even before all the national hoopla over the city commenced, Seattle enjoyed a more quiet literary vitality, found in bookstores such as Elliott Bay Book Company and Red and Black Books, readings such as the Castalia series run by poetry professor Nelson Bentley at the University of Washington, local literary publications such as *Bellowing Ark* and *Seattle Review,* and (even before Starbuck's) a healthy coffeehouse scene, all of which made the city fertile ground for the more recent mushrooming of literary activity. *Invisible Seattle,* billed as "a novel of Seattle by Seattle," stands as one of the more daring literary undertakings from the early (pre-boom) 1980s. The introduction to the final print version of the novel explains that the novel's "characters, plots, and phrases were gathered from citizens in the streets by a dedicated band of Literary Workers, then assembled in a four-day spectacle on the giant computer Scheherezade" at the 1983 Bumbershoot festival. In effect, *Invisible Seattle* was one of the first collaborative hypertext novels, on a scale unimaginable until then, and perhaps an augur of the literary and technological explosion soon to hit the city. Today's *Seattle Stories* web site, part of the larger City Stories Project, which posts tales based on public encounters and occurrences by anyone wishing to contribute them, could be regarded as at least one indirect legacy of the *Invisible Seattle* project.

Reading Seattle demonstrates that a significant and notable body of prose writing about Seattle now exists, even though this writing has accumulated slowly. In San Francisco at the turn of the century, journalists and fiction writers led by Bret Harte and Frank Norris strove to make that city the literary capital of the West, as writers began to recognize the realist possibilities of the city setting. Half a century later, as part of the San Francisco Renaissance, Kenneth Rexroth, Lawrence Ferlinghetti, and many of the Beat writers again turned the city into a major literary center. In Chicago in the 1910s, 1920s, and 1930s, Theodore Dreiser, Sherwood Anderson, James T. Farrell, and others vigorously wrote about that city, establishing it as the Midwest's literary capital. However, among Seattle writers (as the *Fortnightly* columnist hinted and despite Lancaster Pollard's Credo Club), there has been no deliberate and organized campaign to represent the city in imaginative prose. Seattle writers form no movement or school. To the contrary, they have been a rather scattered bunch. As Seattle resident and writer Jonathan Raban says, "There is not much hobnobbing among us." With the occasional exception, Seattle writers have tended to be rather demure in promoting themselves and their writing. Although the city heartily supports the literary arts with book sales, public funding, and attendance at readings, no openly acknowledged Seattle School of writing exists—a lack perhaps befitting Seattleites' reluctance to be collectively identified under a single banner.

At the same time, fiction and nonfiction writers have clearly come to recognize that an alluring opportunity exists to represent and discuss a city of such wide-ranging economic circumstances, mixed racial and ethnic backgrounds, contrasting lifestyles, intriguing history, and varied and colorful neighborhoods. In size and character, Seattle comes very close to resembling, if not the ideal city, then at least, as Jonathan Raban defines it, a "tolerable city": "that intense, sociable, walkable place, big enough to lose oneself in, small enough to generate surprise and coincidence"— the kind of city that is probably more ideal to write about than even the ideal city, if such exists.

While Seattle has seen boom periods before—the gold rush years, the Alaska-Yukon-Pacific Exposition period, and the midcentury Boeing heyday—the boom period of the past two decades has heaped unmatched economic and cultural change upon the city. Yet, when informed people reflect upon Seattle, they consider its pioneer history, its production of jet planes, its role in the digital revolution, its groundbreaking music scene, its World Trade Organization protests, its coffee craze, its majestic scenery, and, most certainly, its rainy weather . . . but odds are that the notion of a Seattle literature rarely appears on people's top-ten list of all things Seattle.

Reading Seattle attempts to correct this oversight. By gathering into one volume a collection of the best prose writing set in Seattle and about Seattle from the past fifty-plus years, the anthology does not intend to serve as a proclamation for any particular movement or school in Seattle writing. Rather, it aims simply to declare that Seattle has joined New York, Chicago, San Francisco, Boston, and New Orleans as one of the nation's great literary cities. As readers, reviewers, and publishers catch on that Seattle is a city teeming with writers, we also recognize that there is now a genuine and vital Seattle literature.

No longer a provincial, out-of-the-way city uncertain about its own self-representation, Seattle has proven itself to be a city that inspires, provokes, and stirs the literary imagination. In addition to celebrating this status, the prose in *Reading Seattle* extends our thinking about urban American literature and gives Seattle writing its due place within that tradition. Beyond this, the fiction and nonfiction here enables us, ultimately, to better experience and understand this remarkable city.

Part 1. Coming into Focus (1930s–1980s)

Northwest Gateway: The Story

of the Port of Seattle

ARCHIE BINNS

Archie Binns (1899–1971) was born in Port Ludlow, Washington. He was one of Seattle's earliest acclaimed novelists and historians and an instructor of creative writing at the University of Washington in 1950. He wrote The Maiden Voyage *(1931),* Lightship *(1934),* The Laurels Are Cut Down *(1937),* The Land Is Bright *(1939),* Mighty Mountain *(1940),* The Timber Beast *(1944),* You Rolling River *(1947),* The Radio Imp *(1950),* Secret of the Sleeping River *(1952),* Sea in the Forest *(1953),* Sea Pup *(1954),* The Enchanted Islands *(1956),* The Headwaters: A Novel *(1957), and* Sea Pup Again *(1965). His nonfiction includes* The Roaring Land *(1942),* Mrs. Fiske and the American Theatre *(1955), and* Peter Skene Ogden: Fur Trader *(1967). The selection below, from* Northwest Gateway: The Story of the Port of Seattle *(1941), lyrically introduces Elliott Bay, Alki Point, the city's seven hills, and the city's own creation myths. On a more solemn note, Binns also provides the historical setting for Chief Sealth's famous speech to Governor Isaac Stevens.*

S teaming south, you open up the fine harbor of Port Madison with its snug inner harbor, and Agate Passage on the west opening into fifty miles of still more-inland waterways. All of them are on the wrong side of the Sound for a great city, though one of them has Bremerton and the Navy Yard.

Still you have not seen one real harbor on the continental side, though

From *Northwest Gateway: The Story of the Port of Seattle,* by Archie Binns. Reprinted by permission of Mrs. Archie Binns and the children of Archie Binns.

the signs keep multiplying. You meet a ferry loaded to its shovelnose with motor cars; a big freighter slides out from behind the headland of West Point and swings toward you. Flying high, an air liner for Victoria passes over your ship. A silver ferry, as streamlined as any car it carries, shuttles across the Sound past Bainbridge Island; a passenger steamer for Alaska plows out from behind the great headland; and a four-motored bomber rumbles overhead on a trial flight from Boeing Field. Between you and West Point, surprisingly, a sightseeing steamer pokes out of the high, yellow bluff and passes confidently between buoys that mark the entrance of the Lake Washington ship canal.

If we were to follow the sight-seer's course in reverse, our big steamship would go comfortably through the Government locks at Ballard and through the ship canal. The canal would open out and we would find ourselves in a mile-long lake in the heart of the city; a lake with wharves, drydocks and yards where new ships are built and older ones are repaired, and mooring grounds where still older ships, steamers and windjammers, lie enchanted in the still dark water, overtaken by the synthetic death of obsolescence.

From Lake Union we would sail on through the city, through the campus of the University of Washington. When it seemed we had already sailed too far and could go no farther, our ship would steam out of the narrow, dredged channel of reedy Union Bay into a deep, freshwater lake on the other side of the city; a lake twenty miles long, surrounded by the city and shipyards and fir forests, sawmills and cabins and homes of elegance with yachts anchored out in front and seaplanes parked in front yards. That would be Lake Washington. In the lake there would be Mercer Island, five miles long and a mile wide, rising to three hundred feet high, with city streets and homes and fir forests. A floating bridge links it with the city and a fixed bridge spans the distance to the opposite shore.

This is part of the harbor of Seattle, with its infinite variety of waterways through land and land in water, and salt water harbors and fresh: canals and lakes and rivers leading from security to security. That is what we would find if we turned in at the door in the yellow bluff and sailed our steamship into the heart of the city and out on the other side.

But we are still in Puget Sound, between Point Jefferson and Spring

Beach, and we are on a more conventional voyage. The wheelhouse clock is striking eight bells, four in the afternoon. Pinch-hitting for your amateur helmsman, you take the lanyard above the wheel and give it eight smart jerks, in pairs. The clangs are answered in deeper tones by the big bell on the fo'c'sle head, and the first officer and a quartermaster step into the wheelhouse. They are coming on their appointed watch, ignorant of the trick you have been playing on history.

The historian relinquishes the wheel to the quartermaster with a sigh of relief. Following you out onto the bridge, he says, "Thank goodness, that's over. I was scared stiff that I might run into some of this shipping, or aground."

"Not aground," you say. "Right here we're in the greatest depth of all, with nearly a thousand feet of water under us."

"Remarkable waters," the historian says, "truly remarkable!"

You stand on the port wing of the bridge as your ship steams around West Point, opening up Elliott Bay, with a great city rising before you. And still the Sound is three miles wide, and better than eight hundred feet deep. Off to the west a freighter is passing close to the beautiful shore of Bainbridge Island, with the smoke from her stack drifting before her in the light southerly blowing out of the Sound. The freighter is a big one of ten thousand tons, but she does not look big or small. Against the high, forested shore she looks a part of nature, comfortably at home, as a ship should look. Above the ship and the wooded hills of the island there is the long range of the Olympic Mountains, blue and crested with snow like long seas breaking in the sky.

To port, that three-hundred-foot cliff, golden in the sunshine, is Magnolia Bluff, crowned with madroña trees. By now there may be magnolias around some of the fine residences, but there were only madroñas when it was named by some amateur botanist who was confused by somewhat similar foliages. Like Appletree Cove back there beyond Point Jefferson. One of Vancouver's men saw dogwood in bloom and predicted apples in the fall. Among discoverers the first to arrive is awarded the palm, even though he has left his glasses at home and accepts it for a pine.

Those madroña trees have never borne magnolia blossoms, but they have done something even more remarkable. Notice how some of them lean out over the edge of the bluff toward the sun and this water of Adriatic blue. Remember their wood is weak and brittle and tremendously heavy. By all laws they should break in the first good breeze. But they do not break, even in a rare gale. They accomplish that by adopting the principles of engineering and growing their trunks in the shape of "I-beam" girders. You are not expected to believe that, but drive out there sometime and look for yourself. As the trees grow older and heavier, their cylindrical trunks flatten on two sides. And as they grow still older and heavier, the flattened sides become concave until the cross section of the trunk has an unmistakable I-beam shape.

The flora is remarkable in other ways. With a good telescope used at the right moment you could make out date palms up there in someone's garden, out of doors the year round and making a go of it. On Queen Anne Hill ahead, you could see fig trees ripening their fruit, and hedges of bamboo. Sometimes roses bloom on Christmas Day. Admittedly, such things are strange in the latitude of Maine.

The warm Japan Current has something to do with it, but the real explanation lies in your own field, Historian. We have it from history that Juan de Fuca invented these mythical waters in Venice. Never having been near the Puget Sound country, he could not be expected to get everything right. It was only natural that some of the trees and flowers of the Adriatic should slip in; and some of the climate; and the color on those golden cliffs and on the deep waters of this gentle northern sea-waters as blue as the Adriatic, forever with the quality of a dream.

There, to port, is Smith Cove Terminal and the Great Northern Docks that were a part of Jim Hill's empire. Not part of the real harbor, but a port big enough for a fair-sized city: piers half a mile long and channels dredged through mud flats. Japanese steamers load there mostly, sometimes a dozen of them at a time, and Smith Cove longshoremen are a breed of their own.

It has a tough sound, Smith Cove, but Henry Smith was another sort. He was a medical doctor and a literary man who wrote good prose and better verse. One was about "Time that blows a wreath of wrinkles to us all. . . ." But that was when he was an old man. When he was young he had his share of adventure. On the night the Indian War broke he rowed out of the cove with his mother in a boat with muffled oarlocks, and escaped to the Seattle blockhouse. Then he came back with two runaway sailors and harvested the crop in his clearing—the crop that the Indians burned along with his house before his harvest sweat was dry. Like the doctor whom they could have killed a dozen times, they had a sense of humor, and they let him garner everything into the house and barn before they fired the flaming arrows. No, Smith wouldn't be surprised to see the freight terminal and those piers. He settled in that wilderness cove in the belief that it would be a railroad terminal—and he lived to see it happen.

Beyond Seattle, protecting the harbor from the south, that long, low headland with the fir trees is Alki Point, where the pilgrims landed. Protecting the harbor from the west, the inner point we see, nose on, is Duwamish Head. Between it and the main city, the Duwamish River is split by Harbor Island, which divides the East Waterway from the West Waterway. Between there and here is the main harbor, with deep water up to five miles of curved harbor shore, finned with piers that lie from east to west. The depth of water is authenticated. The Denny brothers and Boren and Bell took soundings from an Indian dugout before they decided to build a city here. Mary Denny supplied the clothesline, with a warning to bring it back. They had a horseshoe for a sounding lead, and their city was fortunate.

There it is, on its seven hills; a city of upwards of half a million people, with all the trappings of a modern metropolis, and a sky line something like New York's. But its personality is its own. And its history is not like that of any other city, Historian. It is a piece of American mythology. The guardian spirits of the city are two horses that came out of the sea at the beginning: a docile black mare and a milk-white stallion with an unbroken spirit and a disposition toward violence.

That is not folklore. It was such a little while ago that there are men living on those hills, keeping office hours in those skyscrapers, who remember the man who drove Seattle's first horses from the sea. His name was Thomas Mercer. Mercer Street and Mercer Island are named after him. He named Lake Union and Lake Washington, and first proposed the ship canal. Discreet and factual histories mention and praise the docile mare and give her name, which is "Tib." They record that Mercer brought two horses, but they do not say much about the other one, because they want their city to have a good name. But the spirits of those two still gallop over the mighty hills of the city: the impatient, pale stallion and the docile black mare.

. . .

Even in the early days of the village that bore his name Seattle knew that he had made a hard choice of one-sided co-operation. He saw his high-spirited granddaughter bought from her parents by a drunken and brutal white man. He saw her beaten and pursued and brought back and beaten again when she ran away. He could not interfere because he was an Indian, and the whites did not interfere because the girl was an Indian. Presently the girl killed herself by hanging, leaving a son who turned out no better than his father. A white man could do as he pleased with his squaw. But when one of the Indians killed his squaw the white men hung him to a tree.

Neither the Americans nor the Indians were sufficiently advanced in civilization to be able to live together. Chief Seattle saw that early, and he was relieved rather than otherwise when he heard that the Government was preparing to buy the Indians' land and segregate them on reservations.

On a hurried visit to the Territory in 1894 [Governor Isaac] Stevens devoted a month to traveling about the large region west of the Cascade Mountains, "familiarizing" himself with thirty-odd tribes of Indians, "learning their needs" and deciding on the value of their land. The haste was ominous and at best the results could only be tragically superficial. The Governor had been handed a bad situation and he made it worse with haste and bad judgment. He was an ambitious man and he had insisted on having charge of the railroad survey along with his other superhuman tasks. The realization of the railroad was twenty years away and the Indian War only a year, but Governor Stevens made a bad guess. After the hasty survey of his new territory he raced back to Washington, D.C., to fight Jefferson Davis on the routing of the railroad.

In his hurried glance over Indian affairs Governor Stevens visited the village of Seattle, where all the Indians of the Elliott Bay region were called together. The shore was blackened with hundreds of canoes drawn up on the beach, and the narrow forest trails poured out Indians until three thousand of them crowded the village.

The Governor's party arrived in the new Sound steamer *Major Tompkins,* which the canoe-traveling settlers looked on as a miracle of luxury. The small and swarthy Governor addressed the Indians from in front of Doctor Maynard's drugstore-real-estate log cabin. Doctor Maynard was master of ceremonies, and an interpreter hacked and jammed the Governor's English into Procrustean Chinook Jargon. The Governor told them how the Great Chief in Washington loved Indians, and he told them that he loved them as much as if they were the children of his own loins. Because of his love for them he was going to have the Great Father buy their lands and he was going to give them fine reservations and the blessings of civilization, such as schools and blacksmith and carpenter shops.

The Governor made a fine speech, but he was outranged and outclassed that day. Chief Seattle, who answered in behalf of the Indians, towered a foot above the Governor. He wore his blanket like the toga of a Roman senator, and he did not have to strain his famous voice, which everyone agreed was audible and distinct at a distance of half a mile.

Seattle's oration was in Duwamish. Doctor Smith, who had learned the language, wrote it down; under the flowery garlands of his translation the speech rolls like an articulate iron engine, grim with meanings that outlasted his generation and may outlast all the generations of men. As the amiable follies of the white race become less amiable, the iron rumble of old Seattle's speech sounds louder and more ominous.

Standing in front of Doctor Maynard's office in the stumpy clearing, with his hand on the little Governor's head, the white invaders about him and his people before him, Chief Seattle said:

Yonder sky that has wept tears of compassion upon my people for centuries untold, and which to us appears changeless and eternal, may change. Today is fair. Tomorrow it may be overcast with clouds. My words are like the stars that never change. Whatever Seattle says the great chief at Washington can rely upon with as much certainty as he can upon the return of the sun or the seasons. The White Chief says that Big Chief at Washington sends us greetings of friendship and goodwill. That is kind of him for we know he has little need of our friendship in return. His people are many. They are like the grass that covers vast prairies. My people are few. They resemble the scattering trees of a storm-swept plain. The great, and— I presume—good, White Chief sends us word that he wishes to buy our lands but is willing to allow us enough to live comfortably. This indeed appears just, even generous, for the Red Man no longer has rights that he need respect, and the offer may be wise also, as we are no longer in need of an extensive country . . . I will not dwell on, nor mourn over, our untimely decay, nor reproach our paleface brothers with hastening it, as we too may have been somewhat to blame.

Youth is impulsive. When our young men grow angry at some real or imaginary wrong, and disfigure their faces with black paint, it denotes that their hearts are black, and then they are often cruel and relentless, and our old men and old women are unable to restrain them. Thus it has ever been. Thus it was when the white men first began to push our forefathers further westward. But let us hope that the hostilities between us may never return. We would have everything to lose and nothing to gain. Revenge by young men is considered gain, even at the cost of their own lives, but old men who stay at home in times of war, and mothers who have sons to lose, know better.

Our good father at Washington—for I presume he is now our father as well as yours, since King George has moved his boundaries further north— our great good father, I say, sends us word that if we do as he desires he will protect us. His brave warriors will be to us a bristling wall of strength, and his wonderful ships of war will fill our harbors so that our ancient enemies far to the northward—the Hydas and Tsimpsians—will cease to frighten our women, children and old men.

Then in reality will he be our father and we his children. But can that ever be? Your God is not our God! Your God loves your people and hates mine. He folds his strong and protecting arms lovingly about the paleface and leads him by the hand as a father leads his infant son—but He has forsaken His red children—if they really are his. Our God, the Great Spirit, seems also to have forsaken us. Your God makes your people wax strong every day. Soon they will fill the land. Our people are ebbing away like a rapidly receding tide that will never return. The white man's God cannot love our people or He would protect them. They seem to be orphans who can look nowhere for help. How then can we be brothers? How can your God become our God and renew our prosperity and awaken in us dreams of returning greatness? If we have a common heavenly father He must be partial—for He came to his paleface children. We never saw Him. He gave you laws but He had no word for His red children whose teeming multitudes once filled this vast continent as stars fill the firmament. No; we are two distinct races with separate origins and separate destinies. There is little in common between us.

To us the ashes of our ancestors are sacred and their resting place is hallowed ground. You wander far from the graves of your ancestors and seemingly without regret. Your religion was written upon tables of stone by the iron finger of your God so that you could not forget. The Red Man could never comprehend nor remember it. Our religion is the traditions of our ancestors—the dreams of our old men, given them in solemn hours of night by the Great Spirit; and the visions of our sachems; and it is written in the hearts of our people.

Your dead cease to love you and the land of their nativity as soon as they pass the portals of the tomb and wander way beyond the stars. They are soon forgotten and never return. Our dead never forget the beautiful world that gave them being.

Day and night cannot dwell together. The Red Man has ever fled the approach of the White Man, as the morning mist flees before the morning sun. However, your proposition seems fair and I think that my people will accept it and will retire to the reservation you offer them. Then we will dwell apart in peace, for the words of the Great White Chief seem to be the words of nature speaking to my people out of dense darkness.

It matters little where we pass the remnant of our days. They will not be many. A few more moons; a few more winters—and not one of the descendants of the mighty hosts that once moved over this broad land or lived in happy homes, protected by the Great Spirit, will remain to mourn over the graves of a people once more powerful and hopeful than yours. But why should I mourn at the untimely fate of my people? Tribe follows tribe, and nation follows nation, like the waves of the sea. It is the order of nature, and regret is useless. Your time of decay may be distant, but it will surely come, for even the White Man whose God walked and talked with him as friend with friend, cannot be exempt from the common destiny. We may be brothers after all. We will see.

We will ponder your proposition, and when we decide we will let you know. But should we accept it, I here and now make this condition that we will not be denied the privilege without molestation of visiting at any time the tombs of our ancestors, friends and children. Every part of this soil is sacred in the estimation of my people. Every hillside, every valley, every plain and grove, has been hallowed by some sad or happy event in days long vanished.... The very dust upon which you now stand responds more lovingly to their footsteps than to yours, because it is rich with the blood of our ancestors and our bare feet are conscious of the sympathetic touch.... Even the little children who lived here and rejoiced here for a brief season will love these somber solitudes and at eventide they greet shadowy returning spirits. And when the last Red Man shall have perished, and the memory of my tribe shall have become a myth among the White Men, these shores will swarm with the invisible dead of my tribe, and when your children's children think themselves alone in the field, the store, the shop, upon the highway, or in the silence of the pathless woods, they will not be alone.... At night when the streets of your cities and villages are silent and you think them deserted, they will throng with the returning hosts that once filled and still love this beautiful land. The White Man will never be alone.

Let him be just and deal kindly with my people, for the dead are not powerless. Dead, did I say? There is no death, only a change of worlds.

Soon after this meeting Governor Stevens was on his way east, to be gone for months. He returned to the Territory in November and plunged into the business of extinguishing the Indians' title to the land.

The Executioner Waits

JOSEPHINE HERBST

Josephine Herbst (1892–1969) was born in Sioux City, Iowa. Making up her Trexler Trilogy are the novels Pity Is Not Enough *(1933),* The Executioner Waits *(1934), and* Rope of Gold *(1939). Herbst, an associate of Ernest Hemingway and John Dos Passos, wrote four additional novels, a nonfiction book, a biography, and many journalistic accounts, essays, and memoirs concerning the turbulent politics of the early part of the century. In this selection from* The Executioner Waits, *Herbst captures the spirit of the times during Seattle's 1919 General Strike, one of only two such strikes in U.S. history. Viewed by its opponents as an outright Bolshevik Revolution, the Seattle General Strike took place on the heels of World War I and the Russian Revolution. The clash of old and new gender roles for women since the advent of women's suffrage in 1923 and the emergence of modern attitudes permitting women greater freedom generally are revealed here in the differences between the two Wendel sisters and their landlady at the White Elephant, a Seattle boardinghouse.*

THE SIDE LINES

Their mother's plans and optimism were an old story to the Wendel girls. Long ago they had laughed and agreed that Mamma would never sell the White Elephant. They had said it bitterly, when they were forced to contribute for its upkeep during the years when the two youngest wanted to save for college. The White Elephant had never been a cheap monster;

From *The Executioner Waits*, by Josephine Herbst. Reprinted by permission of Hilton Kramer.

it had housed them but it was always demanding paint and repairs. Plumbing went wrong, the furnace didn't work. It was a constant worry and care. Long ago Vicky and Rosamond had shelved the White Elephant as a possible gold mine. If it made Mamma happy, that was all that could be expected. But wages were so high in Seattle that winter, until after the soldiers began coming back and gutting the market with cheap labor, that the girls saved month by month. Even Nancy and Clifford saved, and Clifford began talking vaguely of getting a little business of his own, maybe buying into an automobile agency.

The armistice had let everyone down and, in the boarding house out near the university where the sisters and Clifford had breakfast and dinner, a suspicious nagging crept into the conversation that had been open and gay before the bells rang all night and crowds heaved in the downtown streets yelling and happy. A few business couples eating at the place talked sourly of leaving before the ship yards quit and business began flattening out. Students in the R.O.T.C. felt cheated that they had not got into the excitement. The boarding house lady Mrs. Caspar was worried because now she could not keep on indefinitely telling the story that Mr. Caspar was east on "war work." Sooner or later he would have to return or the boarders would continually wonder why. She would rather drop dead than admit that he had just run off with a stenographer. She would protect her children, if she had to send her husband to Austria, and get him shot, to do it.

Sometimes after a hard day with all her muscles aching she would sit rocking upstairs, seeing herself a widow, in decent black, peered at from behind the neighbor's sympathetic window curtains. "Poor Papa," she would say, showing that handsome scamp's photo that stood in a frame that cost three dollars on the parlor table. If she died for it, she'd keep up her pride and the boarding house was good; business people paid better than students and it was only because she could see the time when they would be leaving that she got so provoked at those two Wendel girls, the single one and that married one, Mrs. Stauffer, for always starting arguments at the table. Still, the men liked it, they fired up and got excited the way you'd think only a leg show would affect them. It was a lesson to her and she felt sometimes as if immorality was going on right at the table when those two girls would start at it, bold as brass, criticizing the world. And the worst was the way they came out defending those Bolsheviks in Russia. Oh what a high-handed way to do things. You'd think they'd show some discretion. The way the war made girls carry on was a caution. If it wasn't running outright with men, it was flaunting opinions that did credit to no decent woman, right in the faces of a whole table of the young and innocent. Why they had the nerve, those girls, to laugh at what everyone knows is true; everyone knows that the revolution was just to national- ize women, so as to give them license. Liberty was one thing, license was another, and she certainly approved of the way the government was round- ing up loose talkers and suspicious characters. Cigarette smoking was one thing she did not approve of in a lady and she had seen, with her two eyes, those two girls on the front porch with two of the best boys, one of them a young lieutenant, smoking. All she could say was that, try as she might, she couldn't help making her spine a little stiller when she served them their pie after that. A girl with her husband at the front—and the other one, who knows how far she carried her high talk?

It was all right as long as people were still singing songs and feeling all bound together in a great common purpose like the war; she could tol- erate a little of that then perhaps, a little talk and so on but now that she felt so terribly let down, with Papa a constant worry and the fear that any day people might begin to insist, "But when is Mr. Caspar coming home from his war work, Mrs. Caspar," her nerves were on edge and she was in no condition to handle a big strike. No indeed. The flu had been bad enough, with one fatality right in the house and several days going by with not more than two boarders showing up at that long table. No one could say she had shirked, she'd been on her feet early and late. Feeding people was no joke, but add to that nursing the sick and you had a bill of require- ments that would shake an ox. And she was no ox, thank you, in spite of her heavy build. She could see, bit by bit, her boarding table split up, first arguments, then high wrangling tones about the Fourteen Points. What a mistake that was, as if we shouldn't punish those Huns, punish them so they couldn't rise again. Why, there was one evening when she had waited in the kitchen absolutely trembling with the pudding in her hand ready to throw it at that Victoria Wendel when she had gone on about

33

the kind of peace that would only make another future war. Prison was too good for a girl like that. What did she know about anything? Wait until her husband walked out right under her nose with a frippery stenographer, and what did she have that his own wife didn't have, what, I ask you? She'd been a good wife, never one to say no to anything, no matter how tired. And what a reward. She clattered the dishes now, glancing over her shoulder at the cook. The roast beef was too rare, the salad lacked that dab of mayonnaise. She was as tired of that dab as of her old hat but what else was there? She watched the plates go into the babbling room and waited.

"What are they talking about tonight?" she said, when Clarence came out in his white coat.

"The strike."

"Is there going to be one?" said Mrs. Caspar.

"You bet your life," said Clarence, stacking up the soup plates and arming himself with the roast beef.

"What's that? Clarence Upstone," said Mrs. Caspar. "What ails you? Why, those men have no right to strike, just selfish, that's all. What right have they? Do I strike? No, I have to go on, day after day, slaving away. Of course," she amended quickly so that he wouldn't get suspicious, "I'm glad to do it, it keeps me busy while my husband is at his war work. I'm glad to contribute to my country." He had gone into the dining room and the voices had subsided with the appearance of food.

When he came out again, she rinsed her plump arms and began arranging the dessert. "What is that they're saying? Is there going to be a strike? Oh, we are in for it. Me, in a business like this, with a general strike." She looked at him scared and furious. "What do they say in there?"

"They don't know anything," said Clarence. "Nobody does but the strikers. The papers say it's pretty bad, food will be scarce, lights will go off. . . ."

"Ooh," said Mrs. Caspar. "Lights. Oh, we'll have robbers and thugs running around breaking in, nothing will be safe, nothing." She clutched her breasts, whirling around to the cupboard. "Coffee, beans, sugar, prunes, flour, eggs, why it will take every cent I've got and can scrape together to lay in food. And lights. Oooh. What can we do?"

"Kerosene," said Clarence cheerfully, hoping they would strike with a vengeance, strike hard, strike Mrs. Caspar and all her kind who were thick-headed and hard of heart. Why, she had bickered with him about his meals and always gave him the leftovers and even tried to slip leftover food from the boarders' plates onto his if he didn't keep an eye open. No wonder her old man had dished her. War work. Pretty good. You had to call it something. He snickered.

"What's that?" said Mrs. Caspar, whirling at him. "I hope I didn't hear a laugh. I surely hope not in a time like this."

"I was only trying to keep from sneezing, I think I'm catching a cold, Mrs. Caspar," said Clarence.

"Take those drops I gave you, I can't afford colds around here not after that siege of flu. If I had to live through that again, I'd say, bury me. But this strike, Clarence, are you *sure*. What right have they? Suppose I struck, what would happen? Can I give myself such a luxury, no, I have to work." She clattered the plates and Clarence began arming himself ready to charge into the dining room. "Give that to those Wendel girls," said Mrs. Caspar indicating two plates with slightly smaller puddings and less sauce. "I miscalculated and it didn't quite hold out." Clarence shouldering his burden pushed into the dining room and plunked the two stingy portions down in front of Mr. and Mrs. Granger. Mrs. Granger eyed her portion critically and sniffed slightly, whispering to Mr. Granger. The Granger portions were placed carefully before Victoria and Rosamond.

"Begin eating," whispered Clarence to Victoria, "before the old lady sticks her nose in the door." Victoria and Rosamond took big bites and when Mrs. Caspar breezed in with, "Everything all right, folks?" Rosamond spoke up with the rest, "Just fine, thank you, Mrs. Caspar."

After dinner Mrs. Caspar asked advice from everyone as to the strike and the boarders were practically agreed that it was plain greed and selfishness that led to strike talk. The Wendel girls and Nancy and Clifford put their wraps on and left without a word. Outside Nancy said, "Can't you two girls be a little more tactful? About this strike particularly. Everyone is worried and worked up, why do you rub it in? I don't think you girls ought to take out your personal grievances on the boarding house like that."

"I don't even know what you mean," said Victoria.

"Yes, you do," said Nancy. "You're just sore because things didn't turn out the way you liked in San Francisco, I know all about it, that Barnes and his family acting so slow, and Rosamond is upset about Jerry. But you girls ought to learn tact. Neither of you used to be this way except that you always were provoking, both of you. Why, when Clare and I used to come home with fellows you darned kids would be at the window flattening your noses."

"I suppose the ship yards men are mad at their sweeties and that's why they are striking," said Rosamond. "I suppose that's it, isn't it, Clifford?"

"That's another thing altogether," said Nancy virtuously, galloping a little ahead of the rest as they came to a corner. "Quite another thing. You girls aren't ship yards workers. Why do you have to stick on their side for? With a whole city against them. I can't understand it." She felt grieved as if they had insulted her personally and spoiled her chances for fun.

"Why don't you read the Seattle *Union Record* instead of the *PI* then and maybe you'd find out," said Vicky.

"*That* paper," said Clifford, laughing.

"Oh laugh," said Rosamond hooking her arm into Vicky's. The street lights paled and the street ahead under the dark trees was very black and shiny.

"Look, the lights are going out, see them blink," said Nancy, taking an extra skip. Something was going to happen at last. "What if the whole place goes dark?"

"We bought candles this afternoon," said Vicky. But the lights were already coming back strong. Then they flickered. Somewhere in the power house someone was about to turn off the lights.

Nancy and Clifford went one way. Rosamond and Vicky another. At their rooming house, their landlady Mrs. Parks had a row of candles waiting on the hall table. "Did you see those lights flicker? I don't know what we're coming to," she said cheerfully. "Oh we're certain to see trouble."

Trouble. Everyone talking of trouble. Caseman had headed north into "trouble." Like as not he was in this city and knew all about the strike. It was more than the two girls knew. Some said it was a protest against sending munitions to Siberia, some said it was against a wage cut, some said it was just plain cussedness on the part of labor. The two girls could only

36

climb the stairs and sit down in their rooms, read a book, darn a few stockings. Outside a rain began gently on the heavy expensive window pane. The Parks had built a very good house. They had put all of Mrs. Parks's little inheritance into their home. The roomers slept on the best beds and paid good prices too. The only thing was that the radiators rarely were as hot as they should be. Mrs. Parks saved on the heat. The house took a great deal of fuel and was, all in all, a Great Expense. Still, it was worth it. What else did they have? "Our little home is all we have," Mrs. Parks often explained. That very afternoon she had laid in a store of food, plenty of candles. Thousands of housewives and hotel keepers and restaurant keepers did the same. Little stores did a sudden business in oldtime kerosene lamps. Every now and then the lights flickered but did not go out.

The rain changed to snow and a soft persistent snow fell for twenty hours. It fell along the street car tracks and piled in little ridges, then it smoothed over into soft drifts. Mrs. Caspar's boarders struggled out into the snow, grieved and sore at the weather. It was another sign from heaven that everything was against them. At a time like this, with returned soldiers beginning to straggle in for jobs, it wasn't safe to stay home. If you got a cut, you took it. What a nerve those ship yards guys had to strike against a cut. Everyone else was getting it in the neck, why not them? The little bevy from Mrs. Caspar's straggled out, grumbling and comparing notes. In the midst of falling snow, scab trucks and jitneys slid alongside charging fifty cents for the ride.

Nancy Radford had been so embarrassed at her sisters the evening before that she went without her breakfast rather than face the boarding house crew. Rosamond and Vicky ate in a stony silence. By evening Nancy decided to face the boarding house again but she asked the girls as a personal favor please not to make themselves conspicuous. The entire table was grimly waiting for terrible events. Someone said chopped glass would be put into food. Poison would be poured in the city water supply.

"I've spiked that," said Mrs. Caspar. "We won't drink a living death in this house. I've filled every bathtub and every utensil in sight. Hardly had a thing left to cook with tonight."

"No baths then," said Mr. Draper.

"No baths, Mr. Draper, if you want water to drink."

37

Clarence in his white coat, the two Wendel girls, and a young man, with a suspicion of baldness looked at one another. Victoria snickered, the young man winked. Clarence dodged into the kitchen.

"In my day when a young girl talked as free as those girls, we knew where to place her. Nice girls didn't talk like that, in my day," said Mrs. Caspar. "Mr. Caspar wouldn't like to hear such talk in this house, not with him away on patriotic war work. I shudder to think of what he would do if he were here." She shrugged her shoulders, a little more certain of herself. That very afternoon she had read a long piece about war work in Austria and how workers were being sent over to Hungary and Armenia to take charge of relief. When she had digested the article she could begin her new story about Papa. Would it be better to send him to Armenia or Vienna? Probably Armenia, it sounded very remote and anything might happen.

Clarence dropped a pan. Mrs. Caspar jumped and looked angry.

"My nerves, goodness no wonder, with revolution in our midst." A loud report from the street brought a little scream from highstrung Mrs. Galveston. "It's only a blowout," said Mr. Draper sarcastically. "Don't worry, we've got plenty of water to drink."

The lights were going strong. The street cars hadn't been running for hours. The power plant was said to be in the hands of the enemy.

"What enemy?" said Rosamond.

"Why the strikers, of course," said Mr. Draper. "Strikers and strikes should be outlawed."

"Enemy to *you*, Mr. Draper," said Rosamond sweetly.

"The newspapers print lies. It's all lies about the ground glass. They just say that to get people worked up."

"I suppose you have Inside Information," said Mrs. Galveston in an angry voice.

"I know it isn't true," said Vicky, "and I know something about newspapers, I knew some newspaper people," she bragged trying to make what she said sound important and impressive, "in San Francisco and they told me that news isn't always the truth by any means." She looked from one angry doubting face to another. "What are you so sore about? The men on strike never hurt you, why do you act so mad at them?" Mr. Granger winked at Mr. Draper. In his opinion modern girls put themselves forward entirely too much.

"Well, Miss Wendel," said Mr. Draper, "we've got water in this house anyhow. We are loaded up with enough water to fill an elephant, so why worry?"

"Talking of worry," spoke up Grandma Elkins, "I was worried sick this afternoon when I thought little Freddie had swallowed a button. One minute he was playing with my workbasket and the next the button was in his mouth. I thought sure he'd swallowed it, but it turned up later."

Talk drifted away from the strike and the Wendel girls, who were marooned, took themselves off for a walk in the rain. "Do you think Jerry will ever come home again?" said Rosamond. "I feel awful. The boarding house hates us and the strikers don't even know we exist. We might as well be on an island."

"I know I'm sick of the rain," said Victoria. "We might as well be wax flowers under glass. Why weren't we old enough to get sent overseas to see things? Seems to me we're always stuck in the wrong place. How much money you got saved?"

"About ninety dollars," said Rosamond. "Why?"

"Oh nothing," said Vicky. "I was just thinking."

Farthest Reach: Oregon and Washington

NANCY WILSON ROSS

Nancy Wilson Ross (1901–1986) was born in Olympia, Washington. After graduating from the University of Oregon, she lived in Germany, New York City, and on Hood Canal in Washington before settling on Long Island in New York. Throughout her life, she was renowned for her friendships and correspondences with artists, actors, writers, and intellectuals throughout the world. Ross published six novels, including Take the Lightning *(1940) and* The Return of Lady Brace *(1957). She also wrote extensively on Buddhism, publishing three books that helped introduce Western readers to the subject. She also wrote several children's books and two books about the Northwest:* Farthest Reach: Oregon and Washington *(1941) and* Westward the Women *(1944).* Farthest Reach *blends history, journalism, and travel writing in a quirky, vivid style. The following selection, from the chapter entitled "Seattle," sizes up the city just prior to the contemporary post–World War II period. Many of Ross's insights accurately anticipate the changes Seattle would undergo in the next half century.*

Seattle is a hybrid. You cannot make it into a single piece no matter how you try. It does not seem to have that homogeneity and that centralized core even the visitor feels in Portland, Oregon. Of the two cities Seattle is certainly more dramatic and even more grandly beautiful with its extravagant display of ranges of snowcaps, the winding waterways of its inland sea, and its scattering of lakes. From any one of Seattle's many hills

From *Farthest Reach: Oregon and Washington,* by Nancy Wilson Ross. Reprinted by permission of Yvonne Rand.

one can see views so stupendous and breath-taking that the sprawling city sinks into insignificance. Nothing can ever take away from Seattle the dramatic splendor of its natural setting, and it is perhaps the challenge of this setting which makes one wish for Seattle a destiny somehow comparable in greatness to the landscape in which it lies.

Although Portland has had its quota of rowdy and glamorous days, the memory of them does not seem to stick as it has stuck to Seattle. From the beginning Portland maintained threads of connection with the world of the eastern seaboard. Even the naming of the two towns is not without significance. Portland was named as the result of a coin-tossing between two New Englanders, one from Portland, Maine, and one from Boston, and the gentleman from Maine won. Seattle was named for the chief Sealth (which ineptness at Indian gutturals soon altered to Seattle), and this kindly old man, who accepted the whites in a spirit of philosophical resignation, had to be persuaded that his body would not turn in its grave every time his name was uttered before he would give consent to the town's naming.

When in 1909 Seattle held its Alaska-Yukon-Pacific Exposition it announced to the world awareness of the elements which should, by geographic placement, determine its development and give it its quality: Alaskans, Indians, Canadians, Eskimos, and Russians, the Pacific Islanders, and the Chinese and Japanese. These were Seattle's neighbors and her business associates. They might also have been her teachers as well as her pupils. Seattle, near the century's turn, gave promise of becoming a really unusual American city.

· · ·

Today the knowing visitor comes to the town famous for its spirit and he comes seeking a romantic mingling of the East and the West, the Indian and the Yankee, the Chinaman, the Norwegian, the Russian and the Jap, the Sandwich islands and the Yukon, and like as not—if he has Seattle friends who take him around—he will go away disappointed. For he will not take kindly to local pride in the quick assimilation of Neon-culture and old world grandeurs. There are plenty of American cities like this! Sometimes if the visitor is articulate, or famous enough to be asked his opinion, he speaks out about his disappointment, and Seattle is peculiarly sensitive to such criticisms. Muriel Draper told Seattle that she had come three thousand miles to see some authentic bit of Americanism and she saw only a synthetic culture, a syndicated ghost of New York. Tabu for her! Lewis Mumford, requested to say what he thought of the way the town was laid out, implied that it was too bad it couldn't be torn down and a fresh start made. Seattle citizens, recalling how the topography of Seattle had been altered with almost god-like will—hills leveled, the dirt used to fill the tidelands, grades changed from thirty-five to three percent—found this criticism galling. When Mumford left for Hawaii a local paper bitterly commented that the critic had sailed for Honolulu "which up to this time has been known as the pearl of the Pacific." When Harold Laski came to deliver lectures at the University of Washington in 1938 there was no dinner table topic for months except the monstrousness of paying for the opinions of a left wing liberal with money from the fund of a deceased capitalist. . . . Sometimes this insistence that all visitors give only praise, leads one to wonder if Seattle is not rather like a human being who has failed to fulfill his potential destiny—abnormally afraid of any intimations of the truth.

Prosperous Seattle citizens pride themselves on the astonishment with which the Easterner visiting their "outpost" views the charming club rooms at the Sunset or the Rainier; the amazement with which he sees a flunkey with a striped vest and brass buttons lurking behind an ivy-grown brick façade; the surprise that awaits him in dining at the Olympic hotel where superior French food is served by stereotyped waiters of approved obsequiousness; his polite awe at restricted residential sections with gatekeepers to ask the destination of the visitor before admitting him to fastness of beautiful timber, magnificent views, pools, tennis courts and a famous golf course, as in the Highlands, or to somewhat less private fastness, but with almost equally imposing façades, as in Broadmoor.

There is real pride in the University of Washington with its ten thousand students attending classes in expensive and cautious stone copies of the period known as Gothic (singularly incongruous on the slopes of the blue Pacific). Near the campus is the Shell House where the famous racing shells of Washington cedar are made by the Pocock family, who have the kind of monopoly of which one can approve. These are the shells which have carried victorious Washington crews across the finish line at Poughkeepsie so many times, and the years of work that a few Seattle men put in to get western crews accepted among the eastern elect leads one to question deeply the meaning of American democracy. It is perhaps the rarer Seattle citizen who would point with pride to the name of Vernon L. Parrington on a campus building—and apologize at the same time for the truly formidable ugliness of this building named in the great man's honor. The visitor is not apt to be spared a reminder to take a ride on the streamlined ferry, the Kalakala. This lovely Indian word means Flying White Bird and many people do not understand why a few other people tear their hair at the idea of a "streamlined ferry" moving at roughly seventeen knots on the Sound between Seattle and Bremerton, with no quality which could be thought of as "flying," since the streamlining was built over the vibrating shell of an old and battered boat. Guides with a sense of flavor will take the visitor up to Harvard Avenue to view the cold stone pile which Samuel Hill built, in the face of one of the most magnificent local views, to entertain the Crown Prince of the Belgians who never came. Now the mansion is the home of a Russian gentleman married to the daughter of Seattle pioneers, and here the Grand Duchess Marie—while in Seattle selling her clothes to a local store—was entertained at a dinner of old world regality. The same guides who tell the visitor these stories may well indulge in a little dramatic contrast and take him down to the Skidroad where sailors are on the prowl, floosies with freshly bleached hair wait at the entrance to shooting galleries, and jobless men with broken shoes and empty eyes look for cigarette butts along the curbs near the totem pole.

Finally, among Seattle sights and matters for impersonal pride (though not for general financial support) is the museum in Volunteer Park, given to the city by Dr. Richard Fuller and his mother, commanding an incomparable outlook over lakes, seas, and snowcaps, guarded by huge stone figures from the Ming tombs, and marred only by unsuitable doors of metal crochet. The museum contains an exceptional collection of Oriental art and makes an admirable attempt to bring itself into vital connection with Seattle community life.

There are in Seattle little back eddies where scraps of the old influences may still be found: Japanese restaurants where excellent *sukiyaki* and good green tea are served in a peaceful room; or Chinese ones where something more exotic than chop suey can be had if you know how to order. There are even remnants of a once picturesque post-war Russian colony, in little restaurants decorated like a Petrouchka set, where dark bread and *shashlik Caucasian* can be had; and there are a few Scandinavian places—though not as many as one might expect in a city where the Scandinavian element is so large that one is told it accounts for Seattle's famous "cold" audiences. Cold they may be, says a prosperous and civic-minded citizen who gives a great deal of time to the Symphony and the Chamber of Commerce, but Seattle is nevertheless the greatest "sucker town" in America, and takes more "series" of concerts by dancers and singers than any other place.

. . .

It is easy to criticize Seattle because one's heart is a little sore at the promise this city had—and has—and the picture it makes today. And one can criticize Seattle full-heartedly because it is not yet crystallized, has still a chance, and thus can take it!

Seattle is enjoying a substantial boom, due in some measure to the threat of war, new activities for expansion and defense at Fort Lewis, the Bremerton Naval Base, and in Alaska. Shipyards are re-opening, airplane factories like the Boeing plant are running full time. Yet for all the bustle there are still jobless men on the Skidroad, and Seattle's shanty town along the railroad tracks is second to none in America for picturesque despair.

Since the problem of seasonal labor, with the resultant restless human tides, has always faced the Pacific Northwest, it was to be expected that a genuine revolutionary spirit would have its inception in Seattle. This spirit flowered in the early days of the I.W.W., the old *Union Record,* and the far-famed Seattle general strike. Some of the most dynamic American liberals are still to be found here, quite unfairly pigeon-holed as "Reds" by the more placid citizens.

Much has been said and written about the local problems of Labor gangsterism and political corruption. Far less attention has been paid to a native cultural growth, pushing its slow way toward expression among a scattered group of musicians, painters, writers, dancers, living on the city's fringes—anonymous and often poor, yet filled with the creative juices that flow into them from the magnificent countryside, still so rich in beauty and vitality. With some community understanding and support Seattle could make a truly indigenous and original contribution to American culture. The question as to whether it will or not is still an open one. Surely no city worthy of the adjective "great" can go on endlessly priding itself on a purely materialistic achievement.

Annie Jordan: A Novel of Seattle

MARY BRINKER POST

Mary Brinker Post (1906–?), the granddaughter of Seattle judge Otis Brinker, grew up in Seattle and attended Garfield High School, where she was Mary McCarthy's classmate and friend. She married their English teacher, Harry Post, and eventually moved to Connecticut. Her novel Annie Jordan: A Novel of Seattle *(1948), about a working-class young girl's coming-of-age in turn-of-the-century Seattle, was staple reading for Seattle school-age girls in the 1950s and 1960s. The following selection from* Annie Jordan *introduces young Annie as she explores her favorite part of the city, its waterfront.*

What Annie liked to do when she could slip away from her mother's sharp eye and demanding voice was to loiter around the docks and see the boats riding at anchor, with the green, oily water washing smoothly against their stained and battered hulls. There were the small, sturdy fishing smacks, reeking of their cargo, the island steamers with their black- and red-banded funnels, the bilge water gushing from their sides. Once in a while a big black freighter came in from Portland or San Francisco and the little girl would sit on a pile, watching with fascinated eyes as the burly longshoremen unloaded her.

Sometimes the sailors called to her and waved and she waved back and wished she could go aboard. Most of all she wanted to go with them when the boats got up steam, weighed anchor, and steamed slowly out of Elliott Bay, their prows cutting a foamy path through the dark water.

She loved the rattle of the anchor chains, the cheerful, blasphemous voices of the sailors, the triumphant blast of the whistle as the boat slowly backed away from the slip. She would stand and wave until the boat was only a tiny black dot in the vast, shimmering expanse of the bay and its plume of smoke a thin, frayed banner trailing behind.

Then she would throw crusts, saved from her mother's kitchen, to the swarming, circling gulls that wheeled boldly above her. They glared at her with red, angry eyes and their hooked yellow beaks opened to laugh their strange, raucous laughter and she could see the curious black tongues. They swooped upon the bread she threw into the water, squabbling and shrieking and beating their strong gray and white wings, lighting upon the water and bobbing gently up and down on the long oily green swells, like little boats themselves.

When they rose with long red legs dangling and wheeled up into the air, they were so beautiful and proud and graceful, her heart ached to see them. The curve of their wings made her think of music, of the organ in the Catholic church where she used to go with Pop when he was alive. But when they lighted on the docks and waddled awkwardly along, they looked pompous and smug, switching their sleek, fat bodies as they walked, and she laughed at them.

When all her bread was gone they would fly over her head, scolding her, demanding more until the cook from one of the boats dumped garbage overboard into the bay and then they would begin to scream greedily and fly away, to swoop upon the bobbing vegetables and refuse. She knew they were greedy and cruel, that they were hated by the fishermen because they picked the eyes out of the salmon that swam too close to the surface, but she loved them. She would have liked to be a gull, with two strong wings bearing up into the blue, free and independent and wild.

After she had fed the gulls she would peer into the dusty, smoke-grimed windows of the ship's chandler shops, staring at the coiled, tarry ropes, the swinging ship lanterns, the heavy anchors, the kegs, the oilskins, the boathooks, the strong brown fishing nets draped from the ceiling. She liked the burly, red-faced, bearded men who swaggered with rolling gait through the doors. They smelled of the sea, of strong tobacco, of rum, of tar and oilskins. Their faces looked as if they'd been chiseled roughly from red rock and their eyes were the hazy blue-gray of distant horizons. They called her "Red" and "Carrot Top," and sometimes they gave her strange gifts—a gold earring, a piece of petrified wood, once a tiny, delicate blue starfish that she could hold in her palm.

On her way home there was still another place of wonders that she could never pass without going in. It was the Old Curiosity Shop on Colman Dock, and the bright-eyed old man in the black skullcap and shiny alpaca jacket who ran it didn't mind how long she stayed, gazing into the glass-topped showcases where all the wonders of the far-flung world were kept.

Over the door was the huge white jawbone of a whale, and in one of the cases was the Lord's Prayer etched on the head of a pin. There were tiny sea horses, fantastic, legendary little creatures out of a dream. There were grinning masks cut by the Alaskan Indians from driftwood. There were spears and dried heads from the South Sea Islands. Baskets and blankets of the Siwashes, totems from Alaska. Exquisite ivories from the Orient. Gongs and temple bells, daggers and headdresses. There were Indian war bonnets, ceremonial masks of the medicine men, tomahawks, wonderful beaded moccasins, feather capes of chieftains.

Annie never tired of looking at them, but she never wanted to possess them. It was enough that they were here for her to see and to wonder about. The shop was dim and dusty and smelled of moth balls, and nobody, not even its owner, knew how much treasure trove it held. It was often full of visitors to Seattle, buying curios and souvenirs, laughing and exclaiming over the curiosities. Annie liked to listen to them, to smell the perfume and sachet of the ladies who swished their long skirts so elegantly. They were part of the great world, too, and Annie was hungry for the world and its wonders.

Long Old Road

HORACE R. CAYTON

Horace R. Cayton (1903–1970) was born in Seattle. His father published the city's first black newspaper, The Seattle Republican. *Cayton attended a YMCA college preparatory school in Seattle and then the University of Washington, from which he graduated in 1931 with a B.A. in sociology. He went on to pursue graduate studies at the University of Chicago. He taught economics at Fisk University from 1935 to 1936 and headed a research unit studying the black community that was funded by the Works Progress Administration. He then wrote his books* Black Workers and the New Unions *(1939) and* Black Metropolis *(1945). Both studies, especially* Black Metropolis, *which won the Anisfield-Wolf Award for 1945, were well received by critics. Cayton also published a number of essays and reviews on black figures such as Richard Wright and Paul Robeson. The following selection comes from his memoir* Long Old Road *(1963; 1970) and recounts his family's history in Seattle and his early encounters with racism in the city.*

We lived in a large, two-story white house on Capitol Hill, the most wealthy residential area of Seattle. It faced a broad avenue with a garden area in the center, which led directly to the water tower in Volunteer Park. We were the only Negro family in that part of town; all our neighbors were white and wealthy. Across from us was the Denny Blane [Arthur Denny and Elbert Blaine] estate. Mr. Blane was one of the wealthy old pioneers for whom an important street of the city had been

From *Long Old Road*, by Horace R. Cayton. Reprinted by permission of Susan Cayton Woodson.

named. As a newspaper editor and publisher, my father was known and respected in the community, and though we were not warm social friends, our neighbors were pleasant and respectful.

Our house was not the most luxurious in the neighborhood but it was well built and beautiful, set on a small hill surrounded by a long terraced lawn. Near the house were banks of flowers, shrubbery, and rose bushes. In back was a stable where our horses were kept and the carriage was stored. Before my parents moved to Capitol Hill, they had owned a house near the center of the city, and as the business area expanded they had sold it at great profit to move into this exclusive area. Both Mother and Dad wanted to live and raise their children in comfort, if not luxury.

. . .

Race prejudice was spreading in Seattle at that time, and many restaurants that had previously served Negroes now began to refuse them service; for some reason my estrangement from the Negro group turned me into its self-appointed champion. I made pilgrimages to restaurants I had heard would not serve Negroes and tried to force them to serve me. Perhaps this crusade was, in part, an attempt to atone for my betrayal of Negroes by wanting to associate with whites. I am no longer sure.

Years later I met a young, rebellious Negro boy in Washington, D.C., who had gone out driving one Sunday morning in nearby Virginia and, on an impulse, stopped at every home along the road that had a little black boy as a decorative hitchingpost, and asked the owner why he or she wanted to poke fun at Negroes. The young man had been arrested, and many people laughed at him, but I understood this kind of compulsion.

At some of the restaurants I was reluctantly served, although many times I was too nervous to eat the food set before me. At others I was refused and made a scene. From still others I would slink away hurt and defeated when the owner shook his head. But my battle against the barrier continued.

There had to be an end to it, of course. When I heard that the Strand Theater, a motion picture house on Second Avenue, was insisting on seating all Negroes in the balcony, I forced myself on unwilling feet to a test. I was accompanied by a Negro friend, but he left me at the door, refusing to participate in my war against segregation.

I told the usher that I would sit downstairs or know the reason why, and this was overheard by the ticket taker, who relayed it to the manager. I ignored the usher and seated myself downstairs. The manager asked me to leave, and when I refused he called the police. I was arrested and taken to jail.

At the police station the desk sergeant, an elderly man with white hair, routinely asked, "What's your name?"

"Cayton."

"The newspaper editor's son? Well, I didn't expect to see his son in trouble. What's the charge?"

When he was informed by the arresting officer that I had caused a disturbance in the theater he asked me, "What kind of a disturbance, son?"

"They wouldn't let me sit downstairs because I was colored. So I sat there anyway, and they had me arrested," I answered hotly.

"Let the boy use the phone to call his father," the sergeant said to one of the officers.

I got Dad on the phone and told him what had happened. He said he was coming right down, so I sat in a chair in the booking office and awaited his arrival.

When he walked into the police station he was greeted by the sergeant, who turned out to be an old friend.

"How are you, Jim?" Dad said. "I've come for my boy."

"There he is. Take him home and tell him to be more careful in the future."

"I'll tell him to obey the law, like I've always told him. But according to his story on the phone, Jim, he's broken no law."

"Perhaps you're right, Cayton, but you know as well as I do that things have changed around town. It's not my fault and it's not yours. It's not like it was years ago, when you and I were pioneers in this town. Anyway, teach your boy a little patience. Things have changed, Cayton."

"I know they have, Jim," Dad replied. "But there's no law that says where a man should sit in a theater in Seattle. We'll change when the law does, but we'll fight any law that takes away our rights. Come on, son. Good night, Jim."

"O.K., Cayton, you're the doctor. But quiet the lad down."

As we walked out of the station, Dad said, "Let's walk home. I want to talk to you, and a walk will do us good."

We started slowly to climb the long, steep Yesler Way hill. It was some time before Dad spoke, and he seemed quiet and reflective, far from the forceful, confident man he had been in the station house. At last he said, "In a way Jim was right, son. Things are changing here and not for the better. I can remember when it didn't matter what color you were. You could go any place and work most any place. But it's different now."

I answered him with emotion. "What are you going to do about it— just take it? You taught us all our lives that we were just like other people, that this was a free country. You and Mother said that we should insist upon our rights. What do you expect me to do now?"

"We've got to fight, son. But not the way you're doing it. Now keep still a while and let me talk."

We walked silently for a few minutes, and then my father began to talk as he seldom did around our home.

"I was born a slave. The property of another man, as was your grandfather. Your mother doesn't like me to mention it at home. It's far more pleasant for all of you to hear about your Grandfather Revels, but you had another grandfather, and a father, both of whom were slaves. And don't forget it— don't forget that most Negroes, all Negroes in this country, came from slaves. It's too bad that you think only of your Grandfather Revels. It pulls you away from your own people, and your fate is still tied up with theirs.

"One of my first memories was hearing the slaves talk about freedom. I was called the Freedom Child. Those were hopeful days, because freedom was coming and we all believed it. When it came, we rejoiced. But many did not know what to do with their new freedom. They were so tied to the slave system that they just stayed on the old plantation, even when they were not given wages for their work. But my father was lucky. Because my mother was white and from a prominent plantation family, he got some land and began to farm for himself. He was among the fortunate few who were successful.

"As a young man in the South, I was as fiery and rebellious as you. When I found that freedom and education didn't mean much in Mississippi, I left the South. It wasn't easy, but I felt that there must be freedom *some place* in this country and I was determined to find it. I went as far from Mississippi as I could, and I found it.

"When I first came out to this territory, a man was as good as his word. I went out in man-to-man competition and was successful. I provided a good home for my family. I had high hopes it would continue that way. I believed in the country. I believed in myself and my ability to compete with any man.

"But now the South has overtaken us, and freedom is only in name— not in fact. I'm defeated; you may not know that, but I seldom forget it, even at home. I have given up any hope of ultimate freedom for myself. It may not even come for you children, but for this I want you to fight all your life. America may not offer much but it is the only country we have or ever will have.

"You have been fighting a senseless, ill-prepared, and single-handed battle. That is not the way to do it. You must prepare yourself to fight in a more sensible and constructive fashion. You must go to school, learn, prepare yourself.

"Perhaps I was wrong in the way I raised you. Your mother and I both told you that you were the equal of anyone. And we made you feel different, superior to most Negroes, especially those who are coming to Seattle now. But it was a mistake that was easy to make in those days, because neither of us ever dreamed that the insanity of the South could catch up with us out here. It's defeated me, but you must prepare yourself to go on fighting.

"You'll have to begin to shape your life, Horace. I'd like you to go back to school and become a lawyer. I can help a little. But, son, you'll either go back to school or find a job."

My father's words were kindly, but I sensed their firmness.

"This is an ultimatum," he said. "Go to school or go to work, and stay out of this senseless trouble between the races."

The next day I was lonely and despondent. Before I realized where I was going I found myself on my way to Mr. Walker's house. He took me into his small, book-lined living room, and immediately I launched into my story.

"Your dad's right, boy. Things are changing, changing so fast we may have to alter our tactics and be patient for a while. The South is reaching out each day to engulf more and more of this country."

"No, I can't wait. I can't be patient. I don't know what to do. I'm lost."

The old man thought for a long time. "You're young, really too young to leave home, but I don't know what else to suggest. Why don't you go to sea for a while, see something of the world. Get out where you can think and ponder these things. When you come back perhaps you'll see things differently."

"And where should I go?" I asked.

"It doesn't matter where," he replied. "Just take a trip."

The next day I wandered down to the waterfront and made my way out onto one of the piers. Maybe I should go to Alaska as Mr. Walker had. He had gone to a new country and had been successful. Maybe I could do the same.

Before I realized what I was doing, I found myself walking up the gangplank of the steamship "Ketchikan." I was stopped on deck by a member of the crew, who asked me what I wanted. I told him I wanted a job, I wanted to ship out. He sent me to the purser.

"How old are you, boy?" the purser asked.

"Eighteen," I lied.

"We need a mess man. Can you handle that?"

"Sure," I answered, not knowing what a mess man was or did.

"O.K., come back in the morning at eight o'clock."

Two days later I sailed on a three months' trip on the Alaska Company's S.S. "Ketchikan."

I stood in the bow of the boat as we crossed Puget Sound and headed for the Strait of Juan de Fuca and the Pacific Ocean. I could see the seven hills of Seattle as they receded in the background and I was elated. I would start anew, maybe even strike it rich like Mr. Walker. My isolation from people was over; I would find a place where I belonged in the great new Territory of Alaska.

Thus I moved from the confusion of youth into the exciting period of young manhood.

How I Grew

MARY MCCARTHY

Mary McCarthy (1912–1989) was born in Seattle and grew up in the city's Madrona neighborhood. After graduating from Annie Wright Academy in Tacoma, she attended Vassar College. During her writing career, she wrote often on political topics for The Nation *and* The New Republic, *and was an editor of the* Partisan Review. *Her novels include* The Company She Keeps *(1942),* The Oasis *(1949),* The Groves of Academe *(1952),* A Charmed Life *(1955),* The Group *(1963; later made into a film),* Birds of America *(1971), and* Cannibals and Missionaries *(1979). In 1957, her autobiographical essays were collected under the title* Memories of a Catholic Girlhood. *In her day, McCarthy, who received the National Medal for Literature, was perhaps America's most renowned writer from Seattle. In this selection from* How I Grew *(1987), a memoir, McCarthy compares Seattle to San Francisco and offers historical insights into the Queen Anne Hill neighborhood.*

Seattle is often compared to San Francisco. It is spread out on hills (First Hill, Capitol Hill, Second Hill, Queen Anne Hill, all told the Roman seven, though some have been leveled) and ringed almost entirely by water (Elliott Bay, Lake Union, Green Lake, Lake Washington, the canal). It has cable cars, Orientals, a skid row, and a Bohemia. The University district, across the canal from the city proper, matches Berkeley, across the Bay Bridge. Both cities grew rich on a gold rush (my grandmother's father, described as a "broker," was a forty-niner in San Francisco); the Klondike

From *How I Grew*, by Mary McCarthy. Reprinted by permission of the Mary McCarthy Literary Trust.

came in 1897, when my grandmother and her sisters were already matrons in Seattle.

Both were ports trading with Japan, China, the Philippines, Hawaii; both harbored a White Russian population, mainly from Harbin in Siberia. Each had had a famous fire. The climates are similar, mild, without a real winter but with plenty of rain—good for the complexion. As a natural wonder San Francisco has the Golden Gate. Seattle has Mount Rainier. Both have good things to eat, in restaurants and on home tables. Seattle's are Dungeness crabs and little Olympia oysters and Columbia River salmon; San Francisco's are sourdough bread and abalone. Both are "wide open" towns—ships in the harbor, sailors in the streets; in my time Seattle had loggers and trappers, too. Both had smart shops, jewelers, furriers, well-dressed women. My grandmother, well off but not rich, owned six fur coats: a mink, a squirrel, a broadtail, a caracul, a moleskin, a Persian lamb, besides a skunk jacket and a suit with copious monkey trim.

Compared to San Francisco, Seattle was hardly cosmopolitan. Yet we had our own new smart hotel, the Olympic, with a palm court and violins playing at tea-time; we had theatres besides the Henry Duffy stock company—at the Moore, in 1907, Laurette Taylor had got her start, playing regular leads. We had the Ladies' Musical Club (with Aunt Rosie as its dynamo), the Seattle Symphony, and, soon to come, "Symphonies under the Stars" in the University stadium (copying the Lewisohn in New York), with Michel Piastro, concertmaster of the New York Philharmonic, conducting. My grandmother, who played the piano but liked her comfort, objected to the cold nights and stone seats. I went with a new friend named Evelyn Younggren (Swedish father, Italian mother, fair silky hair, dark-brown eyes, cloak of soft gray wool buttoning up to the small chin, whose poetic looks I never forgot and borrowed for the heroine of a novel). Under the brilliantly lit skies, I first heard the words "Scarlatti," "saraband," "Couperin," and classical music became romantic to my tone-deaf ear. It was a change from "Valencia," played over and over on the family phonograph, even though I did not follow a single sound the orchestra made, apart from an occasional resemblance to the Gregorian chant I remembered from church. For that reason, surely, I liked early music bet-

ter than the three B's—"You're in modality, not in tonality," a musician
friend told me later, at Vassar.

Our city also had the Cornish School, run by old Miss Nellie Cornish,
where Mark Tobey taught painting and Maurice Browne and his wife, Ellen
Van Vulkenburgh, pioneers of "serious" drama, directed the theatre. Like
San Francisco, we had a Chinese Opera. We had the Pike Street Market,
with stalls of Japanese truck-gardeners and bright colored stands of fish
from river, lake, and sea, and open-air shops of Far Eastern merchandise—
crystals, kimonos, incense-burners, fans. And we had more Jews (a "cosmopolitan element," *vide* Hitler and Stalin) than you would find in South
Bend, Indiana. Yet our only poet, as far as I knew, was a child prodigy
named Audrey Wurdeman, the daughter (I think) of an army colonel;
this girl, no older than I, was *published,* with her picture (not bad-look-
ing) in the paper.

In my mind, Seattle's Bohemia was identified geographically with Queen
Anne Hill, the highest part of the city, formerly a "good" neighborhood
with large old frame houses painted in dark colors and looming up from
overgrown yards. It looked down on Elliott Bay. My grandparents' pale-
gray house was in Madrona, between Cherry and Columbia, looking out
across the Lake toward Fuji-like Mount Rainier. In front we still had a
carriage block engraved "1893," where the horses used to be drawn up to
the curb. On the street side, to the left of the front door a narrow porch
wound around toward the rear, and on the right there was a swelling bay
window two stories high containing on the ground floor an étagère full
of Tiffany glass. In back there were a wide porch and two grass terraces
going past the rose beds and corn and peas and asparagus and artichokes
down to where the red currants grew. Despite my tenure in this paradise,
where ice-cream was churned every Sunday morning on the kitchen porch,
where my grandmother's pearl-gray electric was charged every night in
the stately garage (until she got the Chrysler), where you could watch the
crew races on the lake from the third-floor sleeping-porch outside the
maid's bathroom, restlessness had set me to exploring, by foot, streetcar,
and cable car all the far-flung districts of Seattle, from Alki Point to Lau-
relhurst to Seward Park. And I longed to "come from" Queen Anne Hill.

Not Mount Baker, where my grandfather's partner Mr. Thorgrimson had a new house and a lot of tulips, not Broadmoor, a development centered on a new golf club attractive to successful automobile dealers among the "young marrieds," not The Highlands (Jimmy Agen) next to the Seattle Golf Club, not even that green point of land near the Tennis Club—the old Alexander place, they called it—where, beside a tall poplar, a weeping willow bent over the Lake. No; Queen Anne Hill. A few "early settler" girls from the Sacred Heart (was one of them Eugenia McClellan?) had their houses there, I remembered, but I did not know where. On a dismal afternoon, procuring a transfer, I would take the long streetcar ride up the steep grade just to look at the secretive, half-run-down neighborhood, which had scarcely a soul on the sidewalks; you could not see in the windows, boarded up or with drawn shades or set back behind rambling porches, vines, once-ornamental shrubbery. They said that it was up here that the White Russians lived, but I am not sure it was true.

Anybody Can Do Anything

BETTY MACDONALD

Betty MacDonald (1908–1958), born in Boulder, Colorado, spent much of her life in and around Seattle. She attended the University of Washington, but shortened her studies to assist her husband in realizing his dream of being a chicken farmer on the Olympic Peninsula, experiences she would later recount in her writings. In the late forties, MacDonald began writing a series of juvenile fiction books, Mrs. Piggle-Wiggle, *which are still popular today. Her prose for adults, noted for its wit and flippancy about life's trials and tribulations, is autobiographical. Her books include* The Egg and I *(1945),* The Plague and I *(1948),* Anybody Can Do Anything *(1950),* Onions in the Stew *(1955), and* Who Me? The Autobiography of Betty MacDonald *(1959). In 1947,* The Egg and I *was made into a film with actors Claudette Colbert and Fred MacMurray. It is also the basis of the popular "Ma and Pa Kettle" film series. The following selection from* Anybody Can Do Anything *recounts the author's early efforts at employment in Seattle and showcases the city's famous Pike Place Market circa the 1930s.*

It was fun making calls with Mary but I dreaded the day when I'd have to go alone. I didn't dread it half enough.

On Wednesday morning, Mary gave me a little stack of cards, some briefing and sent me off. My first call was on a Mr. Hemp in an automobile agency. Mary had said, "Sell him that list of Doctors and Dentists—

they're about the only people who can afford cars now. Sell him on the idea of a clever but dignified letter stressing price and mileage per gallon of gas."

I left the office. It was a soft spring morning. The sky was a pale bluing blue and the breeze from the Sound smelled salty and fresh. The automobile company was about fifteen blocks uptown but I decided to walk both to save carfare and because I wanted to delay as long as possible the moment for seeing Mr. Hemp and selling him the clever idea I didn't have.

My route led me up hill, past the dirty gray prisonlike façade of the Public Library, through a shabby cluster of cheap rooming houses that advertised Palm Reading, Mystic Seances and Steam Baths in their foggy limp-curtained windows, past wooden apartment houses with orange-crate coolers tacked to their window sills, and whose only signs of life on this clean sunny morning were a few turbaned and housecoated women scuttling around the corner to the grocery store, and a smattering of pale children listlessly bouncing balls or riding tricycles in small restricted areas, the overstepping of whose boundaries brought immediate shrill admonitions from near-by open windows.

The automobile company's wide front door was propped open with a wooden wedge and four salesmen with their hats pushed to the back of their heads lounged in the sunshine on tilted-back chairs, smoking and looking sad. Timidly I asked one of them for Mr. Hemp. The man gestured toward some offices at the back. All the salesmen watched my progress across the huge showroom, which made me so self-conscious I walked stifflegged and cut a zigzag path across the shiny linoleum floor.

The offices were guarded by a long counter, behind which several girls were talking and laughing. I asked one of them for Mr. Hemp and she said she wasn't sure he'd have time to see me but she'd ask him. She went into a glass-enclosed cell and spoke to a man who was lying back in his swivel chair, his feet on his desk, talking on the phone. He turned around and looked at me and shook his head. The girl came back and said, "Did you want to see him about a job?"

I said, "No, I don't want to see him about a job."

She waited for me to reveal what I wanted to see him about but for some silly reason I was ashamed to tell her and acted evasive and sneaky and as though I were trying to sell something either dirty or "hot."

The girl went in and whispered to Mr. Hemp and I watched him peer at me and then shake his head. When she came back she said, "Mr. Hemp's terribly busy this morning and can't see anybody."

I said, "Oh, that's all right, I'm busy myself, I've got another appointment," and I hurried out leaving my purse on the counter. I missed it after walking a block or two, and when I came back to get it the girl looked at me with such a puzzled look I didn't leave my Advertising Bureau card, which by now was quite bent and sweaty anyway.

My next card was a collection agency. As I walked back downtown, I kept glancing hopefully at my watch, praying for it to be noon or too late to make any more calls. But it was only ten-twenty when I reached the large office building that housed the collection agency.

Waiting in the foyer in front of the elevators, laughing and talking, were men without hats and girls without coats. People with regular jobs just coming back from coffee. I looked at them carefully and tried to figure out where they worked, what kind of work they did, what magic something they had that made them so employable. Only one of the girls was really pretty. She had a tiny waist, a big bun of dark hair, and was laughing with one of the men. The other girls were clean and ordinary and looked as if they might belong to business girls' groups and curl their own hair. In the elevator we all stood self-consciously, silently, staring straight ahead the way you're supposed to in elevators.

I got off at the third floor and walked uneagerly down to room 309. The door was frosted glass. Clutching my notebook of collection letters and taking a deep quivering breath, I turned the knob, pushed open the door and was immediately confronted by a pair of eyes so hard they sent out glances like glass splinters. The owner of the eyes, standing at a counter sorting some cards, said, "Wadda *you* want?" as she slapped the cards down into little piles.

I said, "I'm from the Advertising Bureau. . . ." She said, "We don't want any more of those bum collection letters." I said, "I have a new series. I wrote them myself and I think they're pretty good." She said, "Wadda you mean new series? We already sent out one through five." I said, "Now we have five through ten," and began looking for my notebook. The woman said, "Don't bother gettin' them out. I don' wanna see them. It's all a waste of money." I said, "All right, thank you very much." She said, "Wadda *you* thankin' *me* for?" and laughed. I left.

My next call, in the same building, was on a school for beauty operators. Still smarting from the collection agency woman's laugh, I entered the La Charma Beauty School with the same degree of enthusiasm Daniel must have evinced when entering the lions' den. A woman with magenta hair, little black globules on the end of each eyelash, eyebrows two hairs wide, big wet scarlet lips and a stiff white uniform, was sitting at a little appointment desk. The minute she saw me she shoved a paper at me and told me to sign it. So I did and she said, "Black or brown?" I picked up the paper and it seemed to be a waiver of some sort having to do with La Charma not being responsible if I went blind.

I said, "I don't understand, I'm from the Advertising Bureau." She laughed and said, "Gosh, I thought you was my ten o'clock appointment. An eyelash dye job. Say, hon, Mrs. Johnson wants to see you. She wants a letter to all the girls who will graduate from highschool this June." I almost fainted. Somebody *wanted* to see me. I was going to sell something.

Mrs. Johnson, who looked exactly like the woman at the appointment desk except that she had gold hair, was very friendly, offered me a cigarette and thought my ideas for a letter were "swell and had a lotta bounce." I left with a big order and my whole body electrified with hope. Maybe selling advertising was easier than prostitution after all.

My next call was on a shoe repair shop. I went in smiling but the little dark man said, "Business is rotten. No use throwin' good money after bad. I don't believe in advertisin'. Good work advertises itself. Go wan now I'm busy." So I slunk out and went back to the bureau.

Mary, who was in giving the artist some instructions, was so very enthusiastic about the beauty shop and my first order that I didn't tell her about the other calls. We took our sandwiches, which we brought from home, unless we were invited out for lunch, and walked to the Public Market where for five cents we could get an unlimited number of cups of won-

derful fresh-roasted coffee and the use of one of the tables in a large dining room in the market loft, owned by the coffee company.

The Public Market, about three blocks long, crowded and smelling deli-
ciously of baking bread, roasting peanuts, coffee, fresh fish and bananas,
blazed with the orange, reds, yellows and greens of fresh succulent fruits
and vegetables. From the hundreds of farmers' stalls that lined both sides
of the street and extended clear through the block on the east side, Italians, Greeks, Norwegians, Finns, Danes, Japanese and Germans offered
their wares. The Italians were the most voluble but the Japanese had the
most beautiful vegetables.

The market, offering everything from Turkish coffee and rare books
to squid and bear meat, was the shopping mecca for Seattle, and a wonderful place to eat for those who liked good food and hadn't much money.
It had Turkish, Italian, Greek, Norwegian and German restaurants in addition to many excellent delicatessens and coffee stalls.

The nicest thing about it to me was its friendliness and the fact that
they were all trying to sell *me* something. Everybody spoke to us as we
went by and in spite of the depression, which was certainly as bad down
there as anywhere, everyone was smiling and glad to see everybody. A small
dark fruit-dealer named Louis, who was a great admirer of red hair, gave
us a large bunch of Malaga grapes and two bananas. "Go good with your
sandwiches," he said.

The dining room was three flights up in the market loft, so we climbed
the stairs, got our coffee, climbed more stairs and sat down at the large
table by the windows always saved by our friends and always commanding a magnificent view of the Seattle waterfront, the islands and Puget
Sound. Our friends, mostly artists, advertising people, newspapermen and
women, writers, musicians, and book-store people, carried their sandwiches boldly and unashamedly in paper bags. Others who ate up there
were not so bold.

Bank clerks, insurance salesmen and lawers [*sic*] were lucky because
they had briefcases and could carry bottles of milk, little puddings and
potato salad in fruit jars, as well as sandwiches, without losing their dignity. But accountants and stenographers usually put down their coffee,
looked sneakily around to see if they knew anyone, then slipped their sand-

wiches out of an inside coat pocket, purse or department store bag, as furtively as though they were smuggling morphine.

I must admit that I had false pride about taking my lunch and hated the days when it was Mary's turn to fix the sandwiches and she would slap them together and stuff them into any old thing that came to hand—a huge greasy brown paper bag, an old printed bread wrapping, or even newspaper tied with a string.

Mary, one of those few fortunate people who are born without any false pride, laughed when I went to a Chinese store and bought a straw envelope to carry my sandwiches in. The straw envelope made everything taste like mothballs and incense and squashed the sandwiches flat but it looked kind of like a purse. Mary said, "So we have to take our lunch. So what?" and went into I. Magnin's swinging her big brown, greasy, paper bag.

I forced myself to make calls the rest of that week but I diluted the agony with visits to second-hand book stores. I rationed myself, one call—one second-hand book store. Saturday morning I told Mary that we might as well face the fact I couldn't sell anybody anything.

Skid Road: An Informal Portrait of Seattle

MURRAY MORGAN

Murray Morgan (1916–2000) was born in Tacoma, Washington. A graduate of the University of Washington, he wrote for such organizations as Time *magazine, CBS Radio, the* New York Herald Tribune, *and the* Tacoma News Tribune, *over a publishing career that spanned nearly seventy years. In his honor, The Murray Morgan Bridge serves as a gateway to downtown Tacoma, and each year the Murray Morgan Prize is awarded by the Tacoma Public Library to an outstanding Washington author. Considered the "Dean of Northwest Historians," Morgan published eight volumes of history, including* Skid Road: An Informal Portrait of Seattle *(1951, 1960)*, Puget's Sound: A Narrative History of Early Tacoma and the Southern Sound *(1981), and* The Pike Place Market: People, Politics and Produce *(1982). Skid Road remains a mainstay of Seattle history. The following excerpt, "One Man's Seattle," serves as the book's preface. It offers an overview of the history that the later chapters pursue in detail, but more than this, it presents a descriptive appreciation of Seattle in which Morgan sums up his own keen understanding of the city.*

ONE MAN'S SEATTLE

The hills are so steep in downtown Seattle that some of the sidewalks have cleats. They used to be steeper. Less than fifty years ago Seattle seemed to have reached the physical limit of its growth; it had climbed

"One Man's Seattle," in *Skid Road: An Informal Portrait of Seattle,* by Murray Morgan. Reprinted by permission of Rosa N. Morgan.

the hills as far as a town could go. The streets were so steep that members of the Seattle Symphony, who had to climb three blocks to reach their practice hall from the place where they stored their instruments, arrived winded, and sometimes rehearsals were over before all the horn players caught their breath. The musicians rigged a pulley to carry the instruments uphill, so that strangers in town were sometimes startled to have a cello or a tuba swoop past them on the street. The rest of Seattle's residents couldn't solve their problems with pulleys, and they called in engineers to take the tops off the worst of the hills.

By washing nearly as much dirt from the downtown hills as was moved during the digging of the Panama Canal, the engineers made it possible for a modern metropolis to be built on the half-drowned mountain that lies between Puget Sound and Lake Washington. Seattle has continued to spread out over the hills, and the hills are still steep. A three-block walk through the business district may leave a visitor from flat country panting. If, after making the ascent from Second Avenue to Fifth Avenue, he gasps some depreciation of hills in general and, say, Madison Street in particular, he is unlikely to receive sympathy from a resident. "Oh, they aren't bad," a Seattleite will say about his hills. Or else, "Sure they're steep. But look at the view."

Since most of the city clings to the sides of hills that rise from lake and bay and river, there is always a view. Lake Washington is to the east, at Seattle's back door. It makes a good back yard. It is a long and lovely lake, still marked with the wilderness though highways encircle it and a floating bridge of concrete spans it. The racing shells of the University of Washington practice on it, and estates and mills and small homes and a naval air station stand on the shore. "A mountain lake at sea level," a visitor called it sixty years ago, when most of the shore was still outside the city limits. It still feels like a mountain lake.

The real mountains are thirty miles farther east. The Cascades run north and south across the state of Washington, and the wet winds from the Pacific drop their moisture as they sweep over the mile-high barrier, so that the western slope is dark with evergreens for half the year and for the other half deep with snow. The Cascades shut Seattle off from the eastern part of the state, psychologically as well as physically. Seattleites don't think in the same terms as the people who live across the mountains, where the climate is dry and the trees shed their leaves and wealth is fruit and wheat; Seattle thinks in terms of lumber and deep water. Puget Sound is the town's front yard. The first settlers came there in canoes.

The business district faces west by south. From the office buildings that have grown where the Douglas fir and western cedar stood as tall as sky-scrapers, businessmen look westward across the water at another moun-tain range, the Olympics, wilder and wetter than the Cascades—the Last Wilderness, some call them—a timbered world to be conquered and cut. From their downtown offices executives can watch the streamlined fer-ries that carry commuters to and from the Olympic Peninsula and the islands of the Sound; but they forget the ferries when a freighter glides into Elliott Bay and nudges one of the piers. The freighter reminds them that beyond the mountains is the Pacific, and beyond the Pacific is a con-tinent to trade with and grow rich on. The first settlers called the town "New York–Alki," meaning in Indian jargon "New York by-and-by," and Seattle still hopes to be for Asia what the port of New York is for Europe.

Sometimes war or politics shuts off that continent, but there is always Alaska. The half-million people in Seattle tend to look on Alaska as their very own. "We're the only city in the world that owns a territory," a booster once remarked, and the 128,643 Alaskans agree, though they are not happy about it. Seattle stores display sub-arctic clothing, though Puget Sound winters are usually mild; Seattle curio shops feature totem poles, though no Puget Sound Indian ever carved one; Seattle radio stations carry pro-grams especially for Alaska, though Seattle is as far from the territory as New York is from Hudson Bay.

At the foot of the hills, between the office buildings and the bay, lies a narrow strip of low land: here on the waterfront Seattle's history and Seat-tle's future meet and merge.

To know Seattle one must know its waterfront. It is a good waterfront, not as busy as New York's, not as self-consciously colorful as San Fran-cisco's, not as exotic as New Orleans', but a good, honest, working water-front with big gray warehouses and trim fishing boats and docks that smell of creosote, and sea gulls and tugs and seafood restaurants and beer joints and fish stores—a waterfront where you can hear foreign languages and buy shrunken heads and genuine stuffed mermaids, where you can watch the seamen follow the streetwalkers and the shore patrol follow the sailors, where you can stand at an open-air bar and drink clam nectar, or sit on a deadhead and watch the water, or go to an aquarium and look at an octopus.

The trucks and trains rattle past behind you, but there are sea sounds too, the cries of the gulls, the creak of the lines as the moored ships gently move, the slap-slap of small waves against the sea walls, the splash of a leaping salmon. These have not changed since the day, nearly a hundred years ago, when a young physician and poet named Harry Smith got thoroughly lost while walking the three miles from his cabin on the cove that now bears his name to Doc Maynard's general store, the Seattle Exchange, which was located on the low land where the hills flatten out and run into the tideflats near the mouth of the Duwamish River, an area then called the Sag. At low tide it was possible to walk along the beach from the cove to the Sag, but when the tide came in the water lapped against the clay bluffs and it was necessary to climb the hill and walk through the forest. The trees grew to the edge of the bluff, a thick stand of giant evergreens rising out of a tangle of underbrush—ferns and wild rose bushes and salal and Oregon grape. From a few yards back in the woods it was impossible to see the water; in the deep forest even the sun was hidden from sight. So it was that young Doctor Smith, walking south through the woods that covered the hill now called Queen Anne, lost his way and instead of coming out at the Sag discovered a cabin in a clearing by the water where he was sure no cabin or clearing or water should be, a cabin that proved upon investigation to be his own.

It would be difficult to get lost between Smith Cove and the Skid Road today. From the hill, logged by the pioneers and lowered by the engineers, the city spreads out before you. Seattle is located on the eastern shore of Puget Sound on Elliott Bay. From the top of Queen Anne, the highest of all the Seattle hills, you look down on the harbor; piers slant out into the bay from Smith Cove to the mouth of the Duwamish River; the eastern shoreline is jagged as a sawblade. Beyond the Duwamish the land sweeps back to the northwest. Elliott Bay, which lies within this horseshoe curve, opens onto the Sound, and across the Sound you see the islands—

Vashon, which was named by Vancouver for a British naval captain, and Bainbridge, named for the captain of Old Ironsides. Beyond the islands lie the Olympic Mountains. Looking to the east, you see three lakes. The first, Lake Union, is an industrial lagoon bordered by shipyards, boatworks, and the city gas plant. Hundreds of houseboats, built on floats of cedar logs, are moored to the bank, some of them clammy, one-room shacks, others with as many as six rooms, radiant heat, and specially designed light-weight fireplaces. Green Lake, the city's favorite swimming hole, is surrounded by a small park; and the third is the long lovely stretch of Lake Washington. A canal connects Lake Washington and Lake Union with the Sound; the second largest locks in the world raise ships from salt to fresh water.

The skyscrapers of the business district rise from the western slope of the narrow waist of land that separates Elliott Bay from Lake Washington. Dirt sluiced from the hills has covered the clam beaches along the salt water; even at high tide you can follow the waterfront all the way from the Cove to South First and Washington Streets, where Doc Maynard's store once stood.

As you walk south along Alaskan Way, the city on your left, the water on your right, you pass over the anchorage where in the old days the brigs and the clippers and the lumber schooners dropped their hooks and waited their turn to load lumber at the docks. The *Beaver* anchored here too, the first steamer on the coast, flagship of the Hudson's Bay Company fleet. And the *Major Tomkins,* which was wrecked; the *Traveller,* which sprang a leak and sank; the *Fairy,* which exploded; and the *Water Lily,* which was auctioned off as junk. And there were the great paddlewheelers like the *Eliza Anderson,* which for years served as highway and newspaper and post office to the people of the Sound. You can still see paddlewheelers here. The tan-colored sternwheeler *Skagit Chief* ties up from time to time at Pier 66, and sometimes the *Skookum Chief* comes down from the upper Sound. On rare occasions a sailing vessel, a veritable white-winger, enters the harbor. But most of the vessels are American freighters or Scandinavian cargo-passenger ships, sharp-prowed and fresh-painted, so large that when you lean against the waterfront rail to admire them you have to look up to see the anchors at their bows and to read their names.

On the bluff to your left are the public market, where the descendants of the Indians who once possessed the bay now sell vegetables; the neon-marked headquarters of the International Longshoremen's and Warehousemen's Union, where the lieutenants of Harry Bridges plan their unending war with Dave Beck; the tall white building named Dexter Horton, in honor of a sawmill hand who became the town's first banker; and the block-long red-brick building that James Colman built after the tide and the engineers had covered with dirt the beached clipper bark he used as a home. Most impressive of all is the forty-two-story Smith Tower (named for the typewriter, not the pioneer poet), which towers over the site of the main battleground in Seattle's two-day Indian War.

This is the oldest Seattle. Standing by the Alaska Pier, you look up a street that climbs straight over the hill toward Lake Washington. You walk up it, and two short blocks from the waterfront come to First Avenue, which was called Front Street in the days when it ran along the bluff above the beach. Here stood the mill that, in the fifties, meant Seattle was really a town, not just a hope; and here in the doldrum era of the seventies Val Wildman sold Seattle's first stein of nickel beer.

This is Yesler Way. Once it was called Mill Street, and before that it was simply the skid road, the route along which the ox-teams skidded logs to Yesler's Mill in the Sag. It is a dividing line. A hundred years ago it divided the land claimed by Doc Maynard from that claimed by Carson Dobbins Boren; it marked the center of the narrow strip of land that Boren and Maynard gave to Henry Yesler so that he could build his mill where he wanted to. Fifty years ago Yesler Way was the Deadline, the northern limit of what Seattleites called "our great restricted district"; bawdyhouses and low theaters were expected to stay south of the Line. Today Yesler Way is still a dividing line of sorts: to your left as you climb the steep street are the big new buildings, symbols of Seattle's dominance over a state and a territory and its dreams of controlling the trade of a distant continent; to your right, in the redbrick buildings untopped by neon, along the unswept sidewalks where the rejected men stand and stare, are the symbols of the past, the monuments to men who dreamed the wrong dreams or, like Doc Maynard, the right dreams too soon.

This region south of Yesler Way has been known by many names. For a time it was called Maynardtown, after Doc Maynard; later, when Yesler's Mill had been running long enough for its debris to fill the tidal inlets, the area was known simply as Down on the Sawdust. After its character became established during the seventies it was called variously the Lava Beds, the Tenderloin, White Chapel, and the Great Restricted District. For a while it was referred to as Wappyville, in honor of a chief of police who distinguished himself by the amount of graft he collected there. But the first name, the functional name, has outlasted all the others. When the pioneers rolled logs by hand down to the waterfront, when the ox-teams plodded over the hill dragging logs for Yesler's steam mill, this was the skid road, and it is the Skid Road today. This district south of Yesler Way, this land below the Deadline, has helped fix the word on the American language. The Skid Road: the place of dead dreams.

You see here the things you see on other skid roads in America: men sitting on curbs and sleeping in doorways, doors padlocked for non-payment of rent, condemned buildings, signs that read: "Beds, twenty cents." "Oatmeal, five cents. With sugar, seven cents. With cream, nine cents." "Be Saved by Sister Faye." "A charge of three cents will be made for packages stored more than two days." "Indians who want wine must show documents they are not wards of the government." The *People's World* is sold on the street corners, and secondhand nudist magazines are on sale in cigar stores. There are missions and taverns and wine shops and stores where you can buy a suit for $3.75.

And there are things peculiar to Seattle: a totem pole; cafés with Indian names; a manifesto posted on the wall, which recalls the days when this was a stronghold of the IWW and the One Big Union promised an eight-hour day. "Fellow Workers! Unite for the 4-hour day and the 4-day week. No cut in pay."

Once the people here did find a short cut to riches. From a red-brick hotel down the street, Swiftwater Bill Gates, the Dawson plunger, showered nuggets on the Seattleites who gathered in the streets below. Still earlier Doc Maynard tried to get rich and instead brought wealth to others. Doc was the first of the dreamers along the Skid Road. He was Seattle's first booster, the man who was sure greatness could come; he owned a tract of land worth, city officials guess, a hundred million dollars. Wrapped in his dream of making Seattle grow, he gave it bit by bit to anyone whose presence might help the town expand. Seattle grew, but by the time it was big Maynard was dead and the government had taken most of the property he left to his wife. He died poor, but he was a great man.

This book is the story of Maynard and of the men like him, the ones who weren't quite respectable but helped build the great city of the Northwest. The formal history of Seattle has been written many times over, sometimes well; the sons and daughters of the men who moved north of the Skid Road have lovingly told the story of the folk who dreamed the right dreams at the appropriate times. This is the story of the others, of some who tried and failed and of some who achieved success without becoming respectable, of the life that centered on the mills and on the wharves. That is Seattle from the bottom up.

Nisei Daughter

MONICA SONE

Monica Sone (1919–) was born in the Carrollton Hotel in the Skid Road area of Seattle. As the title Nisei Daughter *(1979) suggests—Nisei meaning second-generation—the work is an autobiographical depiction of what it means to grow up Japanese American. Kazuko's story begins with her comparatively idyllic childhood in Seattle before World War II, the focus of the selection below, and follows her family's life through their internment at Minidoka, a War Relocation Authority camp in Idaho, during the war years.*

A SHOCKING FACT OF LIFE

In January, 1918, their first child was born, Henry Seiichi—son of truth. Shortly after, Father sold his little shop and bought the Carrollton Hotel on Main Street and Occidental Avenue, just a stone's throw from the bustling waterfront and the noisy railroad tracks. It was, in fact, on the very birth site of Seattle when the town began its boisterous growth with the arrival of pioneer Henry Yesler and his sawmill on the waterfront. In its early days, the area south of Yesler Hill, where we lived, was called Skid Road because loggers used to grease the roads at intervals to help the ox teams pull the logs down to the mills. Nearly a hundred years later, the district bore the name Skidrow, a corrupted version of Skid Road, with its shoddy stores, decayed buildings, and shriveled men.

The Carrollton had seen its heyday during the Alaskan gold rush. It was an old-fashioned hotel on the second floor of an old red brick building. It had twenty outside rooms and forty inside ones, arranged in three block formations and separated by long corridors. The hallways and inside rooms were lighted and ventilated by the ceiling skylight windows. During the cold of winter, these inside rooms were theoretically warmed by a pot-bellied stove in the lobby, which was located just at the left of the top stair landing. There was only one bathroom, with a cavernous bathtub, to keep sixty-odd people clean. A separate restroom, FOR GENTS ONLY, eased the bathroom congestion somewhat. For extra service all the rooms were equipped with a gigantic pitcher of water, a mammoth-sized washbowl, and an ornate chamber pot.

When Father took over the hotel in 1918, the building fairly burst with war workers and servicemen. They came at all hours of the day, begging to sleep even in the chairs in the hotel lobby. Extra cots had to be set up in the hallways.

Father and Mother loved to tell us how they had practically rejuvenated the battered, flea-ridden Carrollton by themselves. Father had said firmly, "If I have to manage a flophouse, it'll be the cleanest and quietest place around here." With patience and care, they began to patch the aches and pains of the old hotel. The tobacco-stained stairways were scrubbed, painted and lighted up. Father varnished the floors while Mother painted the woodwork. New green runners were laid out in the corridors. They re-papered the sixty rooms, one by one. Every day after the routine room-servicing had been finished, Mother cooked up a bucket of flour and water and brushed the paste on fresh new wallpaper laid out on a long makeshift work table in the hall.

All the while Father tried to build up a choice selection of customers, for even one drunkard on a binge always meant fist fights and broken furniture. Father quickly found that among the flotsam of seedy, rough-looking characters milling around in Skidrow were men who still retained their dignity and self-respect. There were lonely old men whose families had been broken up by the death of wives and departing children, who lived a sober existence on their meager savings or their monthly pension allotment. Father also took in sea-hardened mariners, shipyard workers, airplane workers, fruit pickers and factory workers. He tried to weed out petty thieves, bootleggers, drug peddlers, perverts, alcoholics and fugitives from the law. At first glance it was hard to tell whether a stubble-bearded, wrinkled, and red-eyed man had just returned from a hard day's work or a hard day at the tavern. Father had a simple technique. If the man smelled of plain, honest-to-goodness perspiration, he was in. But if he reeked of wood alcohol or bay rum, the office window came crashing down in front of his nose.

Shortly after the Armistice of World War I was signed, I was born and appropriately named Kazuko Monica, the Japanese name meaning "peace." (Mother chose Monica from her reading about Saint Augustine and his mother, Saint Monica.) Two years later Kenji William arrived, his name meaning "Healthy in body and spirit." Mother added "William" because she thought it sounded poetic. And two years after that, Sumiko, "the clear one," was born.

. . .

So we lived in the old Carrollton. Every day, amidst the bedlam created by four black-eyed, jet-propelled children, Father and Mother took care of the hotel. Every morning they went from room to room, making the beds and cleaning up. To help speed up the chores, we ran up and down the corridors, pounding on doors. We brutally woke the late sleepers, hammering with our fists and yelling, "Wake up, you sleepyhead! Wake up, make bed!" Then someone would think of pushing the linen cart for Father and the rest of us would rush to do the same. We usually ended up in a violent tussle. One of our favorite games, when neither Father nor Mother was looking, was "climbing the laundry." We vied with each other to see who could climb highest on an ill-smelling mountain of soiled sheets, pillowcases and damp towels, piled high to the ceiling. Henry always reached the top by giving himself a running start halfway down the hall. He flew light-footed up the mound like a young gazelle. He hooted scornfully when I scrambled up, red faced and frantic, grabbing at the sheets and tumbling down when I snatched a loose pillowcase. Kenji and Sumiko squealed happily at the foot of the linen pile and slapped each other with the sopping wet towels. Whenever Mother discovered us, she shrieked in dismay, "*Kita-nai, mah, kita-nai koto!* It's dirty and full of germs. Get right out of there!"

Yes, life to us children was a wonderful treat—especially during hot summer nights when Father slipped out to a market stand down the block and surprised us with an enormous, ice-cold watermelon. It was pure joy when we first bit into its crisp pink succulence and let the juice trickle and seeds fall on old newspapers spread on the round table in the parlor. Or sometimes on a wintry evening, we crowded around the kitchen table to watch Father, bath towel–apron draped around his waist, whip up a batch of raisin cookies for us. It wasn't everybody's father who could turn out thick, melting, golden cookies. We were especially proud that our father had once worked as a cook on romantic Alaska-bound freighters.

Life was hilarious whenever Mother played *Jan-ken-pon! Ai-kono-hoi!* with us. This was the game played by throwing out paper, scissors, and rock symbols with our hands, accompanied by the chant. The winner with the stronger symbol had the privilege of slapping the loser's wrist with two fingers. Mother pretended to cry whenever our small fingers came down on her wrist. With her oval face, lively almond-shaped eyes, and slender aquiline nose, Mother was a pretty, slender five feet of youth and fun.

I thought the whole world consisted of two or three old hotels on every block. And that its population consisted of families like mine who lived in a corner of the hotels. And its other inhabitants were customers— fading, balding, watery-eyed men, rough-tough bearded men, and good men like Sam, Joe, Peter and Montana who worked for Father, all of whom lived in these hotels.

It was a very exciting world in which I lived.

I played games with a little girl I liked, Matsuko, who lived in Adams Hotel, two blocks away. Sometimes Henry and his friends Dunks and Jiro joined us to explore dingy alleys behind produce warehouses, looking for discarded jars of candies. Sometimes we fished from Pier Two, dipping a long string with bread tied to its end in the briny, moldy green water. It was pleasant to sit on the sun-warmed old timber which creaked with the waves, and bask in the mellow sun, waiting for the shiners to nibble.

Our street itself was a compact little world, teeming with the bustle of every kind of business in existence in Skidrow. Right below our living quarters was a large second-hand clothing store. It was guarded by a thin, hunchbacked, gray woolly-bearded man who sat napping on a little stool at the entrance. Its dust-misted windows were crammed with army and navy surplus clothes, blanket bathrobes, glistening black raincoats, stiff lumber jackets which practically stood up by themselves and a tangled heap of bootery from romeo house slippers to hip-length fishing boots. Oddly, the shop was very susceptible to fire, and every now and then smoke would seep up through our bedroom floor boards and we would hear fire engines thundering down our street. After each such uproar, the old man would put up huge, red-lettered signs: MAMMOTH FIRE SALE . . . PRAC-TICALLY A GIVEAWAY!

Next to the clothing store was the tavern, the forbidden hall of iniq-uity, around which we were not supposed to loiter. The swinging door was sawed off at the bottom, but with our heads hanging down we man-aged to get an upside down view of it. All we could see were feet stuck to brass rails. A nickelodeon played only one song, day in and day out, a melancholy, hillbilly tune of which we could make out just one phrase. "When they cut down that old pine tree . . ." It was drowned out by the heaven-splitting songs from the mission hall next door, which was filled with hollow-eyed, graying old men, sitting impassively with battered hats balanced on their knees.

Next to our hotel entrance, Mr. Wakamatsu operated the Ace Café. We liked him, because he was such a tall, pleasant-mannered, handsome man. He had a beautiful clear tenor voice which floated out into the alley up to our kitchen as he called out, "Veal, French fries on the side . . . !" Mr. Wakamatsu's window display was always a splendid sight to see. There would be a neat row of purple strawberry shortcakes, or a row of apple pies shining with the luster of shellac, or a row of rigid, blood-red gela-tin puddings planted squarely in the center of thick white saucers.

Next to the Ace Café was Dunks's father's small barbershop. Then was the little white-painted hot-dog stand where we bought luscious hot dogs and hamburgers smothered with onions and the hottest of chili sauce which brought tears brimming to our eyes. The hot-dog man was con-stantly swatting flies on the meat board, and I hate to think how many mashed flies were in the red ground meat.

Then came another forbidden place, the burlesque house. A brunet-haired woman with carefully powdered wrinkles sat in the ticket booth, chewing gum. She always winked a shiny purple eyelid at us whenever we passed, and we never knew for sure whether we should smile back at her or not. The theater marquee was studded with dingy yellow light bulbs, spelling out the "Rialto," and the doors were covered with the life-size paintings of half-naked girls, about to step out from behind feathers, balloons and chiffon scarves.

On the corner of Occidental and Washington Street stood a small cigar shop. We were sure that the storekeeper, who constantly rattled dice in a dirty leather cylinder box, had been a big-time gambler in the past. He was just the type, with his baggy eyes, cigar stuffed in his mouth, and his fingers covered with massive jeweled rings.

Just around the corner was a teamsters' union office. Hairy-armed, open-shirted, tattooed men clomped continually in and out of the smoke-filled room. Twice a day, a man hustled out of there carrying a wooden cratebox. He beckoned to the men loafing on the corner to gather near and listen to what he had to say. We stood watching on tiptoes at the fringe of the crowd until the orating man had worked himself into a passion, alternatingly purring at and berating his apathetic audience.

"... tell me, my friends, what the hell are you anyway ... men or beasts? To the goddamned capitalist, you're nothin' but beasts! Are you going to grovel under their feet the rest of your life? CRUMBS! That's all they give you ... CRUMBS! Are you going to be satisfied with that? I say 'NO!' None of that for us anymore. We have to break them now ... now!"

"Hallelujah," someone would respond dryly.

Across on the opposite corner there was another small crowd, gawking at a man with flowing, silver-white hair and full beard. Tears would be rolling down his uplifted face and disappear into his beard as he pleaded with his audience to "repent before it is too late." Listening to him, I always felt the urgency to repent before it was too late, but I was never sure which of my sins was worth confessing.

The Salvation Army was always there, marching along the street, keeping in time with the brass drum. Wheeling expertly into semicircle formation near the curb, the uniformed men and women would lift their bugles and trumpets and blare out a vigorous hymn. When the tambourine was passed around for our offering, we would move on guiltily, having already spent our nickels for hot dogs.

This was the playground where I roamed freely and happily. And when I finally started grammar school, I found still another enchanting world. Every morning I hurried to Adams Hotel, climbed its dark flight of stairs, and called for Matsuko. Together we made the long and fascinating journey—from First Avenue to Twelfth Avenue—to Bailey Gatzert School. We always walked over the bridge on Fourth Avenue where we hung over the iron rails, waiting until a train roared past under us, enveloping us completely in its hissing, billowing cloud of white, warm steam. We meandered through the international section of town, past the small Japanese shops and stores, already bustling in the early morning hour, past the cafés and barber shops filled with Filipino men, and through Chinatown. Then finally we went up a gentle sloping hill to the handsome low-slung, red-brick building with its velvet green lawn and huge play yard. I felt like a princess walking through its bright, sunny corridors on smooth, shiny floors. I was mystified by a few of the little boys and girls. There were some pale-looking children who spoke a strange dialect of English, rapidly like gunfire. Matsuko told me they were *"hagu-jins,"* white people. Then there were children who looked very much like me with their black hair and black eyes, but they spoke in high, musical singing voices. Matsuko whispered to me that they were Chinese.

And now Mother was telling us we were Japanese. I had always thought I was a Yankee, because after all I had been born on Occidental and Main Street. Montana, a wall-shaking mountain of a man who lived at our hotel, called me a Yankee. I didn't see how I could be a Yankee and Japanese at the same time. It was like being born with two heads. It sounded freakish and a lot of trouble. Above everything, I didn't want to go to Japanese school.

No-No Boy

JOHN OKADA

John Okada (1924–1971) was born in Seattle near Pioneer Square. He graduated from Broadway High and the University of Washington and later earned a master's degree at Columbia University. As a Nisei, *or second-generation Japanese American, Okada faced the questions put to every male of Japanese descent during World War II in the U.S. Selective Service questionnaire: Was he willing to serve the United States? And was he willing to forswear allegiance to the Japanese emperor? Those answering negatively to both questions were called "no-no boys" by fellow Japanese Americans. Unlike the protagonist in his novel* No-No Boy *(1957; 1979), Okada answered yes to these questions, was inducted into the Army Air Corps, and served in the Pacific theater. After President Franklin D. Roosevelt's 1942 signing of Executive Order 9066, Okada's family, like more than 120,000 other Japanese Americans, were interned at a War Relocation Authority camp. After Okada was discharged from the Army, he returned to Seattle, married, and had two children. During this time Okada worked at the Seattle Public Library and wrote his sole published novel,* No-No Boy, *which was poorly received by both the Asian-American community and the general American reading public, each of which for its own reasons was unready to read Okada's story at the time it first appeared. In the novel, the protagonist Ichiro is deeply ambivalent about his community and his country.*

Two weeks after his twenty-fifth birthday, Ichiro got off a bus at Second and Main in Seattle. He had been gone four years, two in camp and two in prison.

Walking down the street that autumn morning with a small, black suitcase, he felt like an intruder in a world to which he had no claim. It was just enough that he should feel this way, for, of his own free will, he had stood before the judge and said that he would not go in the army. At the time there was no other choice for him. That was when he was twenty-three, a man of twenty-three. Now, two years older, he was even more of a man.

Christ, he thought to himself, just a goddamn kid is all I was. Didn't know enough to wipe my own nose. What the hell have I done? What am I doing back here? Best thing I can do would be to kill some son of a bitch and head back to prison.

He walked toward the railroad depot where the tower with the clocks on all four sides was. It was a dirty looking tower of ancient brick. It was a dirty city. Dirtier, certainly, than it had a right to be after only four years.

Waiting for the light to change to green, he looked around at the people standing at the bus stop. A couple of men in suits, half a dozen women who failed to arouse him even after prolonged good behavior, and a young Japanese with a lunch bucket. Ichiro studied him, searching in his mind for the name that went with the round, pimply face and the short-cropped hair. The pimples were gone and the face had hardened, but the hair was still cropped. The fellow wore green, army-fatigue trousers and an Eisenhower jacket—Eto Minato. The name came to him at the same time as did the horrible significance of the army clothes. In panic, he started to step off the curb. It was too late. He had been seen.

"Itchy!" That was his nickname.

Trying to escape, Ichiro urged his legs frenziedly across the street.

"Hey, Itchy!" The caller's footsteps ran toward him.

An arm was placed across his back. Ichiro stopped and faced the other Japanese. He tried to smile, but could not. There was no way out now.

"I'm Eto. Remember?" Eto smiled and extended his palm. Reluctantly, Ichiro lifted his own hand and let the other shake it.

The round face with the round eyes peered at him through silver-rimmed spectacles. "What the hell! It's been a long time, but not that long. How've you been? What's doing?"

"Well . . . that is, I'm . . ."

"Last time must have been before Pearl Harbor. God, it's been quite a while, hasn't it? Three, no, closer to four years, I guess. Lotsa Japs coming back to the Coast. Lotsa Japs in Seattle. You'll see 'em around. Japs are funny that way. Gotta have their rice and saké and other Japs. Stupid, I say. The smart ones went to Chicago and New York and lotsa places back east, but there's still plenty coming back out this way." Eto drew cigarettes from his breast pocket and held out the package. "No? Well, I'll have one. Got the habit in the army. Just got out a short while back. Rough time, but I made it. Didn't get out in time to make the quarter, but I'm planning to go to school. How long you been around?"

Ichiro touched his toe to the suitcase. "Just got in. Haven't been home yet."

"When'd you get discharged?"

A car grinding its gears started down the street. He wished he were in it. "I . . . that is . . . I never was in."

Eto slapped him good-naturedly on the arm. "No need to look so sour. So you weren't in. So what? Been in camp all this time?"

"No." He made an effort to be free of Eto with his questions. He felt as if he were in a small room whose walls were slowly closing in on him. "It's been a long time, I know, but I'm really anxious to see the folks."

"What the hell. Let's have a drink. On me. I don't give a damn if I'm late to work. As for your folks, you'll see them soon enough. You drink, don't you?"

"Yeah, but not now."

"Ahh." Eto was disappointed. He shifted his lunch box from under one arm to the other.

"I've really got to be going."

The round face wasn't smiling any more. It was thoughtful. The eyes confronted Ichiro with indecision which changed slowly to enlightenment and then to suspicion. He remembered. He knew.

The friendliness was gone as he said: "No-no boy, huh?"

Ichiro wanted to say yes. He wanted to return the look of despising hatred and say simply yes, but it was too much to say. The walls had closed in and were crushing all the unspoken words back down into his stomach. He shook his head once, not wanting to evade the eyes but finding it impossible to meet them. Out of his big weakness the little ones were branching, and the eyes he didn't have the courage to face were ever present. If it would have helped to gouge out his own eyes, he would have done so long ago. The hate-churned eyes with the stamp of unrelenting condemnation were his cross and he had driven the nails with his own hands.

"Rotten bastard. Shit on you." Eto coughed up a mouthful of sputum and rolled his words around it: "Rotten, no-good bastard."

Surprisingly, Ichiro felt relieved. Eto's anger seemed to serve as a release to his own naked tensions. As he stooped to lift the suitcase a wet wad splattered over his hand and dripped onto the black leather. The legs of his accuser were in front of him. God in a pair of green fatigues, U.S. Army style. They were the legs of the jury that had passed sentence upon him. Beseech me, they seemed to say, throw your arms about me and bury your head between my knees and seek pardon for your great sin.

"I'll piss on you next time," said Eto vehemently.

He turned as he lifted the suitcase off the ground and hurried away from the legs and the eyes from which no escape was possible.

Jackson Street started at the waterfront and stretched past the two train depots and up the hill all the way to the lake, where the houses were bigger and cleaner and had garages with late-model cars in them. For Ichiro, Jackson Street signified that section of the city immediately beyond the railroad tracks between Fifth and Twelfth Avenues. That was the section which used to be pretty much Japanese town. It was adjacent to Chinatown and most of the gambling and prostitution and drinking seemed to favor the area.

Like the dirty clock tower of the depot, the filth of Jackson Street had increased. Ichiro paused momentarily at an alley and peered down the passage formed by the walls of two sagging buildings. There had been a door there at one time, a back door to a movie house which only charged a nickel. A nickel was a lot of money when he had been seven or nine or eleven. He wanted to go into the alley to see if the door was still there.

Being on Jackson Street with its familiar store fronts and taverns and restaurants, which were somehow different because the war had left its mark on them, was like trying to find one's way out of a dream that seemed real most of the time but wasn't really real because it was still only a dream. The war had wrought violent changes upon the people, and the people, in turn, working hard and living hard and earning a lot of money and spending it on whatever was available, had distorted the profile of Jackson Street. The street had about it the air of a carnival without quite succeeding at becoming one. A shooting gallery stood where once had been a clothing store; fish and chips had replaced a jewelry shop; and a bunch of Negroes were horsing around raucously in front of a pool parlor. Everything looked older and dirtier and shabbier.

He walked past the pool parlor, picking his way gingerly among the Negroes, of whom there had been only a few at one time and of whom there seemed to be nothing but now. They were smoking and shouting and cussing and carousing and the sidewalk was slimy with their spittle.

"Jap!"

His pace quickened automatically, but curiosity or fear or indignation or whatever it was made him glance back at the white teeth framed in a leering dark brown which was almost black.

"Go back to Tokyo, boy." Persecution in the drawl of the persecuted.

The white teeth and brown-black leers picked up the cue and jigged to the rhythmical chanting of "Jap-boy. To-ki-yo; Jap-boy, To-ki-yo . . ."

Friggin' niggers, he uttered savagely to himself and, from the same place deep down inside where tolerance for the Negroes and the Jews and the Mexicans and the Chinese and the too short and too fat and too ugly abided because he was Japanese and knew what it was like better than did those who were white and average and middle class and good Democrats or liberal Republicans, the hate which was unrelenting and terrifying seethed up.

Then he was home. It was a hole in the wall with groceries crammed in orderly confusion on not enough shelving, into not enough space. He knew what it would be like even before he stepped in. His father had described the place to him in a letter, composed in simple Japanese characters because otherwise Ichiro could not have read it. The letter had been purposely repetitive and painstakingly detailed so that Ichiro should not have any difficulty finding the place. The grocery store was the same one the Ozakis had operated for many years. That's all his father had had to say. Come to the grocery store which was once the store of the Ozakis. The Japanese characters, written simply so that he could read them, covered pages of directions as if he were a foreigner coming to the city for the first time.

Seattle, Past to Present

ROGER SALE

Roger Sale (1932–) was born in New Haven, Connecticut. He graduated from Swarthmore College in 1953 and from Cornell University with an M.A. in 1954 and a Ph.D. in 1957. He has been a professor of English at the University of Washington since 1960 and has written many articles and reviews for periodicals, including the New York Review of Books, *the* New York Times Book Review, *the* Hudson Review, *the* New Republic, *the* Antioch Review, *and the* Seattle Post-Intelligencer. *In addition to publishing widely on English literature, he has published two works about Seattle:* Seattle, Past to Present *(1976) and* Seeing Seattle *(1994). In this selection from* Seattle, Past to Present, *Sale reflects on the theme of Seattle's perceived shortcomings and great potential.*

A t the end of *Northwest Gateway,* Archie Binns sounds the uneasy note that is also played at the end of almost every other good piece of writing about Seattle:

> The city offers great opportunity for the enjoyment of life, with its lovely summers and mild winters, its surrounding mountains and forests, and its infinite variety of salt water and fresh, and water and land interpenetrating. Seattle people enjoy life as much as they can, and more than most people, but some ingredient is missing, or there is too much of too many things, and life falls short of its possibilities. There is so much loveliness, and so little peace and security for enjoyment.

Murray Morgan says much the same thing, as do Nancy Wilson Ross and Constance McL. Green. I know no one, native or newcomer, who has not been touched deeply by Seattle who has not felt this sense of life falling short of its possibilities even as there is so much that is enjoyed.

Bourgeois from its first breath, Seattle has had to struggle with finding out what that means. For a long time it has meant rich possibilities for private life: homes, gardens, recreation, feasts for the eyes and the fingertips, all enhanced by those lovely summers and mild winters. Only slightly more recently it has meant ways of letting business and labor live in relative harmony with each other. More recently it has meant possibilities for the shared urban experience of good commercial streets and centers, crowds, places where the sights are people as well as forests, mountains, and water. If the sixties and early seventies of this century were a crisis like the years of World War I, it can be said that now there is less mistrust and more sense of possibility than there was then. In yesterday's *Seattle Times,* on a single page, were stories of François Kissel's newly opened City Loan Pavilion restaurant, of turnaway crowds every night at Shelley's Leg discotheque and gay bar, of Shorey's antiquarian book store getting a new lease on life as it moves to larger quarters at First and Union. One simply cannot overlook these things, or underrate their potential importance.

The one major virtue of a city like Seattle that is apt to go unstated or be played down in the usual summing up is the energy created by its other virtues. One reason for this, surely, is the prolonged reaction against the city boosters who once lauded the Seattle Spirit as though it were something that could be bottled and sold as insurance against any future: just remember the Mercer Girls, the May Day picnic of 1874 that laid the first Seattle and Walla Walla track, just remember the fire or the Alaska Gold Rush. But all that sense of spirit has gone either into faint nostalgia or into the less interesting or laudable desire to become a big league city. More enduring and interesting is what one feels in the making of the Cornish School, or Yesler Terrace, or the Metro plants, Group Health, the Market initiative, the revitalized Pioneer Square. One can go back before any of these and point to the original founding of the university, to the creation of the still lovely park and boulevard system, to R. H. Thomson's regrades. All these are public actions of private citizens either ignoring government or making it suit their immediate needs. All these seem the result of people working from a sense of possibility, or occasionally alarm, generated by their sense of satisfaction with what they already have. Hope seems liveliest in Seattle when based on people feeling, first individually and then collectively, the riches and content of their past.

But these all are spurts of energy, and so they tend to die rather quickly. As a result, most of what has been done best in Seattle has been that which could be done rather quickly, in a year or a few years rather than over a long period of time. When energies lapse, often little is left to take their place until they rise again. Seattle is not a place that builds enduring structures. It has very little hierarchical sense of its society or of its land. It has consistently refused to organize itself into political parties, and has as a result saddled itself with a ridiculous tax structure and a generally weak government. Its response to ethnic diversity has been to seek homogeneity rather than structures of diverse groups. Its sense of neighborhood is fluid rather than organized, and its neighborhood organizations, like most of its public commitments and achievements, tend to be ad hoc rather than permanent. It has large public rituals, like hydroplane races and Husky football and summertime in Seattle Center, where strangers meet, but it has very little in the way of street or neighborhood rituals where acquaintances and friends renew their common experience.

All this would be more alarming but for the persistence of the fact of the energies, spurting here and lapsing there, throughout the city's history. If there are insufficient structures to create solutions to nagging problems, like the public schools and the ghetto, there have been enough created by one spurt or another that have endured to make the city demonstrably a fuller place as time goes on. It would take only one such spurt, for instance, to bring down the Alaskan Way viaduct and re-create the land between First Avenue and the waterfront, and once it was done it would be done, as Metro's cleanup of the lake was done, as the parks and boulevards were done. All, or almost all, that was best in Seattle's past is still here, and can remain indefinitely. Its very lack of structures means that while it can lapse into quiet fairly easily, it probably will remain resistant to demagogues or other violent forces capable of really doing permanent harm. "Seattle is a success," wrote Murray Morgan twenty-five years ago at the end of *Skid Road*, "but the city has yet to achieve the assurance of success." That may still be true, but it is much less so than it was in 1950, and this is a process which will continue, if only in the fits, starts, and fallings off that are Seattle's characteristic way of getting things done.

. . .

In 1917, when the Hiram Chittenden Locks were opened to connect Lake Union and Puget Sound, all the freshwater lakes and bays were lowered by as much as twenty feet. Union Bay, which extended west from Lake Washington, became partly a marsh, near the university arboretum on its south end and to the east of the university campus on its north end. Within a few years the marsh had developed its own ecological system of cattails, blackbirds, beavers, and ducks. Someone coming new to Seattle in the mid-1920s might imagine the marsh had always been there, the creation of nature only.

Later the city and the university, which owned the land on the north end of the bay, worked out an agreement whereby the city could use that part of the marsh as a dump. When the land was full, the university would regain possession. At the extreme north end of the marsh a viaduct was built down Northeast 45th Street and, on land once owned by a Japanese truck farmer, a shopping center was built (rumor has it the land was confiscated when the truck farmer was incarcerated during the war). Then, in the late 1950s, a second bridge was built across Lake Washington and its road was extended westward across Foster's Island and the south end of the Union Bay marsh, through a tip of Montlake, on across Portage Bay and up to Capitol Hill, where it joined the I-5 freeway. Unfinished extensions south from that bridge were to connect with another expressway, the R. H. Thomson, which was planned to come down from the north end and go either over or under Union Bay. Shortly thereafter the Army Corps of Engineers and the Seattle Garden Club built a trail extending through the marsh from Foster's Island to the Montlake Cut just across from Husky Stadium. Meanwhile the university began building on its filled-in land: new tennis courts, an enormous parking lot, a series of athletic fields, a golf driving range, a group of buildings in which the Art Department could teach ceramics.

It may seem that here, as with so many other places where people got busy in the 1950s and early 1960s, that God had proposed well and man had disposed badly. But no. However it acquired its land, University Village became the finest shopping center in the city. The new courts, driving range, and playing fields became part of an admirable renewed awareness that one doesn't have to be on an intercollegiate team to play hard or stay in shape. The University Canal House, on the edge of Union Bay, rents canoes, and from there one can take trips, often in astonishing quiet, to both ends of the marsh. The marsh walk itself is a wonder. Many of its clients are joggers and cyclists going past signs saying NO JOGGING OR CYCLING. They and the others get a chance to see what no one on foot could know about before, the endless subtle shifts in the marsh life as the seasons and weather change. Finally, though the R. H. Thomson expressway was scrapped during the antifreeway activity of the early seventies, the unfinished extensions remain, and from them kids dive into the water at the north end of the arboretum. Part of the deliciousness of this irony is that the kids are a scruffy lot indeed, youth with a vengeance, given to drink to make them rowdy, drugs to make them unresponsive, and to wearing no clothes.

Top to bottom, this sequence is one of the finest things in Seattle, and one of the city's most characteristic expressions of itself. Nature created, to be intruded upon and then to change and endure, needing both itself and the intruders to mix into a landscape of wonderful and incongruous variety. It is good enough as it is, but, like almost everything else vital in a city, it becomes more absorbing and more poignant as its history is known and understood. The sight of cliff swallows nesting underneath the freeway is enough by itself to convince one of the inscrutable fascinations of time passing, tempting the curiosity, rebuking the doctrinaire conclusion, yielding an enduring sense that the urban creations of land and labor are among the most wonderful things we can know.

Digressions of a Native Son

EMMETT WATSON

Emmett Watson (1918–2001) was the consummate Seattle chronicler. Born and reared in Seattle, he began writing for the Seattle Star *in 1944. In 1946, he went to work for the* Seattle Times *and four years later began his thirty-three-year stint as an item columnist for the* Seattle Post-Intelligencer. *In 1983, he returned to writing for the* Seattle Times. *Watson made an art of hammering out 1,500 words a day about Seattle. He often promoted his semi-serious movement Lesser Seattle in his column as a way of discouraging people from moving to Seattle after it was designated the nation's most livable city in 1979. In 1982, Watson published a memoir,* Digressions of a Native Son, *followed by two collections of his columns,* Once Upon a Time in Seattle *(1992) and* My Life in Print *(1993). Never sentimental about a topic, Watson was always true to his observations and opinions. His style is clear and unpretentious, amused and self-effacing, informed and perceptive. Rarely one to use superlatives when discussing Seattle, he always maintained that the city was simply "a pretty good place to live." Emmett Watson is often at his best when writing about Seattle's people, as in the following excerpt from* Digressions of a Native Son.*

By his own reckoning, Rudi weighed seven stone eleven and stood nineteen hands high; certainly he was huge. He was bearded, burly and strong, and he had a deep, rich voice that sometimes shook the receiver when you picked up the telephone. He looked the way Paul Bunyan pictures did in my primary school books. To me, Rudi was the quintessential Seattleite.

Rudi Becker loved the salt air, Puget Sound, and the city which bred him. He was born in the Zindorf Apartments up at Seventh and James, one of those old buildings that barely escaped annihilation by the downtown freeway. Rudi knew every back alley, crevice, side street, offbeat place in the city. His father had worked as a waiter and maitre d' in most of the city's once-famous restaurants, places like Manca's, Chauncey Wright's, Blanc's and the Rathskeller—all of them gone, long gone. Rudi himself was many things. He was a tugboat skipper, a camp counselor, a contractor and builder, and for ten years he ran Harbor Tours on the waterfront. His friends were rich, big, small, poor, ordinary and often nutty. He liked newspaper guys and that was why he kept phoning in news items and ideas for my column.

These were not stories that would help him at all. He phoned in stuff about other people—a nice bartender, a business friend, a waitress down on her luck, a kid who needed help, or a cause worth mentioning. It went on, weeks and months, of almost daily phone calls from Rudi. Everywhere I went, people would say, "Hey, I saw that blurb in your column about the waterfront. You've been talking to Rudi again." Finally I couldn't stand it anymore, so I invited Rudi to lunch. "I'll pick you up," he said. He arrived in a six-year-old pickup truck; he was wearing a plaid shirt, boots and he had a drink in his hand. In this truck he had a glass holder, the kind that tilts, the kind they use on boats.

We settled in down at Ivar's and I asked him, "Why the hell do you do all this, all this phoning stuff?" "I like to have a part in getting other people's stories in print," he said. "Maybe I'm a frustrated journalist. It must have started when I was a kid and got run over by a *P-I* delivery truck."

We became friends that day. Whenever I think of Rudi I remember Auntie Mame's great line, "Life is a feast, and most poor sons of bitches are starving to death!" Rudi said it differently: "It's a wonderful world, and anybody who doesn't like this life is crazy." And to Rudi Becker, the world was a wonderful place. He lived a sort of roaming life of fulfillment (God knows when he worked; he supported himself with some kind of siding and pre-fab business) in the back alleys and side streets of Seattle.

He knew where to get things fixed, where to find a left-handed monkey wrench, how to get a friend out of jail; he knew the tides, the weather, the texture and the feel of the city. Ivar Haglund called him "some kind of genius. It was not that he knew so much about a little, but that he knew so much about so many things."

He was the "honorary mayor" of Carkeek Park, where he lived with his wife, Kay. Their home was a crazy, lovely hodgepodge of nautical collectibles, and it included many things Rudi had hand-crafted himself. But he was, even in his advancing age, a child of the streets—of the waterfront, the bars, the boats and the beaches. He roamed everywhere, missing nothing, lusting for precious fragments of joy the way some men collect jade, roaring with laughter at his own mischievous pranks.

Thus the phone would ring: "This is Rudi. I'm down here under the viaduct and some guy has scrawled a message on a pillar. It says, 'Joshua Green uses Medicare.' See ya later." One of Rudi's hobbies, if you can call it that, was what he called "giving people the mental hotfoot." He said he just "did things that were fun," but in his case, "fun" was a flexible word. He despised loud discourtesies, any form of boorish behavior, and his particular objects of scorn were people who impatiently honk horns behind you the instant a traffic light changes.

In one case, Rudi found himself stuck on the Ballard Bridge as cars lined up to await the passage of a boat. When the drawbridge barrier was lifted, one of the Unspeakables behind Rudi laid heavy on the horn. Calmly, Rudi (remember, he was seven stone eleven and stood nineteen hands) got out of his car and walked back to the honker's car. He deftly raised the fellow's hood, reached in and methodically ripped off the wires that connected the horn. Then he walked back to the spluttering driver. Towering above the honker he announced pleasantly: "There. Your horn was stuck, but now it's all fixed."

He had another method of enforcing courtesy among horn-honkers. Rudi used to drive a Packard convertible and this he equipped with a huge, old-fashioned blunderbuss, a fearsome looking weapon. Somehow he rigged it up to a very loud air horn. Not long after, at a downtown intersection, an impatient fellow in a top-down convertible behind, let go an angry blast at Rudi just as the light turned green. Rudi stood up in his own convertible. He reached down and picked up the gun. Deliberately and carefully, he held the gun high, squinted along the sights, then brought it slowly, methodically to dead aim on the horn-honker's chest.

The victim, of course, recoiled against his seat, a look of uncomprehending horror on his face. Then Rudi pulled the trigger. What resulted— a great loud air horn blast—shook up pedestrians for blocks. Rudi calmly sat down, put his car in gear, and drove off—leaving the poor wretch in a pallid state of near seizure. "Some people have to be taught to be nice to other people," he said later.

Most of Rudi's practical jokes had a message. Like many of us, he wearied of prattle about the "sportsmanship" and "responsibility" of experienced hunters. Scraping up a deer's head and hide (he knew exactly where to find them), he set out to prove a point. On the night before hunting season opened, he drove out along the highway, from which it is patently illegal to shoot at anything. Inside his deer head and hide he inserted the huge blade of an obsolete circular saw. At dawn, Rudi placed himself safely away from what he knew would be a line of fire. What followed was little short of carnage. "I damned near caused traffic accidents," he recalled. "Cars would screech to a stop and guys would jump out and start firing. Every clean shot let off a loud, metallic 'ping!' I counted fifteen bullet marks in that saw. Let 'em tell me about sportsmanship."

He once spread some Sea Dye along downtown Second Ave., and this being Seattle, he did not have to wait long for rain. Rudi happily watched the amazed faces around him as Second Ave. was transformed into a bright, glorious green. He used to carry raisins in a jar of soda water because he discovered that raisins, for some reason, move up and down in soda water.

"These," he would announce in a bar, or to some passerby on the street, "are very rare Chinese diving oysters. You see, the thing about Chinese diving oysters is that they feed by raising up and down in the water, collecting plankton." To his pleasure, he found a brisk market in selling Chinese diving oysters, charging what the traffic would bear. "It's funny," he reflected, "but I sure filled up a lot of Milk Fund bottles."

Back in 1976, Rudi said he would be checking into a hospital. We didn't hear from him for a few days so Carol Barnard, the column's curator and den mother, checked in at Rudi's house to see how he was doing. "Rudi

Part 2. Many Voices (1980s–1990s)

Still Life with Woodpecker

TOM ROBBINS

Tom Robbins (1936–)was born in Blowing Rock, North Carolina, but left the South and made his way to the Pacific Northwest, as he has said, to escape the conservatism of his family. He now lives in La Conner, Washington. His fiction is marked by humor, imagination, and brilliant irreverence seemingly dedicated to making the most of the freedom the author has found in the Pacific Northwest. Besides Still Life with Woodpecker *(1980), he is the author of eight other novels, at least five of which are better, in his opinion, than* Still Life With Woodpecker. *They include* Another Roadside Attraction *(1971),* Even Cowgirls Get the Blues *(1976),* Jitterbug Perfume *(1984),* Skinny Legs and All *(1990),* Half Asleep in Frog Pajamas *(1994),* Fierce Invalids Home from Hot Climates *(2000), and* Villa Incognita *(2003). These works typically involve extraordinary characters influenced by powerful ideas and circumscribed by highly convoluted plots. The following selection, from* Still Life with Woodpecker, *emerges from a plot as thick, and thus undistillable here, as the profusion of blackberry vines the author imagines as smothering the city of Seattle.*

Blackberries.
Nothing, not mushrooms, not ferns, not moss, not melancholy, nothing grew more vigorously, more intractably in the Puget Sound rains than blackberries. Farmers had to bulldoze them out of their fields. Homeowners dug and chopped, and still they came. Park attendants with flame

throwers held them off at the gates. Even downtown, a lot left untended for a season would be overgrown. In the wet months, blackberries spread so wildly, so rapidly that dogs and small children were sometimes engulfed and never heard from again. In the peak of the season, even adults dared not go berry picking without a military escort. Blackberry vines pushed up through solid concrete, forced their way into polite society, entwined the legs of virgins, and tried to loop themselves over passing clouds. The aggression, speed, roughness, and nervy upward mobility of blackberries symbolized for Max and Tilli everything they disliked about America, especially its frontier.

Bernard Mickey Wrangle took a yum approach.

To the King, during tea, Bernard had advocated the planting of blackberries on every building top in Seattle. They would require no care, aside from encouraging them, arborlike, to crisscross the streets, roof to roof; to arch, forming canopies, natural arcades, as it were. In no time at all, people could walk through the city in the downpouringest of winter and feel not a splat. Every shopper, every theater-goer, every cop on the beat, every snoozing bum would be snug and dry. The pale green illumination that filtered through the dome of vines could inspire a whole new school of painting: centuries from now, art critics might speak, as of chiaroscuro, of "blackberry light." The vines would attract birds. Woodpeckers might not bother, but many birds would. The birds would sing. A bird full of berry pulp is like an Italian full of pathos. Small animals might move into the arches. "Look, Billy, up there, over the Dental Building. A badger!" And the fruit, mustn't forget the fruit. It would nourish the hungry, stabilize the poor. The more enterprising winos could distill their own spirits. Seattle could become the Blackberry Brandy Capital of the World. Tourists would spend millions annually on Seattle blackberry pies, the discerning toast of the nation would demand to be spread with Seattle blackberry jam. The chefs at the French restaurants would dish up duck in purplish sauces, fill once rained-on noses with the baking aromas of *gâteau mûre de ronce*. The whores might become known, affectionately, as blackberry tarts. The Teamsters could try to organize the berry pickers. And in late summer, when the brambles were proliferating madly, growing faster than the human eye can see, the energy of their furious growth could be hooked up to generators that, spinning with blackberry power, could supply electrical current for the entire metropolis. A vegetative utopia, that's what it would be. Seattle, Berry Town, encapsulated, self-sufficient, thriving under a living ceiling, blossoms in its hair, juice on its chin, more blackberries—and more!—in its future. Consider the protection offered. What enemy paratroopers could get through the briars?

The King's heart had rattled like spook chains in a horror show. Trembling, he had changed the subject to basketball.

"Oh-Oh, spaghetti-o," muttered Tilli under her breath.

Had the ink remained upright in its bottle, had the carpet's innocence been preserved, it was still doubtful if Bernard would have been invited back to the palace.

Now, following Chihuahua slaughter and publicized arrest, it was futile for Leigh-Cheri to expect sympathy from her parents, let alone help. She wept against Gulietta's bricklike breasts. And when the tear barrel was finally empty and every available frog had been consulted, she made-up, dressed-up, and caught a bus into town. She was going to keep an appointment with Bernard's attorney. She was embracing the blackberry as her emblem, her symbol, her exemplar, her muse. In other words, she would persist to the wildest lengths of persistence. She was going to blackberry her way to her man.

The suburban bus let her off on First Avenue, a street as old as the city itself, though far younger than the tawdry commerce that for many Seattleites the very name of the street implied. A slim, steady rain was falling. Neon reflections on the wet concrete gave First Avenue the appearance of an underwater burial ground for parrots. As Leigh-Cheri walked south, the mood of the avenue grew increasingly rowdy. Mouth holes of saxophones and pistols gaped at her from pawnshop windows. "Adult" bookstores and porno cinemas promised further gapings. Smells of stale hot dogs and soaked mackinaws wafted by on zephyrs of exhaust. If she had drunk just one beer in each of the taverns she passed, she could have consumed a case in a very few blocks, but though beer, in its foamy neutrality, may have been the perfect beverage for the last quarter of the twentieth century, Leigh-Cheri did not drink beer and wouldn't have drunk it in the Born to Lose Tavern, the Broken Jaw Tavern, or the Sailors Have More Fun Tavern if she did.

Passing a tattoo parlor, she paused to window-shop the mermaids, screaming eagles, and macabre tributes to Mom. Through the raindrops that streaked the plate glass, she saw that phrase again, *Born to Lose,* this time on the tattoo artist's flash card: Born to Lose, a slogan so expressive, so deeply relevant that men have it permanently etched into their hides, and she thought of her own flaccid biceps, imagining the slogan stenciled there. She wondered if one lost one's royal privilege if one had one's royal epidermis inscribed. She did know that once tattooed one could no longer expect to lie for all eternity in an orthodox Jewish cemetery. They wouldn't even bury women with pierced ears. A strange theory of mutilation from the people who invented cutting the skin off the pee-pee.

The Princess walked on.

She met sailors who hunkered. She met lumberjacks who cursed. She met the original cast of the Food Stamp Opera, who tried to lure her up to their three-dollar hotel rooms, where the light bulbs were dying and the wallpaper was already dead. She met many winos. They were at various stages of wino development. Invariably, however, they seemed to have made peace with the rain, as if the wino ambassador had negotiated a treaty with the rulers of rain, a compromise henceforth known as the Tokay Accords. The Indian winos, in particular, were unhurried by the weather, and she recalled that Bernard had said, "White men watch clocks, but the clocks are watching the Indians."

The Princess was wearing a yellow vinyl slicker with matching hat. It looked great with her red hair. She walked on.

First Avenue lay on an incline. Steeper toward the north. Traveling south, she moved downhill. Like the rainwater. Like the twentieth century. At the foot of First, where it crossed Yesler Way, there was a small cobblestoned square, watched over by the several wooden eyes of a totem pole. There, at Pioneer Square, the mood changed abruptly. Once as rough and raunchy as upper First Avenue, Pioneer Square had been hit by restoration. Now, art galleries, boutiques, and discos were replacing the storefront churches, and the *déclassé* luncheonettes were giving way to restaurants that featured imported mineral waters and a gay waiter behind every fern.

In Pioneer Square, where the seedy collided with the chic, was where Nina Jablonski had her law office. Being somewhat of radical temperament, Nina Jablonski had volunteered to defend Bernard Mickey Wrangle against the United States of America, although Mrs. Jablonski did not fully share her client's view that he against the United States of America was a fair match. Actually, the Woodpecker regarded the contest a bit one-sided in his favor, and he would have liked to take on Japan, East Germany, and the Arab nations as well.

Nina Jablonski had red hair. Not as red as Bernard's or Leigh-Cheri's, but definitely red, and the Princess was certain that it was on account of Jablonski's hair, and perhaps the fact that she was seven months pregnant (he maintained a residue of regret about destroying the prospective male pill), that Bernard had agreed to allow her to defend him. Leigh-Cheri had to confess that she, too, was irrationally assured by Mrs. Jablonski's tresses—a fellow victim of sugar and lust? another ally against Argon and the sun?—but the swell of the attorney's belly merely reminded her that she herself hadn't had a period since she left for Maui, an omission that made her as nervous as the Queen's lapdog. Ah, but there was good news! Jablonski, whose features were so strong that no amount of freckles could burden them, had been successful in her petition to have Bernard's rights to be visited restored. Leigh-Cheri could go see him on the following Sunday, three days away.

"There are conditions, however," said Jablonski, handing the Princess a tissue to mop up her happy tears. "Conditions set not by the court but by Mr. Wrangle and me."

"Like what?" asked Leigh-Cheri.

"My dear, you must realize that your conversation will be bugged. For some reason, Mr. Wrangle is suspected of being involved in an international plot to return your father to the throne. Anything you might say regarding your family, or, for that matter, your personal relationship with Mr. Wrangle, might be misconstrued in such a manner as to deepen those suspicions, which would hurt our chances for a minimal sentence. I wanted to establish some safe guidelines for your conversation. Mr. Wrangle went one step further. He doesn't feel it would be emotionally beneficial—for either one of you—to converse at all. He feels that poignant dialogue will merely make your separation all the more difficult. And he certainly doesn't believe the CIA should be privy to the private tenderness you share. He does very much want to see you. And he longs to hear your voice. But he desires that nothing in the way of personal conversation pass between you."

"But—what'll I do? I can't just sit there and talk about the rain on the fucking blackberries. What'll I say?" (Tears of joy, exit stage right. Tears of bewilderment, enter stage left; advance to footlights.)

"Mr. Wrangle suggests that you tell him a story."

"What? A story?"

"Yes, a story of some sort. He wishes to look at you. He wishes to hear you speak. You'll have ten minutes. Just tell him a story. I'm sure you'll think of something."

Leigh-Cheri stared at the antinuclear posters on the office wall. Nuclear power was one of the most sinister frauds ever perpetrated on the American people, and yet its implications meant little to her now.

Mrs. Jablonski removed her fashionably large spectacles and stood. "I asked Mr. Wrangle what you were like. He said you were hornet juice and rosebuds in a container of gazelle meat. He does speak colorfully, doesn't he?"

Leigh-Cheri pulled on her dripping slicker and departed. As she sped back up First Avenue in a taxi—she was not in the mood for any more Born to Lose—she thought, "A story? I do know one story. I know one story. It'll have to do."

The Rainy City

EARL W. EMERSON

*Earl W. Emerson (1948–) was born in Tacoma, Washington, and gradu-
ated from Principia College, in Elsah, Illinois, in 1967 and from the University of Washington in 1968. Since 1978, he has been a lieutenant in the Seattle
Fire Department. He received the Private Eye Writers of America Shamus
Award in 1985. Since 1985, he has published seventeen novels, most of which
have been part of either the Thomas Black or Mac Fontana mystery series.
His writings depict Seattle's neighborhoods and streets with detail and a sense
of immediacy. Emerson's* The Rainy City *(1985), from which the following
selection derives, includes familiar locales known to the city's pedestrians, bicy-
clists, and drivers, whose interests do not always coincide.*

No matter how long I live in Seattle, I am constantly amazed at the
variety of the city. The Crowells resided on the waterfront in West
Seattle. It took five minutes and a good map to pinpoint the precise location. It took another twenty minutes of prowling around on pitch black,
rain-spattered streets before we found it.

Melissa's parents lived on a numbered street smack dab on the water.
The road came down off a hill, dropping a good hundred and fifty feet in
elevation as it approached the select community. We descended through
three-quarters of a mile of virgin woods inside the city limits before we
found it. The dead-end road was narrow and pitted, mired in spots, partially blocked by small mud slides, doubling back upon itself twice.

We discovered five houses on the beach. Guard dogs yapped at our headlights. One streetlight wobbled on a pole in the wind. None of the houses looked as if they could even be discussed for less than a million.

Angus Crowell's place was a sprawling stucco ranch-style house, baroque iron grillwork barring all the street-side windows and doorways. What was he expecting? The Nez Perce had been peaceful for more than a century. The grillwork alone undoubtedly cost more than my entire house.

My best guess was that the nearest house, except for the four others on the beach, was about half a mile away, through the moss-covered trees and up the slimy hill.

The last storm off the sound had toppled a maple at the end of the block. Some industrious soul had chainsawed it into pieces and carted most of it away.

"Maybe I'll just sit in the truck," volunteered Kathy, peering out at the dark house as she listened to the throaty guard dogs up the street. "Besides, I look like a strumpet."

"Yes," I said. "But your heart is pure gold."

. . .

He was in a shark-gray Dodge, and he was good. He intentionally lagged far enough behind so that I wouldn't recognize him.

He followed and I let it ride. I let him tail me down Seventeenth Northeast right through the University of Washington campus and out the other side by the football stadium, although I could have foiled his plans at any point. I knew a dozen choice footpaths I could have detoured onto. By the time I crossed the Montlake Bridge, I knew who he was and I had a good idea what he wanted.

When I zigzagged through some residential streets, I lost him momentarily, but he picked me up again after the industrial museum, just shy of the Arboretum. The Arboretum road was over a mile long, narrow and twisty. The area spawned a lot of crime. Pedestrians were rare and houses were nonexistent. Today, there was little traffic.

Pedaling against a moist southerly wind, I wasn't making very good time. The Dodge paced me. Twice, he crept closer, gunning the engine once, as if to make a move, but at each attempt, a car approached us from the other direction, putting a temporary halt to his plans.

It was Holder, Julius Caesar Holder, and I would have bet my life that his game was bump and run. He knew if he sabotaged the truck I'd eventually ride the bike. And he also knew how vulnerable a man on a bicycle was. He figured he could bounce me into the ditch and motor away, nobody the wiser. It was a neat ploy. He made his move in front of the Japanese tea gardens, and strangely enough, he missed on his first pass. He wasn't trying to kill me. He could have easily run right over me. Instead, he tried to sideswipe my bicycle and knock me for a loop. He must have figured that wouldn't be murder. He was in trouble now. He wasn't just one motorist trying something funny. He was the culmination of hundreds of sloppy, thoughtless motorists that I had run up against in the last few years. It was rare that you caught one. It was even rarer to have a gun on you when you did. My temper got the better of me.

Suddenly, I felt the cold metal of his car brushing my hip. I had been waiting for it. I slammed the caliper brakes on. The Dodge catapulted in front of me as I decelerated.

Slowing down so that he could attempt it a second time was his big blunder.

Instead of pedaling by on the passenger side the way he expected, I swung behind the Dodge and pulled around into the oncoming lane. Sitting up and steering with one hand, I dragged the .45 out from under my windbreaker.

I took careful aim, placing a slug through his side window, as close to his face as I could manage without actually hitting him.

Tires screeched like dying animals, brakes squealed, and the Dodge veered right, bounding up over the high curb and scraping the underbelly with shrill metallic yowls.

I didn't even get off the bicycle. Riding up to the glassless window, I rammed the muzzle of the .45 into Holder's face.

I spoke evenly. "Say your prayers, bastard."

Sisters of the Road

BARBARA WILSON

Barbara Wilson [Sjoholm] (1950–), born in Long Beach, California, founded Seal Press in Seattle in 1976. She is also a co-founder of Women in Transla-tion Press. She has published numerous mystery novels, including the Pam Nilsen series and the Cassandra Reilly series. She has also published several short story collections, including Walking on the Moon: Six Stories and a Novella *(1983) and* Salt Water and Other Stories *(1999). She has also trans-lated the work of such writers as Ebba Haslund, Liv Finstand, and Cecelie Hoigard. She is the author of the memoir* Blue Windows: A Christian Sci-ence Childhood *(1997), among other nonfiction works. Wilson has received the Crime Writers Association Award and the Lambda Literary Award and in 1997 was a PEN Center USA West nominee for* Blue Windows. *Wilson writes crime and detective stories about female protagonists who confront gender, racial, and national and international political issues. This selec-tion, from* Sisters of the Road *(1986), a Pam Nilsen mystery, describes Seat-tle's Sea-Tac strip as it evokes the grisly serial Green River murders from the 1980s and 1990s.*

I got into my Volvo in the airport garage and let it warm up. For six years it had been a trusted friend—now, like seemingly everything else in my life, it was kicking up. Burning oil and burping wounded little noises whenever I went over forty. The Volvo hadn't wanted to come to the air-port tonight at all, and now it was rebelling against going home. It

wanted gas too; I'd better stop at a station outside the airport. I wished
June had driven with me, and not only because she was so good in auto-
motive emergencies. I could have used the company.

All the gas stations were off the freeway on Pacific Highway South, also
known as the Sea-Tac Strip—a long necklace with a jewelled cluster of
Hyatts and Hiltons at the center and tawdry pearls and rhinestones of
cheap motels, taverns, go-go dancer bars and Burger Kings strung out a
mile in either direction. The street that was so often mentioned as the "last
place seen." The last place a girl or young woman had been seen before
she turned up as a heap of bones and teeth to be identified in some wooded,
desolate spot nearby.

They called them the Green River murders because the first remains
had been discovered by the Green River. In the months and years since
then, boy scouts, hikers and picnickers had found almost three dozen
corpses or skulls and bones all over the area south of Seattle, and more
women were missing. Some estimates ranged in the seventies. The investigation had bogged down over and over, but whenever a new set of
remains was found the newspapers regurgitated the whole story and sometimes printed a list of the murdered. Wendy Lee Coffield, Debra Lynn Bon-
ner, Opal Charmaine Mills. They all had three names, with a number from
fifteen to twenty-five after them. Their ages. They were runaways and prostitutes, the papers said, and went on with touching articles about their
foster parents or their single mothers, who all said they didn't know where
the girl had gone wrong. None of the dead were women that I or any of
my friends knew. We didn't know any prostitutes.

At the station I filled the tank, put in oil and looked into the engine—
not that I could have figured out what was wrong. I decided that if the
Volvo lasted until spring I'd sell it. Maybe I should even sell it now, while
it was still running.

Back inside the car I drove up what looked like a main street and went
a couple of blocks before I realized I was going in the wrong direction to
get back to the freeway. There was nothing up here but cheap motels advertising adult channels and waterbeds; most of them were too shoddy even
to be lurid and they all had vacancies. The snow was falling faster now
and it was difficult to see. I pulled into an apartment complex to turn

around. It was a badly illuminated, sinister set of buildings with a peeling sign that said Bella Vista: Deluxe Suites Available.

Reversing, the car stalled and died. The wet snow began to pile up on the windshield, on the passenger side where the wiper didn't work as well.

Don't panic, I told myself sternly. Just two blocks away, the benevolent yellow neon of a Denny's restaurant gleamed at me. Where there's a Denny's, there's twenty-four-hour safety. I'd give the Volvo a couple of tries and then call June if it wouldn't start. She'd be home in ten minutes.

But, grumbling, the car came to life again and I began to back up. Out of a gap to my right, behind me, between two of the dimly lit apartment buildings, stepped two figures, one supporting the other and both of them weaving drunkenly. They seemed to be making towards me, and I kept reversing as far to the left as I could. As I went past, the taller one, the one who was supporting the other, gestured to me to stop. I had an impression—but no, they were both wearing hats—it was too dark and thick with snow to see clearly—but even if they were women—to pick up two drunks—in this part of town . . . I kept staring at them as the car reached the sidewalk. The one had slumped over and the other was trying to drag her. Yes, they were women, they looked quite young, they looked like teenagers.

I put on the brakes and skidded slightly, then began to accelerate cautiously forward again. When I got alongside of them I could see that one was Black and one was white and they were only about sixteen or seventeen, wearing hats and thin leather jackets and tight jeans and, of all incredible things on this night, high-heeled shoes with thin straps.

I leaned over and rolled down the passenger window, shouting, "Hurry up before you freeze to death. There's a blanket in the back. Get in and tell me where you want to go."

The Black girl fell into the back seat and immediately passed out. The taller white girl, her face pinched and ghastly under heavy makeup, said breathlessly, "We want to go to downtown Seattle, to a place we're staying on Second Ave."

I nodded, still not sure if I should have picked them up—what if they mugged me?—and said, "What's the fastest way to the freeway entrance? Can you point it out?"

"Go back to the airport and get on that way. Could you hurry, please?" she asked in a strained and urgent voice. "We really want to get back. Rosalie isn't feeling too well."

Great. She was going to puke in my car; that should certainly add to its saleability. My voice sounded sharp and prim as I answered, "I'll drive as fast as it's safe to."

She didn't say anything. She wrapped the blanket closely around her sagging companion and stroked her shoulder.

"My name's Pam. What's yours?"

"Trish," she said reluctantly. In the rearview mirror she looked younger than I'd first imagined. The black felt hat was pulled down over a triangular face with widely-set, black-ringed eyes and two patches of blusher like red gauze pasted on her cheeks. Strands of wet hair streamed below the hat, and earrings made of many thin chains hung down past her pointed chin.

I found the freeway at last and entered slowly. The traffic was moving erratically, divided equally between drivers who were determined to pretend that nothing out of the ordinary was happening, that this really wasn't a snow storm and that they could still drive as fast as they wanted, and those like me, weather cowards, who were practically holding their cars by the hand and walking them.

I turned up the heater, which was fortunately working tonight, and fiddled with the radio, which wasn't. Static and irritating gusts of country-western music. No news or weather reports. I probably didn't want to hear about the hazardous driving conditions anyway.

"Please," came a small, insistent voice from the back seat. "Can't you go any faster?"

"No," I said shortly. "I don't know what your hurry is. Your friend can sleep it off just as well here in the car as anywhere else."

"She's not sleeping," Trish said, and now I caught her panic. "I can't wake her up. She was, somebody, I mean, she's hurt. . . ."

I turned around with a jerk just as Trish raised Rosalie's head for me to see. Blood was running from somewhere under her hat, running down her neck and inside her jacket. There was a thin trickle coming from her mouth too, and her eyes rolled under half-closed lids.

"Shit!" I said, then gripped the wheel firmly and stepped on the gas.

Seattle's Son

DAVID GUTERSON

David Guterson (1956–) was born in Seattle and earned a B.A. in English and an M.A. in creative writing from the University of Washington. His first book, The Country Ahead of Us, the Country Behind, *a collection of short stories, was published in 1989. In 1992 he published* Family Matters: Why Home-Schooling Makes Sense, *a collection of essays about family and education. His 1994 novel* Snow Falling on Cedars *was a best-seller and winner of the PEN Faulkner Award and was later made into a film. His most recent novels include* East of the Mountains *(1998) and* Our Lady of the Forest *(2003). He has published essays in* Esquire, Sports Illustrated, *and* Harper's. *The following essay, "Seattle's Son," appeared in* Architectural Digest *in 1998. A third-generation Seattleite, David Guterson recounts here his personal Seattle history and examines his bittersweet relationship to the city.*

I was born in Seattle in 1956, when the city had neither freeways or sky-scrapers. The first white settlers had arrived in the area only 105 years earlier, and Seattle had burned almost entirely to the ground 67 years before my birth, leaving few buildings older than my grandfather. My grand-mother's Uncle Dave had seen the razing of the city and once told me that all those cinders had driven his family north to Whatcom.

At the founding of Seattle in 1851, New York was already more than 225 years old. New Orleans was more than 130 years old, and the other major cities of the American West Coast, Los Angeles and San Francisco, had been thriving for about 75 years. Seattle was young when I was a child, a small town by today's standards, innocent and provincial in most ways. A backwoods outpost in the far Northwest, it was far from anything that mattered.

My namesake and great-grandfather, David Taylor, had his shop on Seneca Street between First and Second—Taylor The Tailor, it was called. My Grandfather Ben sold cigars at Keiter & Bernbaum's, inside the Savoy Hotel. My mother's parents sold secondhand clothing on First Avenue South in Pioneer Square, until my grandmother was killed by a speeding truck not far from the shop's door.

The house of my childhood, in the north end of the city, stood close to dairy farms, blackberry brambles, deep ravines and remnants of the forest that had once been everywhere. The poet Gary Snyder, who was born twenty-six years before me and grew up in a tar paper house not far from mine, remembers north Seattle as "the aftermath of a giant clear-cut," a place of cedar and Douglas fir stumps, blackberry, madrona and cascara. I, too, recall enormous stumps, vestiges of the old forest, in certain backyards and blackberry thickets overrunning the train tracks along Lake Washington.

The houses on our block were humble brick boxes in the Colonial Revival and Prairie School styles; later we moved northwest a few blocks to a new street of split-level ranch houses put up in the soil of Mr. Girolamo's truck farm. For the most part our neighborhood looked banal, slapped up out of plywood and two-by-fours with little thought given to history or design, grace or the eye's pleasure. As far as I knew, there was no such thing as architecture, except that when I accompanied my father to a rank landfill on the shore of Lake Washington, where seagulls wheeled and shrieked overhead, I could see, in the distance, Husky Stadium, with its impossibly cantilevered steel roof and monumental spiral ramps. I was also impressed, early, by the Seattle Art Museum in Volunteer Park—its huge, windowless façade was utterly terrifying, and the inference I made pondering it was that the building housed instruments of torture.

My mother was a perennial student at the University of Washington, which I later attended, as did my four siblings. The campus's Central Plaza, colloquially known as Red Square, included a pair of soaring campaniles built, I assumed as a child, to make use of leftover paving bricks. My father, a criminal attorney, kept an office in the Hoge Building, on the site of the first house built in Seattle, the Carson Boren cabin. He sometimes took me there on Saturday mornings, when he would catch up on his dictation. At such times the building was deserted, except for a uniformed attendant in the lobby who would unlock the front door and call the elevator. I recall the decorative plaster of the lobby, the stately pace of the elevator, the wainscoting in my father's anteroom and the worn marble bathroom floors. I also recall the federal courthouse, where my father now and again tried a case—its formal landscaping and austere façade suggested to me, at a very young age, the severity and majesty of the law.

Across the street and south of the Hoge Building stood the city's most obvious landmark, the Smith Tower: My Grandfather Ben, before he sold cigars, ran one of its elevators. When it was built in 1914, the Smith Tower was the tallest building west of the Mississippi, a fact every child in Seattle once seemed capable of reciting. The Space Needle's construction at the north end of downtown made it possible to view the city from the west as poised between two prominent spires, one a futuristic monstrosity, the other—the stolid, antiquated Smith Tower—echoing Sienese palazzi. There were no tall buildings in between until the black monolith of the Seattle First National Bank went up at Fourth and Madison.

Across from the Four Seasons Olympic Hotel, on the southwest corner of Fourth and Seneca, there is now a Starbucks coffeehouse on the site of my aunt and uncle's former drugstore and fountain. While their business thrived, I had only to walk through the glass doors to earn the gift of a model airplane and a chocolate malt or sundae. Equally exciting was the Seattle World's Fair, which opened after much anticipation when I was six years old. Though its vision of the future seems laughable now, like something out of Buck Rogers, it was no laughing matter at the time. I went to the fair with dread and excitement—exhilarated by the modernity of things but suspicious that some sinister objective stood behind it all. The fair's Space Needle dominated my consciousness—like most children, I thought it would fall—but more thought-provoking were the neo-Gothic arches of the Pacific Science Center. They rose gracefully from pools and fountains and suggested the flying buttresses and transverse arches of cathedrals I'd seen in picture books.

Yet the entire city paled in comparison with the mountains surrounding it. From my junior high school, on the crest of a hill, I could see both the Cascade and Olympic ranges, and I hiked into them often enough to know some of their ridges and valleys. I stood on summits with a view of mountains rolling endlessly toward other mountains and crossed snowfields from where, on a clear day, a climber could look back over his shoulder toward Seattle's meager skyline, more trivial than anything on the landscape.

My sense of grandeur was inspired, early, not by magnificent buildings but by the splendid view of Mount Rainier from so many places in the city. It could be seen lined up behind Drumheller Fountain, a place of coaxial paths and rose gardens; it was visible through the granite doughnut—Isamu Noguchi's finely sculpted *Black Sun*—in front of the art museum. The mountain's mythology was so powerful that I often contemplated, with a disturbed mind, the implications for the city of an eruption. Perhaps downtown would be inundated by mudflows, the avenues buried in hot ash.

Summers we crossed the mountains eastward, to Soap Lake in central Washington, and stayed in flea-ridden, mouse-infested rooms close to the muddy shore. The sagebrush terrain was sun-seared and alien, and I always felt relieved when, driving home, we crossed Lake Washington on the floating bridge to reenter the city underneath this message, etched in concrete low-relief: City of Seattle: Portal to the North Pacific. My third-grade teacher had once warned that while the floating bridge was anchored to the lake bottom, nothing guaranteed that it wouldn't sink in a windstorm of sufficient magnitude. It gave me something to fret about, presciently, since the bridge sank in 1990.

As I grew older, my sense of wonder shrank, and the city began to stale. Like most Seattle teenagers of my era, I longed to be somewhere else. Twenty-five years before the city was fashionable, the capital of grunge music and coffeehouse culture, it was the rainy, mildewed capital of nowhere—the portal to the North Pacific—and this I felt acutely. The chief industry was the manufacture of airplanes, and the adult citizenry lacked flair of any sort, soberly marching through the workweek. There was nothing of any consequence present, and later—when I started to write—nothing to write about. Fate had cast me up on these shores, where all was pedestrian, irrelevant.

Looking back over the fictions I've written, published and unpublished, short and long, I see that after twenty-two years of work there is still very little of Seattle. It is the setting for two early practice novels, the setting for two of sixty stories, but after that, either nonexistent or a vague presence in the background.

Why? I confess that after all this time, I have not come to terms with the city of my birth or found the means to imagine it. My visits there now are furtive and muddled, filled with niggling resentments. The changes everywhere gall me, and I feel no connection to Seattle's new culture, so consciously hip and so generic I could be anywhere.

Finally, I'm saddened by Seattle. Its streets are haunted by the feel of another time I cannot readily explain. The city, for all its understated beauty, is lost to me now, in most ways. Or perhaps, like many people, I confuse place and being. I cannot separate myself from the city. Perhaps I simply miss my childhood.

The Good Rain: Across Time

and Terrain in the Pacific Northwest

TIMOTHY EGAN

Timothy Egan (1954–), born in Seattle, graduated from the University of Washington in 1980. He is the Pulitzer Prize–winning chief and correspondent for the Seattle bureau of the New York Times. *Aside from numerous jouralism articles, he has published* The Good Rain: Across Time and Terrain in the Pacific Northwest *(1990),* Breaking Blue *(1992), and, most recently,* Lasso the Wind: Away to the New West *(1998). By mixing ecology and cultural history, Egan's writings powerfully chronicle both the hopes and ecological failings of those settling and developing the Pacific Northwest. In the following passage from* The Good Rain, *Egan views Seattle from the vantage of the kayak he paddles to work and thereby evokes the historical backdrop for the stunning Seattle skyline he observes.*

WITH PEOPLE

Here we have a city: black and beige and boxy up front, the towers of Chicago or Tokyo planted in soil that once held a glacier and fed a forest. Such bulk, piled on land so rumpled, pinched by an enormous lake on one side and an inland sea on the other. It's all very new, and all very tentative, for Seattle is a city that can't decide what to wear. The city has changed its look three times in the last thirty years, and half a dozen times in the last century. The hills that once rose steeply from the central water-front—they've been cut in half. The Black River, a salmon stream that

flowed from Lake Washington to the Duwamish and into Puget Sound—
it's gone. And the tidelands which nurtured a bouillabaisse of sea life—
buried. Still, the city is not finished; every wave of fresh tenants wants to
remodel. So, the flat-topped hills of downtown, minus their natural summits, are sprouting new skyscrapers by the month, and the forested edge
of the city is leveled for Weyerhaeuser's newest product: the instant neighborhood. When humorist Fran Lebowitz recently visited Seattle, she was
asked what she thought of the city. "It's cute," she replied. "Why are they
tearing it down?"

In the spirit of earlier inhabitants, I approach Seattle by kayak, entering Elliott Bay on a weekday morning; it's like landing at O'Hare Airport
on a kite. Overwhelmed by ship traffic, I hug the shoreline, trailed by sea
birds looking for French fries. The wake of a passing container ship, four
city blocks in length, gives my small craft a muscular nudge. Rainier floats
atop the southern skyline, a hooded cone above the industrial congestion
of the Duwamish Valley. There is the Kingdome, a cement cavern without sufficient daylight to adequately support a baseball team, plopped on
fill-dirt that used to be tidelands. Farther south is Boeing Field, where the
Duwamish River was straightened and its old bed leveled to provide a runway for newly hatched jumbo jets. Towering over downtown is the
Columbia Center. A thousand feet high and black as a charred forest, it's
stuffed with enough lawyers to replace nearly half the attorneys in Japan.

Looking around, I see a few hints of traditional life in the temperate
zone: a rock crab scrambling over exposed pilings, some loose kelp, a cormorant riding a northern breeze. At the entrance, Elliott Bay is nearly as
deep as the Space Needle is high, a depth of six hundred feet that hides a
half-blind octopus of three hundred pounds which paralyzes its prey with
a toxic squirt. In these waters live squid twenty-four feet long, century-
old clams with necks of pornographic dimensions, starfish bigger than
an extra-large pizza—in all, more than two thousand kinds of inverte-
brates. All of that is below me, out of sight. What I see when I paddle into
Elliott Bay is the dominance of one species.

I try to imagine George Vancouver, who was the first to pencil Puget
Sound onto a map that showed no such thing. For one month in the spring
of 1792, at the age of thirty-four, he had the feeling of God during Cre-

ation Week. Traveling up the Pacific Coast, the *Discovery* and the *Chatham* took a right turn at the Strait of Juan de Fuca and proceeded east toward an immense volcano anchored in the North Cascades, which Vancouver promptly relieved of its native name, Koma Kulshan, and replaced with that of his cartographer, Joseph Baker, the "undistinguished biped" cursed by Winthrop. Then south, to an inland sea and an even bigger volcano at its southern end, which he named Rainier. He passed through Admiralty Inlet, the weather clear, the water calm, the mountains polished on either side of him. All around, the land rose up in storm-sculpted detail, the islands carpeted by forests, streams leaping out of steep canyons. The air opened his sinuses and expanded his imagination. Vancouver, already ill with a mystery disease that would kill him before his fortieth birthday, was in the Northwest to map and chart a course for future commerce. A detail man, humorless, he would flog his men in front of other sailors to make his disciplinary point. But when he entered Puget Sound something happened, as if he'd tossed his old spirit overboard in a rush of spring euphoria. The first thing he did was give his men a holiday, their only day off since they'd passed Cape Horn at the toe of South America. From then on, his journals started to sing.

To Vancouver and other British explorers, wild land was evil land, bad until proven civilized. That attitude changed when he came upon the garden of Puget Sound. It was perfect as it was. Vancouver wrote: "As we had no reason to imagine this country had ever been indebted for any of its decorations to the hand of man, I could not possibly believe that any uncultivated country had ever been discovered exhibiting so rich a picture." Farther down the sound, he anchored off Bainbridge Island, just across the water from the future city of Seattle. Vancouver then penned what is perhaps his most famous passage:

> To describe the beauties of this region, will, on some future occasion, be a very grateful task to the pen of a skillful panegyrist. The serenity of the climate, the innumerable pleasing landscapes, and the abundant fertility that unassisted nature puts forth, require only to be enriched by the industry of man with villages, mansions, cottages, and other buildings, to render it the most lovely country that can be imagined.

In short order, the place would be full of villages and mansions and cottages, but their inhabitants felt compelled to assist nature. In Seattle, they nearly overwhelmed it.

On that spring evening in 1792, a six-year-old native boy by the name of Sealth is said to have looked out across the water at the *Discovery,* surely a vessel that could not have been assembled with any product of nature. The Olympics were topped by the gold trim of sunset, the Cascades dark blue in repose. Never again would such a view belong to one band of people. Sealth was the son of a native slave woman taken in one of the periodic raids which the Coast Indians engaged in to replenish the tribal stock of females. The city that was built around Elliott Bay was named for Sealth, changed to *Seattle* because the original pronunciation (See-alth) made the speaker sound as if he had a lisp. But that came much later, more than a half-century after Vancouver passed by.

When Winthrop visited Puget Sound, Washington Territory had just been carved from the Oregon Country and contained fewer than four thousand whites. It was a wilderness twice as large as New England, stretching from the Columbia River to the Canadian border and east to Montana. Like Vancouver before him, he felt this land would need no customizing from humans to improve it; instead, things should work the other way, with the land reshaping its inhabitants—Winthrop's central prophecy. Already the cities of the East, some of them two hundred years old and falling into industrial mayhem, were not working. The nation was torn by slavery; seventy-seven years after the start of the American Revolution, a class system was still in place in many parts of a country where the theory of democracy and the practice of same were an ocean apart. Strange religious cults, centered around leaders who traded in ecstasy and redemption, sprang up in New England, New York and the new states of Ohio and Illinois and Indiana. Here in the Far West, in a maritime valley between two mountain ranges, was a fresh chance for a new nation to live up to its promise. Starting over is the oldest American impulse.

From my kayak today, I look one way at the forest of new skyscrapers and the other way, just beyond Bainbridge Island, to a grassy opening in the trees where Sealth is buried. There is a white cross atop his stone grave; in his later years, he converted to Christianity, and the first historians of

Seattle treated him well as a result. Had he remained true to his native religious beliefs, he would have burned every day he heard his name mentioned in relation to the ever-expanding city in his midst. Once a person died, his name was supposed to go with him, evoked by mortals only on the most solemn of occasions. Sealth had always been one to compromise; some would say he sold out, early and often. He was tall and tough. A warrior in his younger days who owned eight slaves at one point and eventually freed them after Abraham Lincoln did the same thing for blacks in the South. He lived to be a very old man, going from aboriginal king of Elliott Bay and the river that drained into it, to a withered curiosity on the muddy streets of what would become the largest city in the country named for a Native American.

Hunting Mr. Heartbreak:

A Discovery of America

JONATHAN RABAN

Jonathan Raban (1942–) was born in England and now resides in Seattle. He is best known for his works of nonfiction prose and critical literary studies, which include, among others, The Technique of Modern Fiction: Essays in Practical Criticism *(1968),* Soft City *(1974),* Arabia: A Journey through the Labyrinth *(1979),* Old Glory: An American Voyage *(1981),* Coasting *(1986),* For Love and Money: A Writing Life, 1969–1989 *(1989),* Hunting Mister Heartbreak: A Discovery of America *(1990),* Bad Land: An American Romance *(1996), and* Passage to Juneau: A Sea and Its Meanings *(1999), which concerns a sailing voyage from Seattle to Alaska. He has also written several plays and the novel* Waxwings, *set in Seattle. Raban has received the Thomas Cook Award and the Heinemann Award. In 1997, he won the National Book Critics Circle Award for Nonfiction and the Murray Morgan Prize for* Bad Land. *The following selection, from* Hunting Mr. Heartbreak: A Discovery of America, *chronicles the author's initial discovery of Seattle and the promise it offered him and other immigrants to the city.*

GOLD MOUNTAIN

On that particular morning, in hotels and motels, in furnished rooms and cousins' houses, 106 other people were waking to their first day as immigrants to Seattle. These were flush times, with jobs to be had for the asking, and the city was growing at the rate of nearly 40,000 new residents a year. The immigrants were piling in from every quarter. Many were out-of-state Americans: New Yorkers on the run from the furies of Manhattan; refugees from the Rustbelt; Los Angeleños escaping their infamous crime statistics, their huge house prices and jammed and smoggy freeways; redundant farm workers from Kansas and Iowa. Then there were the Asians—Samoans, Laotians, Cambodians, Thais, Vietnamese, Chinese and Koreans, for whom Seattle was the nearest city in the continental United States. A local artist had proposed a monumental sculpture, to be put up at the entrance to Elliott Bay, representing Liberty holding aloft a bowl of rice.

The falling dollar, which had so badly hurt the farming towns of the Midwest, had come as a blessing to Seattle. It lowered the price abroad of the Boeing airplanes, wood pulp, paper, computer software and all other things that Seattle manufactured. The port of Seattle was a day closer by sea to Tokyo and Hong Kong than was Los Angeles, its main rival for the shipping trade with Asia.

By the end of the 1980s, Seattle had taken on the dangerous lustre of a promised city. The rumour had gone out that if you had failed in Detroit you might yet succeed in Seattle—and that if you'd succeeded in Seoul, you could succeed even better in Seattle. In New York and in Guntersville [Alabama] I'd heard the rumour. Seattle was the coming place.

So I joined the line of hopefuls. We were everywhere, and we kept on bumping into each other and comparing notes. At breakfast in the hotel dining room I noticed that the woman at the next table was doing exactly what I was doing myself: circling ads on the Property page of the *Post-Intelligencer* with a ballpoint pen. I was on *Downtown;* she was roaming round the city, going from *University* to *Queen Anne* to *Fremont, Magnolia* and *Capitol Hill.* She had the old-money equestrienne look—the boots, the khaki slacks, the hacking jacket, white silk blouse and gold chain that I'd once coveted for myself. Her expression, as she ploughed through the small print, was avid: she was rolling the telegraphese of *3-bed, 2-ba* round in her head as if it were lines from Wallace Stevens.

"I got to find somewhere fast," she said. "Flew in last night. My furniture's all in store in Denver, Colorado, and that *costs.*"

For a minute or two, her eyes went back to the paper. She sucked on the end of her pen. Then she looked up from the advertisements in order to deliver a non-stop ten-minute advertisement for herself.

Yesterday was her birthday, her 31st birthday—she'd always said she was going to change her life when she was 31—and it was on her chart; an astrologer had told her she was a Scorpio—Scorpios were great decision-makers—she'd had her own business back in Denver—real estate—and a big house—and a car, a silver BMW 520i—she'd sold the business—and the house—and the car—and just *come to Seattle.*

She was the heroine of an adventure story, and she was telling it like the Ancient Mariner.

"I was up here five days last year—I got friends over in West Seattle. I took one look at this city and I knew. Right then I said, 'Susan, here's where you're going to spend your 30s.' I had this gut-feeling. Well—here I am."

It was hard to slide a word in edgeways, but there had to be some as yet unconfessed reason for this audacious and arbitrary move. Love, maybe? If so, why was she spending her first day here alone in a hotel?

"Susan . . . tell me. I still haven't got it. Why here? Why Seattle?"

I was violating her right to tell her own tale. She blinked at the question and shook her head in an impatient swirl of lacquered chestnut hair. "Oh—the quality of the lifestyle, the good environment, the real-estate values; *you* know."

I had misjudged her. She was just a typical domestic flier with a low specific gravity.

Half an hour later, I was lodging a jacket and a pair of trousers with a dry cleaner's a block away from the hotel. The face of the man who took charge of them was a worried knot. He gave the clothes an empty, shell-shocked smile and said, "No problem." Then again, holding up the trousers by one leg, "No problem."

"Don't you want to make out a slip for them?" I said.

His gaze was distraught. "Thank you. Thank you. Yes, thank you."

A woman came out from behind the carousel of hanging garments and said something to the man in what I took to be Chinese. He scampered.

"Oh, I am sorry," she said. "He is only in America two weeks. He not understanding English good. He learning very slow."

"Where is he from?" I asked.

"Inchon, in Korea. He start work yesterday. We train him as presser. But do not worry! We not let him loose on your pants yet, not this week." She laughed and touched her temple. "Jet lag. No 'on the ball.'"

"You're from Korea, too?"

"Yes, Seoul. But I am in America 13 years. August 28, 1976."

The greenhorn was listening, peering out at us through a fringe of skirts and dresses. He was close to my own age, but his infancy in English gave him the facial expression of a fractious toddler. When I caught his eye, he ducked out of sight.

"And you like it here?"

"In America? Oh, yeah! It's good. It is so big! So green! So wide—wide—wide!"

. . .

Looking for somewhere to live, I quartered the city at the wheel of a new rental—a cherry-coloured Spectrum with California plates and a painfully weak stomach. The steep little hills of Seattle made the car break wind with a sickly rumbling in its bowels. When I floored the gas pedal, the engine gave a shuddering sob and stalled.

The realtors turned up their noses at me. *No way,* they said, with lordly smiles, when I described what I had in mind. This was a sellers' market; house prices were up 30 percent on last year; the realtors didn't have time to talk even to *buyers* with less than a quarter million, cash in hand, and they certainly had no time to waste on me.

"Do you know where you're at here? This is boomtown, U.S.A."

I drove on, through a cloud of pink dust. One could tell that Seattle was on a winning streak by the number of men in cranes who were trying to smash the place to bits with ballhammers. The pink dust rose in explosive flurries over the rooftops and coloured the low sky.

Pitched on a line of bluffs along Puget Sound, with Lake Washington at its back, Seattle had ships at the ends of its streets and gulls in its traffic. Its light was restless and watery, making the buildings shiver like reflections. It felt like an island and smelled of the sea.

It was a pity about the ballhammers, for the city they were knocking down was an American classic; a survivor of the Theodore Roosevelt age of boosterish magniloquence. Where the high-toned buildings of Alabama had been cotton planters' daydreams of Ancient Greece, Seattle looked like a free-hand sketch, from memory, of a sawmill-owner's whirlwind vacation in Rome and Florence. Its antique skyscrapers were rude boxes, a dozen to 15 storeys high, fantastically candied over with patterned brick and terracotta mouldings. Their façades dripped with friezes, gargoyles, pilasters, turrets, cornices, cartouches, balustrades and arabesques. Every bank and office block was an exuberant *palazzo.*

The whole thing was an exercise in conscious theatre. All the most important buildings faced west, over the Sound, and Seattle was designed to be seen from the front. You were meant to arrive by ship, from Yokohama or Shanghai, and be overwhelmed by the financial muscle, the class (with a short *a*), the world-travelled air of this Manhattan of the Far West. If you had the bad taste to look at Seattle from the back, all you'd see would be plain brick cladding and a zig-zag tangle of fire escapes.

Until very recently, it seemed, Seattle had got along well enough with its turn-of-the-century Italian Renaissance architecture; but now the terracotta city was beginning to look dingy and stunted beside the 60- and 70-storey towers that were sprouting over its head. Some were still just steel skeletons, with construction workers in hard hats swarming in their rigging like foretopmen. Some were newly unsheathed, with racing clouds mirrored in their black and silver glass. More were in the chrysalid stage, obtected in rough shells of scaffolding and tarpaulins. Then there were the holes in the ground, the ballhammer jobs, the moulded garland going into smithereens.

I was having little luck. A "furnished executive suite" turned out to be a low-ceilinged room, as small as Alice's, in a new block, at a rent of $1400 a month. *No way.* A promising one-bedroom apartment on First Hill at $550 was for non-smokers only.

"Even if I do it out the window?"

"Even if you do it out the window."

I asked around the bars. It was possible, apparently, to rent a room in a rooming house in the International District for $60 a month.

"But they're kind of funny. They're Vietnamese. I don't think they take Caucasians."

I was told about the Josephinum Residence at a bar, where it was variously reported to be an apartment block, a Catholic shelter for low-income families, an old people's home and a hotel. But it was generally agreed that, whatever it was, the place was so big that it must have empty rooms.

The building was a richly encrusted pile on Second Avenue, three blocks back from the waterfront. Inside, it looked like the Medici tomb. Its vaulted ceiling, 40 feet up, was tricked out in flaky gold; huge veined marble pillars supported a balustraded cloister on the mezzanine floor. A 15th-century merchant prince might have found it homely, but it was hard to fit this heroic essay in the architecture of power and money to the people who now occupied the Josephinum's lobby. Shrunken, bald, leaning on sticks and planting walking frames ahead of them, they limped and clicked across the marble hall. Crayoned notices, in big round letters, advertised Bingo, Flu Shots, the arrival of the Bookmobile and Mass at 3 P.M. in the chapel. It had the institutional smell of Lysol and overboiled cabbage.

At the desk I apologised for making a mistake; but no, said the manager, there was indeed a vacant room, and she'd be happy to show it to me. No, you didn't have to be old—it was just that at this time of day most of the other tenants were at work. Nor did you have to be a Catholic, nor a non-smoker; she was neither herself.

We stepped into the elevator with a spry centenarian whose black wig was a little askew on her head.

"She's as old as the state of Washington, aren't you, dear?" the manager said. "And you got a special telegram on your birthday from the President, didn't you?"

"Sure did," said the woman. "From the President."

"Mr. Bush."

"Lot of wind out there today." She tugged at her wig, bringing it down over her eyes.

"Oh, she could tell you a few things about Seattle; she's seen it all in her time, haven't you, dear?"

"Huh? Maybe," the woman growled. Being 100 looked like a job that she had long grown bored with. As the elevator climbed the shaft, I watched her going through her flight-check routine: *wig*—okay; *afternoon paper*—

okay; *specs*—roger; *room key*—where's that tarnation key? Yup, you got it. It's in your other hand.

On every floor we stopped at, a robed figure was waiting at the elevator doors. The first time this happened, I mistook him for a resident, then saw that he was St. Francis, with bluebirds, cast in plaster in the school of Dante Gabriel Rossetti. The centenarian got out at Joseph the Carpenter; we went on up to 13, Christ of the Sacred Heart. His beard was chipped, his blood had oxidised to chocolate; He was blessing the brassbound rococo Cutler mail chute.

A long dark corridor led to an enormous room, empty of furniture but full of light. The air tasted as if it had been left to cook for many months, and there were some curious stains on the yellow shagpile carpet, but the view from the uncurtained windows was serene. The room looked out over turreted flat roofs to Puget Sound: beyond the cowled air vents, plants in tubs, fire escapes and satellite dishes, ships were on the move in Elliott Bay, whose wind-damaged water looked like knapped flint. A car ferry was coming in to dock from a suburban island; a big container vessel, flying a Japanese flag, was being taken in hand by a pair of shovel-fronted tugs.

"You want to see the bathroom?"

I was busy with the fishing boats over by the West Seattle shore, the shipyards, the line of buoys pointing the way in to the Duwamish Waterway. At this window, one could spend all day far out at sea, with the city laid out under one's feet. It was a cormorant's perch.

"If you want a phone, the plug's right here."

The light was changing, the water turning from grey to a pellucid iceberg-green. The ferry sounded its diaphone. The note, way down at the bottom of the tuba range, reverberated in the glass of the windowpane.

"It's a hell of a view."

"You'd better enjoy it while it lasts. It probably won't last long. We're lucky here. We're saved. They were going to pull us down, but we just got our official designation. We're a historic landmark as of last month."

The building had been put up in 1906, at the height of the craze for Italianate magnificence. It had been the New Washington Hotel, Seattle's grandest. Theodore Roosevelt himself was one of its first guests—and the gilded swank of the New Washington, its triumphant Americanism, was a perfect embodiment of the Roosevelt presidency. It had stayed in business as a hotel until 1962, the year of the Seattle World's Fair, when Elvis Presley had lodged in a suite on the penthouse floor. Then it had been taken over by the Little Sisters of Mercy, who'd run it as a home and hospital for the elderly.

Although the Josephinum was still owned by the archdiocese, it had caught the 1980s virus of free market economics. As the old died in their rooms or were packed off to nursing homes, younger and richer people were being recruited to fill their places. New tenants had to pass a means test to prove that they earned at least 60 percent of the "median income" of $17,000 a year, and some well-heeled out-of-towners had begun taking rooms in the Josephinum as their Seattle pieds-à-terre. It was still a cheap place to live by middle-class standards—this big studio, with dressing room and bathroom, cost $425 a month—but the building was steadily hoisting itself out of the reach of the people it had housed for the last quarter-century.

When I went down to the lobby, all conversation stopped. Walking frames came to a squeaky halt; dog-eared magazines were lowered and eyes raised over the tops of half-moon specs. I was shaken to see that on every face there was an expression of frank antipathy to the appearance of the latest cuckoo in the Josephinum nest.

I saw—and saw too clearly for comfort—the man who was reflected in the old people's eyes: a guy in a loud pink denim suit, with a foreign accent and money to burn. He was a sign of the times. When the papers talked about the great Seattle boom, about clogged freeways and massive rent-hikes, this was the man they had in mind: a paunchy stranger waving a chequebook and driving a car with California plates.

. . .

It was something in the disposition of the landscape, the shifting lights and colours of the city. *Something.* It was hard to nail it, but this something was a mysterious gift that Seattle made to every immigrant who cared to see it. Wherever you came from, Seattle was queerly like home.

The Scandinavian fishermen and loggers who had formed the original backbone of Seattle's working population, and who still held the suburb of Ballard as a Nordic fastness, had felt immediately comfortable here. It was fjord-country, with wooden houses reaching down to the edge of half-wild, half-tame water. On Puget Sound at night, looking across to the lights of Winslow and Suquamish, one might easily be on the Oresund at Hälsingborg, with Elsinore twinkling on the far shore. The forest, the sea, the lakes were things that were already memories in the imagination of the rawest newcomer. In Seattle for the first time, he knew that he'd been here before.

Koreans kept on telling me that they found it "just like Korea." Japanese immigrants looked up at Mount Rainier and saw Mount Fuji there. Out on Fourth Avenue under my umbrella, I walked through London rain, at a London temperature. In Guntersville, I had mentioned to George Kappler that I was thinking of going to Seattle. He said, "You may laugh now, but I bet, when you get there, that Seattle will remind you of Guntersville. . . ." Now I saw exactly what he meant: its wateriness, its green hills, its bridges, its houses hidden in the trees *were* like northern Alabama, but a kinder, gentler northern Alabama, without the sleepy heat and the poisonous snakes.

It was an extraordinarily soft and pliant city. If you went to New York, or to Los Angeles, or even to Guntersville, you had to fit yourself to a place whose demands were hard and explicit. You had to learn the school rules. Yet people who came to Seattle could somehow recast it in the image of home, arranging the city around themselves like so many pillows on a bed. One day you'd wake up to find things so snug and familiar that you could easily believe that you'd been born here.

Black Planet: Facing Race

during an NBA Season

DAVID SHIELDS

David Shields (1956–) is a professor of English at the University of Washington. He graduated from Brown University with a B.A. and from the University of Iowa with an M.F.A. His fiction includes the novels Heroes *(1984) and* Dead Languages *(1989) and the short story collection* A Handbook for Drowning *(1991). His nonfiction includes* Remote *(1996),* Black Planet: Facing Race during an NBA Season *(1999),* "Baseball Is Just Baseball": The Understated Ichiro *(2001), and* Enough about You: Adventures in Autobiography *(2002). His essays and short stories have been published in numerous periodicals, and he has received numerous awards and fellowship for his writing, including the James Michener Fellowship, the James D. Phelan Literary Award, and the National Endowment for the Arts Fellowship. The following selection comes from* Black Planet, *which recounts the author's year of following the Seattle Sonics basketball team as a means of reflecting on issues of race in Seattle and America.*

I take a curious pride in *Sports Illustrated*'s calling the Sonics the "NBA's most impudent team," because the ruling ethos of Seattle is forlorn apology for the animal impulses. According to a political talk-show host, "Seattle is almost an entirely different market than the rest of the country. There's a very polite approach here. In other cities, callers get much more acerbic. People here are civilized. You don't have to be abrasive or rude or say things in a boisterous, loud way to make your point." A cheerleader at the University of Washington named Robb Weller, who is now a game-show host, is credited with having started the Wave. In his review of *Cat on a Hot Tin Roof,* the drama critic for the *Seattle Post-Intelligencer* explained that he left at intermission because he can't waste his time any-more on theater that glamorizes dysfunctional families and alcoholism. When I castigated a carpenter for using the phrase "Jew me down," he returned later that evening to beg my forgiveness, and the next week he mailed me a mea culpa and a rebate. An editorial in the *Post-Intelligencer* argued that the authors of a *Harvard Law Review* parody of a murdered law professor's work should have been severely disciplined, and concluded: "The First Amendment simply cannot extend to expression which dimin-ishes another's self-esteem." Kenny G. is from Seattle. "Louie, Louie" is often on the verge of being named the state song. When the *Seattle Times* published a front-page photograph of Kurt Cobain's dead body after his suicide, the executive editor wrote an interminable column about how the picture was not in fact sensationalistic (it wasn't). Seattleites use their seat belts more, return lost wallets more often, and recycle their trash more than people in any other city. Once a year, for twenty-four hours, thousands of people gather in the Kingdome to visualize world peace. In one of her weekly columns in the *Seattle Times,* psychologist Jennifer James explained that "women used to be attracted to big men because they could bring home meat and defend us against marauders," but "women are less likely to be battered by small partners," so she encouraged her readers to "reverse the current genetic trend and save the universe" by marrying "thoughtful lit-tle people." When people don't give money to beggars, they frequently say, "Sorry—no change today." When a restaurant closed, it put a sign in the window that said, "After twenty years of service to the community, we regret to inform our customers that we will be closed indefinitely"—twenty years of *service.* The most recent Republican (losing) candidate for mayor was a man who claims to have invented the happy face . . .

And what I love about the Supes, of course, is that they are not like this at all. So what does that make them? What does that make me in rela-tion to them?

. . .

The Sonics' small-forward Detlef Schrempf's new tattoo is a 3" × 3" design over his heart: an eagle, a lake, a forest, a sun, mountains. "Each symbol stands for something," Schrempf explains. He was born and raised in Leverkusen, West Germany, though he attended high school in central Washington and played college ball for the University of Washington. "It's something I wanted to keep for the rest of my life. It shows some things that I believe in. It has more to do with inner strength. If I do have some doubt about certain things, I can look at myself and get the reassurance of what I believe in." He also says, "I'm not a trash-talker. It's important for us [the Sonics] not to have that label. Trash-talking can only hurt you. It can never help you, with the referees, the crowd, anything. You can't take away the vocal part of Gary [Payton]'s game. But there is a positive way of doing it. Instead of directing it toward the opposing bench, he can talk to himself or his teammates." Schrempf is such a Seattleite: *nature is the one true source; impolite conversation is bad for you.*

. . .

In a hurry at the supermarket, I go careening around an aisle with my shopping cart, and when I nearly bump into a checker stocking shelves, he says, with a completely straight face and expression. "Sorry—." Is this Northwest irony? If so, it's dry as dirt.

Riding home on the bus with my groceries, I notice two punky kids standing in the gutter, waiting for the light to change in their favor. Instead of just continuing past them—he has plenty of room to drive by—the bus driver makes a particular point of braking, opening his window, informing them that he has the green light, and then driving on.

Four blocks from my house, I'm holding my bag of groceries, standing a foot from the curb, waiting for the light to change. Although the light is with her, the driver screeches to a halt, virtually commanding me— via an exaggerated hand gesture—to cross in front of her. The gesture conveys so much: she's never in a rush, she has no will, no ego; if my self-discipline is that poor, if my needs are that pressing, she'll help me out. I refuse to go. Instead, I practically scream at her until she eases the car forward, "What are you waiting for? *You* have the green light. Just go!"

Seattle's passive-aggressiveness intrigues as well as aggravates me; it is a kind of daily riddle.

. . .

11.18.94—How to explain the general tendency of Seattle motorists to refuse to pull over for ambulance, fire, and police sirens? In larger cities, there's never any room, so no one even pretends to try to get out of the way; here, the traffic is only occasionally that congested, and yet cars rarely edge to the right curb, let alone stop. I'm ecstatic about this weird contradiction of the Northwest's polite humanitarianism, until Laurie comes up with a simple and convincing explanation: everybody has the music in their cars cranked so loud that they can't hear the sirens.

. . .

12.21.94—While I'm standing on my back porch, separating newspapers and magazines and bottles into their proper recycling containers, a black man walks past the house and, in proper Seattle fashion, nods and smiles. I almost never acknowledge such greetings—my deepest dread is becoming a true Seattleite—but I don't want him to think that I'm being unfriendly or wary to him because he's black, so I nod and smile at him. Entering or exiting a store, I don't usually go wildly out of my way to hold the door open for the person behind me, but if the person is black, I never fail to; so, too, if the bus driver is black. I thank him—a Seattle custom— when I get off at my stop, whereas I would never think of doing this if the driver were white. Are black people conscious of how excruciatingly self-conscious white people have become in their every interaction with black people? Is this self-consciousness an improvement?

Maybe not, because I'm thinking of people in categories rather than as people, which is a famously dangerous thing to do. I once mentioned to Laurie that in my experience black people tend, as a rule, not to tip very much—*we've been, over time, charged enough.* Laurie, who waitressed her way through college, responded, "Well, your proud race tends not to tip very well, either."

"What do you mean—like, ladies who lunch?" I said, thinking Judaism is a religion, not a race.

"No," she said, "in general," at which point I understood as I hadn't before the problematics of generalization.

. . .

Paul e-mails me: "Have you heard about the latest idea to print domestic violence warning labels on all marriage licenses issued in the state of Washington? Now pending in the legislature! Also, did you see William Arnold's recent review in the *P-I* [*Post-Intelligencer*] of *My New Partner*— a pretty funny comedy about on-the-take cops in Paris in which he concluded that the film was terrible because 'police corruption isn't funny'? And then there are the new public-service announcements urging people to report their friends and neighbors for any infractions or suspicious-seeming events, of which my own favorite is the Dial-000-HERO campaign, whereby we're encouraged to report observed commuter-lane violators on the freeways to the state police." All my friends love to struggle against the Seattle ethos, and what we love to struggle against is its assumption of the perfectibility of humankind. As the locally popular bumper sticker has it, MEAN PEOPLE SUCK; someone finally came along with the necessary rejoinder: NICE PEOPLE SWALLOW.

. . .

A late-middle-aged white man is wearing a hat that has AMERICA'S CUP '95 on the brim, a gold watch, Dockers, a flowered shirt. The post-office supervisor—a short, stocky, middle-aged black woman—explains to him that the postal scales are calibrated every month.

"But you're charging the public money," he says. "If the scales aren't correct, it isn't right."

She asks him to come with her into her office, so he won't hold up the rest of the line, but he says, "I'd just as soon be out here." Who knows what nefariousness she might have planned for him back there? "You should certify the scales," he reiterates.

"We do certify them," she explains again.

"Someone else should certify them—an independent agent, not a government employee. That's a flaw in the system, when you're charging the public money."

Finally, he asks for her card and her name and the name of her supervisor.

"I'm the supervisor," she says. "I am in charge of this postal branch."

They stare bullets at each other for an eternity until she pivots to return to her office. The man slams the glass door against a garbage can on his way out, nearly shattering the glass. When he's gone, everybody waiting in line breaks into applause for the supervisor. I find that, at least for the moment, I really do sort of love Seattle.

Emerald City: Third & Pike

CHARLOTTE WATSON SHERMAN

Charlotte Watson Sherman (1958–) was born in Seattle and graduated from Seattle University in 1980. She has worked in Seattle as an emergency housing coordinator, a social worker, a mental health specialist, and a writing workshop instructor. Her writings include a collection of short stories, Killing Color *(1992), and the novels* One Dark Body *(1993) and* Touch *(1996), the most recent about an African-American artist who works as a hotline counselor at a Seattle clinic. Sherman is the editor of the anthology* Sisterfire: Black Womanist Fiction and Poetry *(1994). She has received the King County Arts Commission Publication Award, the Seattle African-American Women's Achievement Award, and, for* Killing Color, *the Great Lakes College Association Award. "Emerald City: Third & Pike," from* Killing Color, *uses the occasion of the narrator's encounter with a street person to explore questions of African-American identity in Seattle.*

This is Oya's corner. The pin-striped young executives and sleek-pumped clerk-typists, the lacquered-hair punk boys and bleached blondes with safety pins dangling from multi-holed earlobes, the frantic-eyed woman on the corner shouting obscenities, and the old-timers rambling past new high-rise fantasy hotels—all belong to Oya even though she's the only one who knows it.

Oya sits on this corner 365 days of the year, in front of the new McDonald's, with everything she needs bundled inside two plastic bags by her

From "Emerald City: Third & Pike," in *Killing Color,* by Charlotte Watson Sherman. Reprinted by permission of Calyx Books.

side. Most people pretend they don't even see Oya sitting there like a Buddha under that old green Salvation Army blanket.

Sometimes Oya's eyes look red and wild, but she won't say anything to anybody. Other times her eyes are flat, black and still as midnight outside the mission, and she talks up a furious wind.

She tells them about her family—her uncle who was a cowboy, her grandfather who fought in the Civil War, her mother who sang dirges and blues songs on the Chitlin Circuit, and her daddy who wouldn't "take no stuff from nobody," which is why they say some people got together and broke his back.

"Oh yeah, Oya be tellin them folks an earful if they'd ever stop to listen, but she don't pay em no mind. Just keeps right on talkin, keeps right on tellin it."

One day when Oya's eyes were flat and black and she was in a preaching mood, I walked down Third & Pike, passed her as if I didn't know her. Actually I didn't. But Oya turned her eyes on me and I could feel her looking at me and I knew I couldn't just walk past this woman without saying something. So I said, "Hello."

Oya looked at me with those flat black eyes and motioned for me to take a seat by her.

Now, usually I'm afraid of folks who sit on the sidewalks downtown and look as if they've never held a job or have no place to go, but something about her eyes made me sit.

I felt foolish. I felt my face growing warm and wondered what people walking by must think of me sitting on the street next to this woman who looked as if she had nowhere to go. But after sitting there for a few minutes, it seemed as if they didn't think more or less of me than when I was walking down the street. No one paid any attention to us. That bothered me. What if I really needed help or something? What if I couldn't talk, could only sit on that street?

"Don't pay them fools no mind, daughter. They wouldn't know Moses if he walked down Pike Street and split the Nordstrom Building right down the middle. You from round here?"

I nodded my head.

"I thought so. You look like one of them folks what's been up here all they lives, kinda soft-lookin like you ain't never knowed no hard work."

I immediately took offense because I could feel the inevitable speech coming on: "There ain't no real black people in Seattle."

"Calm down, daughter, I don't mean to hurt your feelings. It's just a fact, that's all. You folks up here too cushy, too soft. Can't help it. It's the rainwater does it to you, all that water can't help but make a body soggy and spineless."

I made a move to get up.

"Now wait a minute, just wait a minute. Let me show you somethin."

She reached in her pocket and pulled out a crumpled newspaper clipping. It held a picture of a grim-faced young woman and a caption that read: DOMESTIC TO SERVE TIME IN PRISON FOR NEAR-MURDER.

"That's me in that picture. Now ain't that somethin?"

Sure is, I thought and wondered how in the world I would get away from this woman before she hurt me.

"Them fools put me in the jail for protectin my dreams. Humph, they the only dreams I got, so naturally I'm gonna protect em. Nobody else gonna do it for me, is they?"

"But how could somebody put you in jail for protectin your dreams? That paper said you almost killed somebody."

I didn't want to seem combative but I didn't know exactly what this lady was talking about and I was feeling pretty uneasy after she'd almost insulted me then showed me evidence she'd been in jail for near-murder, no less.

"Now, I know you folks up here don't know much bout the importance of a body's dreams, but where I come from dreams was all we had. Seemed like a body got holt of a dream or a dream got holt of a body and wouldn't turn you loose. My dreams what got me through so many days of nothin, specially when it seemed like the only thing the future had to give was more of the same nothin, day after day."

She stopped abruptly and stared into space. I kept wondering what kind of dream would have forced her to try to kill somebody.

"Ain't nothin wrong with cleanin other folks' homes to make a livin.

Nothin wrong with it at all. My mama had to do it and her mama had to do it at one time or nuther, so it didn't bother me none when it turned out I was gonna hafta do it too, least for a while. But my dream told me I wasn't gonna wash and scrub and shine behind other folks the rest of my life. Jobs like that was just temporary, you know what I mean?"

I nodded my head.

"Look at my hands. You never woulda knowed I danced in one of them fancy colored nightclubs and wore silk evenin gloves. Was in a sorority. Went to Xavier University."

As she reminisced, I looked at her hands. They looked rough and wide, like hands that had seen hard labor. I wondered if prison had caused them to look that way.

Oya's eyes pierced into mine. She seemed to know what I was thinking. She cackled.

"Daughter, they'd hafta put more than a prison on me to break my spirit. Don't you know it takes more than bars and beefy guards to break a fightin woman's spirit?"

She cackled some more.

"Un Un. Wouldn't never break me, and they damn sure tried. I spent fifteen years in that hellhole. Fifteen years of my precious life, all for a dreamkiller."

I looked at her and asked, "But what did you do? What did they try to do to your dreams?"

Oya leaned over to me and whispered, "I was gonna get into the space program. I was gonna be a astronaut and fly out into the universe, past all them stars. I was gonna meet up with some folks none of us never seen before, and be ambassador of goodwill; not like the fools bein sent out there now thinkin they own the universe. I was gonna be a real ambassador of goodwill and then that woman I scrubbed floors for had the nerve to tell me no black maid was ever gonna be no astronaut. Well, I could feel all the broken dreams of my mama and my grandmama and her mama swell up and start pulsin in my blood memory. I hauled off and beat that fool over the head with the mop I had in my hands till I couldn't raise up my arms no more. The chantin of my people's broken dreams died down and I looked and there was that dreamkiller in a mess of blood all over the clean floor I'd just scrubbed. And they turned round and put me in jail and never did say nothin bout that old dreamkiller. Just like my dreams never mattered. Like I didn't have no dreams. Like all I could ever think bout doin was cleanin up after nasty white folks for the rest of my life.

"Humph!" She snorted, and I almost eased to my feet so I could run if I had the cause to.

"You got any dreams, daughter?" Oya asked with a gleam in her eye.

I knew I better tell her yes, so I did.

"Well I don't care if you is from up here, you better fight for your dreams!"

Slowly, I reached out and held one of her rough hands. Then I asked, "But was your dream worth going to prison for all them years?"

Oya looked at me for a long, long time.

"I'm still gonna make it past all them stars," she said as she freed her hand and motioned for me to get to getting.

"Right now, this street b'longs to me and don't *nobody* mess with me or my dreams!" She was still shouting as I walked toward Pine Street.

Seattle and Vicinity

COLETTE BROOKS

Colette Brooks (1952–) was born in Seattle and currently lives in New York City. Her literary and cultural essays have appeared in many publications, among them the New York Times, The New Republic, Partisan Review, *and* The Georgia Review. *She has taught at Harvard University, Columbia University, and New School University in New York City. Her book* In the City: Random Acts of Awareness *(2002) won the 2001 PEN/Jerard Fund Award for a distinguished work of nonfiction. Brooks attended Ravenna Elementary School, John Marshall Junior High, Roosevelt High, Reed College, and the Yale School of Drama. The following selection comes from her essay "Seattle and Vicinity" (1992).*

THE MAP

*M*ukilteo, Suquamish, Puyallup, Pt. Defiance, Driftwood Key, Shilshole, Bothell, Commencement Bay: the map of the city of Seattle and its surroundings, like the maps of other territories to which travelers have laid claim, is studded with thousands of names, thousands of tenuous links in a cartographer's network, each insistently etched, all locked in enduring relation. Seen up close, at 0.68 miles to the inch, the city seems a delicate, ordered abstraction, its areas laced with an infinity of lettered and numbered lines, its names pinned onto those lines precariously, as though the whole would float away were it not for the encompassing red grid that restrains it, latitude and longitude employed to hold both water and land in place. Seen from farther out, at a scale of 3:1, the city becomes a small white block ringed by bands of blue, these now tiny areas themselves dwarfed by the yellows and greens of larger areas seeping yet farther out. The county lines, newly visible from this vantage point, are drawn with dashes that sometimes bisect the waters circumjacent to the city, as though to suggest that any entity can be bounded, once named, and constraint imposed upon fluidity. At this distance, however, what distinguishes the city from its environs is less apparent than in the first view; it seems as if the city, though marked off in myriad ways, still cannot truly be separated from what surrounds it.

I believe that lives are like cities in this regard.

Phyllis, Miss, Phil, Doll, Mom, Lady, Maam, Sis, Dear: I once knew a woman who spent most of her life in one city, who spoke often of "taking off" but never did, who reacted to the tumult of that life by screaming, in what became an incantation, "I could write a book about it," but never did, who until the moment of her death was restive and unsettled and, I think, still screaming, still trying to take off. The woman was my mother, and the city she lived in was the one that I left, long ago. I can no longer summon up the sound of her voice, though it once seemed as if I would never forget it, but I sense her vividly *in situ,* framed against the city and spaces we shared. *Pioneer Square, Jacobsen Road, Roosevelt Way, Wallingford, Sea-Tac, Northgate, the floating bridge, Lake Washington, The Door, The Alley, Alki:* This is the story of places and experiences that will be for me forever interwoven, as maps and lives are forever linked.

. . .

WALLINGFORD

My grandparents, over the years, lived in two houses, one on the water and one in Wallingford, a neighborhood where schools and shops and services abounded, and where they chose to raise their children. They would acquire, as time went on, other pieces of property, modest houses and lots that had suddenly come on the market and seemed a prudent investment, but the Wallingford house remained, always, the center and very focus of the family. It was where my mother grew up, and it was where she would often return, as an adult, to find it unchanged, its rooms arranged as they had been when she was a child, its furnishings virtual artifacts, passed down to and older than my grandparents themselves. We celebrated "the folks'" fiftieth wedding anniversary in that house, and we fully expected to watch them mark off another fifty years together, as though they would live forever, all laws of nature suspended within those walls. My mother's house, in contrast, stood as though exposed, precariously, to the elements; with each rise in the wind its only slightly worn façades and interiors would seem to be swept away, to be replaced by new decors and landscapes, these in turn uprooted and supplanted by something else. Over the years, in what seemed to be fantastically accelerated cycles, turquoise color schemes would turn to beige, and beige to lavender, and lavender to yet another shade; linoleum gave way to wood, and paint to wallpaper, and three windows to one, and rugs to carpeting, and open cabinets to enclosed, and wooden shingles to aluminum siding, and on. She called the house her "Ponderosa." I got used to the changes and enjoyed repainting and redecorating alongside her. As I grew older, I began to suspect that the house was sturdy enough, despite appearances, to withstand all manner of gales and such from without; it was, however, no match whatsoever for the rising storm within.

. . .

THE FLOATING BRIDGE

One day, when I was fourteen, my mother took my grandparents and me out for a Sunday drive, our destination the wilderness terrain due east of us. To get there we had to get past a lake, a lake that stretched the length of the city, as though to buffer in its watery body all shocks from without which might threaten that thin strip of land. The lake was too long to drive around, but it was spanned by a bridge that floated on the water's surface, the water itself seeming to slap up against the cars as they too floated, suddenly amphibious. On days when the weather was good, the sun out and sky clear, crossing the bridge was like gliding through space, neither air nor water resisting; on bad days, when the rain washed down and the waves rose, it was of a different order altogether, the once effortless passage now not simply difficult but sometimes treacherous, the bridge tossing as though to shake off the tiny vehicles that had suddenly become so burdensome. I was drawn to this bridge, though wary of it, its changeable nature seeming to me to bespeak an almost willful instability. And in that, of course, lay much of its attraction. "The floating bridge structure is the most interesting feature of the bridge," a local guidebook declared, as if to affirm and sanction such thrill-seeking. "Each floating unit is securely anchored and weighs 4,558 tons." And so we were said to be safe, regardless of appearances, the bridge engineered to resist disturbance, its quicksilver temper only an illusion.

On the day of our drive it was beautiful out, the air clear and calm. We could see the two chains of mountains that encircled the city, whitened, remote, suspended in the distance, as if to suggest that drive as we might we would never reach them, our progress infinitesimal by cosmic measure. We had been riding along, silently, for some minutes when I realized that something was amiss; we didn't seem to be slowing for stoplights, and my mother was paying less than her usually-minimal attention to other drivers. We were, in fact, on a roller coaster ride, gathering speed with each loop and dip in the road, skimming its surface, the whole city suddenly our private amusement park. And we were headed for the bridge. My grandparents began to clear their throats, quietly, hoping perhaps that this odd turn of events might prove the result of lapsed attention rather than caprice; I could only chime in with a "hey," knowing that soon, panic impending, I might not be able to speak at all. She responded to our imprecations by stepping on the gas, handling the car with the exaggerated grace that comes to those who cross over the line, from impulse to action, believing their resolve to be irrevocable and themselves freer than ever before. Soon, we all fell silent, for we had moved onto the bridge, beyond recall, and were weaving through traffic, the metallic river parting before us as if by divine intercession. I thought we would never reach the other side, but we did. My grandfather insisted that she pull over, and she did, and he and I got out while my grandmother, in steely self-possession, stayed put. Grandpa and I flagged down a bus going in the opposite direction and rode back to the city. When we got to the house they were already there, safe and sound, as though nothing had happened, but I knew better; for the look in her eyes I had seen in the car persisted, and it warned me away.

Years later, when she was working in an east side suburb, she had to drive that bridge twice a day and it spooked her, especially when the weather was bad. On those days she took extra time and arrived home very late, still shaken. I never knew whether she had forgotten the crazed ease of that earlier ride or remembered it all too clearly. By that time, however, my own fear of the bridge had diminished, for I had realized that the narrow strip of land that supported the city was also a bridge, and was also floating, and that nothing in either realm could ever be said to be securely anchored. And the thought did not much disturb me, anymore.

LAKE WASHINGTON

Each year, during the summer Seafair festival, the city held a hydroplane race on Lake Washington, and boats with names like "Miss Budweiser" and "Old Oly" swept around the lengthy course at speeds of 180 miles per hour or more. The Gold Cup, as it was called, took a whole day to run, and those who could not get to the lake themselves could watch it on television, all national programming preempted for this beloved local event. We lived several miles from the race site, but I could hear the roar of the hydros from our house, and I followed the race with intense interest. Some years, I made mock-ups of the event, using construction paper and cardboard to simulate, crudely, the topographical conditions of the course. I would cannibalize other games to find the dice and spinning arrows that would enable me to move my markers forward in orderly but competitive sequence. Lastly, I would fashion the tiny boats themselves, taking care to re-create the fins and other oddly shaped elements that distinguished hydroplanes from conventional craft. When I finished with this reconstruction, I would run my race, keeping an eye on the actual event as it unfolded; if the real Miss Budweiser capsized or lost her engine, I would ruthlessly retire my Miss Bud, mimicking the swift irruptions of fate that befell those in that larger world, deserving or not. At times, the development of this scale-model scenario would begin to diverge from that of its life-sized source, and I would have to make minute adjustments of pace or position among the markers. Too free a field, and my race would lose all relation to the events that were playing out in actuality; too faithful a re-creation, and I would not really be playing by any rules at all, merely replicating the happenstance and immediacy of fact, and that wasn't much fun. So I worked away until I found a method of counterpoising these parallel worlds, a principle of play through which I proposed and disposed as I pleased, while remaining faithful to the spirit and essence of the event.

Then, I was playing; now, I see that I was also learning, learning of the power of containment, of the beauty of the minutely delineated, of the clarity of vision that comes from rendering experience on a scale that offers in compressed force what it lacks in lived amplitude.

. . .

THE ALLEY

As a girl, I used to watch Nightmare Theatre on late night television, every weekend, with a friend and fellow horror film fan who lived down the block. On Friday night one of us would sleep over at the other's house, sleeping bags, potato chips, and soda pop carefully arrayed in front of the set, our object to scare ourselves as fully as possible during the film and then intensify our dread in whispered discussion after it had ended. The quickest way to get from one house to the other was up the alley that ran through the middle of the block, bordering garages and back yards. We would always escort one another, in the evening's ritualistic prelude, claiming that it took two to carry the sleepover stuff, knowing in fact that we were each already frightened, well in advance of the film's start, and half expected Frankenstein or Dracula to step out of the alley's shadows and sweep us away, with no one the wiser until it was too late for rescue. Alone, we were vulnerable; together, we could fend off any creature, at least long enough to scream for help from adults who were sitting in the well-lit kitchens and living rooms lining the route. Our precautions were effective, it seems, for in the many trips we made up the alley no monster ever once dared to detain us. Years later, when I was sixteen or so and far too sophisticated to remember those childish fears, I would walk up that alley all the time, without a thought about it. One evening at twilight, as I was approaching my house, the bogeyman appeared, unbidden, in human form. He was shorter than Frankenstein, less verbal than a vampire, but just as determined to sweep me up and carry me off. I screamed, and struggled, and the adults poured out of their houses, as I had imagined they might, years earlier, and I escaped unharmed. My attacker flew off, never to be found.

And what I remember most about that night is the sensation of surprise. I had always considered it "my" alley; though I held no proper title, years of use and familiarity had made it mine, as distinct from the hundreds of other alleys in the city towards which I took no proprietary stance. And in "my alley" nothing could happen that I didn't countenance. But now a stranger had proved that it was his, too, and had shown just how insubstantial my claims of dominion actually were.

I learned, then, that the boundaries of lives, like those of places, are permeable, and that the truly fearsome inheres not in the exotic, but in the utterly familiar.

A Good Man

REBECCA BROWN

Rebecca Brown (1956–) was born in San Diego and lives in Seattle. She graduated from George Washington University and later from the University of Virginia with an M.F.A. She has published three collections of short stories and four novels, including Gifts of the Body *(1994),* What Keeps Me Here *(1996), and* The Dogs: A Modern Bestiary *(1998). In 2003, her nonfiction book* Excerpts from a Family Medical Dictionary *was published by the University of Wisconsin Press, and her collection of thirteen linked stories, essays, and "rants,"* The End of Youth, *was published by City Lights Books. Brown has also published fiction and nonfiction in numerous literary reviews, magazines, and newspapers. She has been the Washington State Arts Commission writer-in-residence and a MacDowell Fellow. In addition, she has received the Lambda Literary Award for Fiction, the Boston Book Review Award for Fiction, the Pacific Northwest Bookseller's Association Award, and the Washington Governor's Writers Award. This selection from the short story "A Good Man," which appears in* Annie Oakley's Girl *(1993), depicts the loving friendship between a gay man suffering from AIDS in a Seattle hospital and a lesbian woman.*

Jim calls me in the afternoon to ask if I can give him a ride to the doctor's tomorrow because this flu thing he has is hanging on and he's decided to get something for it. I tell him I'm supposed to be going down to Olympia to help Ange and Jean remodel their spare room and kitchen.

He says it's no big deal, he can take the bus. But then a couple hours later he calls me back and says could I take him now because he really isn't feeling well. So I get in my car and go over and pick him up.

Jim stands inside the front door to the building. When he opens the door I start. His face is splotched. Sweat glistens in his week-old beard. He leans in the door frame breathing hard. He holds a brown paper grocery bag. The sides of the bag are crumpled down to make a handle. He looks so small, like a school boy being sent away from home.

"I'm not going to spend the night there," he mumbles, "but I'm bringing some socks and stuff in case."

He hobbles off the porch, his free hand grabbing the railing. I reach to take the paper bag, but he clutches it tight.

We drive to Swedish Hospital and park near the Emergency Room. I lean over to hug him before we get out of the car. He's wearing four layers— T-shirt, long underwear, sweatshirt, his jacket. But when I touch his back I feel the sweat through all his clothes.

"I put these on just before you came." He sounds embarrassed.

I put an arm around him to help him inside. When he's standing at the check-in desk, I see the mark the sweat makes on his jacket.

Jim hands me the paper bag. I take his arm as we walk to the examination room to wait for a doctor. We walk slowly. Jim shuffles and I almost expect him to make his standard crack about the two of us growing old together in the ancient homos home for the prematurely senile, pinching all the candy stripers' butts, but he doesn't.

He sits down on the bed in the exam room. After he catches his breath he says, "Nice drapes."

There aren't any drapes. The room is sterile and white. Jim leans back in the chair and breathes out hard. The only other sound is the fluorescent light. He coughs. "Say something, Tonto. Tell me story."

"—I . . . uh . . ."

I pick up a packet of tongue depressors. "Hey, look at all these. How many you think they go through in a week?"

He doesn't answer.

I take an instrument off a tray. "How 'bout this?" I turn to show him but his eyes are closed. I put it back down. When I close my mouth, the room is so quiet.

I can't tell stories the way Jim can.

A doctor comes in. She introduces herself as Dr. Allen and asks Jim the same questions he's just answered at the front desk—his fevers, his sweats, his appetite, his breath. She speaks softly, touching his arm as she listens to his answers. Then she pats his arm and says she'll be back in a minute.

In a few seconds a nurse comes in and starts poking Jim's arm to hook him up to an IV. Jim is so dehydrated she can't find the vein. She pokes him three times before one finally takes. Jim's arm is white and red. He lies there with his eyes closed, flinching.

Then Dr. Allen comes back with another doctor who asks Jim the same questions again. The doctors ask me to wait in the private waiting room because they want to do some tests on Jim. I kiss his forehead before I leave. "I'm down the hall, Jim."

Jim waves, but doesn't say anything. They close the door.

Half an hour later, Dr. Allen comes to the waiting room. She's holding a box of Kleenex.

"Are you his sister?"

I start to answer, but she puts her hand on my arm to stop me.

"I want you to know that hospital administration does not look favorably upon our giving detailed medical information about patients out to non-family members. And they tend to look the other way if family members want to stay past regular visiting hours."

"So," I say, "I'm his sister."

"Good. Right. OK, we need to do some more tests on Jim and give him another IV, so he needs to stay the night." She pauses. "He doesn't want to. I think he needs to talk to you."

She hands me the box of Kleenex.

Jim is lying on his back, his free elbow resting over his eyes. I walk up to him and put my hand on his leg.

"Hi."

He looks up at me, then up at the IV.

"I have to have another one of these tonight so I need to stay."

I nod.

"It's not the flu. It's pneumonia."

I nod again, and keep nodding as if he were still talking. I hear the whirr of the electric clock, the squeak of nurses' shoes in the hall.

"I haven't asked what kind."

"No."

He looks at me. I take his sweaty hand in mine.

"I don't mind going," he says, "Or being gone. But I don't want to suffer long. I don't want to take a long time going."

I try to say something to him, but I can't. I want to tell him a story, but I can't say anything.

Because I've got this picture in my head of Jim's buddy Scotty, who he grew up with in Fort Worth. And I'm seeing the three of us watching "Dynasty," celebrating the new color box Jim bought for Scotty to watch at home, and I'm seeing us getting loaded on cheap champagne, and the way Scotty laughed and coughed from under the covers and had to ask me or Jim to refill his glass or light his Benson & Hedges because he was too weak to do it himself. Then I'm seeing Jim and me having a drink the day after Scotty went, and how Jim's hands shook when he opened the first pack of cigarettes we ever shared, and how a week later Jim clammed up, just clammed right up in the middle of telling me about cleaning out Scotty's room. And I think, from the way Jim isn't talking, from the way his hand is shaking in mine, that he is seeing Scotty too.

Scotty took a long time going.

Jim stays the night at Swedish. The next night. The next.

He asks me to let some people know—his office, a few friends. Not his parents. He doesn't want to worry them. He asks me to bring him stuff from his apartment— clothes, books. I ask him if he wants his watercolors. He says no.

I go to see him every day. I bring him the *Times*, the *Blade*, *Newsweek*. It's easy for me to take off work. I only work as a temporary and I hate my jobs anyway, so I just don't call in. Jim likes having people visit, and lots of people come. Chubby Bob with his pink, bald head. Dale in his banker's suit. Mike the bouncer in his bomber jacket. Cindy and Bill on their way back out to Vashon. A bunch of guys from the baseball team. Denise and her man Chaz. Ange and Jeannie call him from Olympia.

We play a lot of cards. Gin rummy. Hearts when there are enough of us. Spades. Poker. We use cut-up tongue depressors for chips. I offer to bring real ones, but Jim gets a kick out of coloring them red and blue and telling us he is a very, very, very wealthy Sugar Daddy. He also gets a big kick out of cheating.

We watch a lot of tube. I sit on the big green plastic chair by the bed. Or Dale sits on the big green chair, me on his lap, and Bob on the extra folding metal chair: We watch reruns, sitcoms, *Close Encounters.* Ancient, awful Abbot and Costellos. Miniseries set between the wars. But Jim's new favorites are hospital soaps. He becomes an instant expert on everything—all the characters' affairs, the tawdry turns of plots, the long-lost illegitimate kids. He sits up on his pillows and rants about how stupid the dialogue is, how unrealistic the gore:

"Oh come on. I could do a better gun-shot wound with a paint-by-numbers set!"

"Is that supposed to be a bruise?! Yo mama, pass me the hammer now. Now!"

"If that's the procedure for a suture, I am Betty Grable's legs."

He narrates softly in his stage aside: "Enter tough-as-nails head nurse. Exit sensitive young intern. Enter political appointment in admin, a shady fellow not inspired by a noble urge to help his fellow human. Enter surgeon with a secret. Exit secretly addicted pharmacist."

Then during commercials he tells us gossip about the staff here at Swedish which is far juicier than anything on TV. We howl at his trashy tales until he shushes us when the show comes back on. We never ask if what he says is true. And even if we did, Jim wouldn't tell us.

But most of the time, because I'm allowed to stay after hours as his sister, it's Jim and me alone. We stare up at the big color box, and it stares down at us like the eye of God. Sometimes Jim's commentary drifts, and sometimes he is silent. Sometimes when I look over and his eyes are closed, I get up to switch off the set, but he blinks and says, "I'm not asleep. Don't turn it off. Don't go." Because he doesn't want to be alone.

Then, more and more, he sleeps and I look up alone at the plots that end in nothing, at the almost true-to-life colored shapes, at the hazy ghosts that trail behind the bodies when they move.

Jim and I met through the temporary agency. I'd lost my teaching job and he'd decided to quit bartending because he and Scotty were becoming fanatics about their baseball team and consequently living really clean. This was good for me because I was trying, well, I was thinking I really ought to try, to clean it up a bit myself. Anyway, Jim and I had lots of awful jobs together—filing, answering phones, xeroxing, taking coffee around to arrogant fat-cat lawyers, stuffing envelopes, sticking number labels on pages and pages of incredibly stupid documents, then destroying those same documents by feeding them through the shredder. The latter was the only of these jobs I liked; I liked the idea of it. I like being paid five bucks an hour to turn everything that someone else had done into pulp.

After a while, Jim got a real, permanent job, with benefits, at one of these places. But I couldn't quite stomach the thought of making that kind of commitment.

We stayed in touch though. Sometimes I'd work late xeroxing and Jim would come entertain me and play on the new color copier. He came up with some wild things—erasing bits, then painting over them, changing the color combos, double copying. All this from a machine that was my sworn enemy for eight hours a day. We'd have coffee or go out to a show or back to their place so Scotty could try out one of his experiments in international cuisine on us before he took it to the restaurant. Also, Jim helped me move out of my old apartment.

But Jim and I really started hanging out together a lot after Scotty. Jim had a bunch of friends, but I think he wanted not to be around where he and Scotty had been together so much: the dinner parties and dance bars, the clubs, the baseball team. So he chose to run around with me. To go out drinking.

We met for a drink the day after Scotty. Then a week later, we did again. Over the third round Jim started to tell me about cleaning out Scotty's room. But all the sudden he clammed up, he just clammed right up and left. He wouldn't let me walk home with him. I tried calling him but he wouldn't answer.

Then a couple weeks later he called me and said, "Wanna go for a drink?" like nothing had happened.

We met at Lucky's. I didn't say anything about what he had started to talk about the last time we'd met, and he sure didn't mention it. Well, actually, maybe he did. We always split our tab, and this round was going to be mine. But when I reached for my wallet, he stopped me.

"This one's on me, Tonto."

"Tonto?"

"The Lone Ranger." He pointed to himself. "Rides again."

He clinked his glass to mine. "So saddle up, Tonto. We're going for a ride."

Lying in Wait

J. A. JANCE

J. A. Jance (1944–) was born in Watertown, South Dakota. She received her B.A. from the University of Arizona in 1966, her M.Ed. at American College in 1970, and her C.L.U. at Bryn Mawr in 1980. Mystery novelist J. A. Jance's best-known stories are about Seattle police detective J. P. Beaumont. Her many novels frequently contain gritty and detailed descriptions of Seattle. She is a member of Sisters in Crime and past president of both the Denny Regrade Business Association and Seattle Free Lances. In Lying in Wait *(1994), from which this selection is taken, Seattle appears in the vivid yet menacing aspect common to noir fiction writers the world over. Here Jance depicts crime scenes particular to Seattle's maritime ties.*

I didn't get much sleep that night. I was up early the next morning. Standing on my twenty-fifth-floor terrace, I was drinking coffee when the fall sun came creeping up over the tops of the Cascades. The previous day's rainstorm had blown away overnight, pushed eastward by the arrival of a sudden high-pressure system. The storm had left behind it a layer of low-lying, moisture-heavy fog that clung to the ground like an immense down-filled comforter.

Looking out across Seattle's skyline from that height, I found that the city's streets were shrouded and invisible, as were most of the surrounding low-rise buildings. I could hear the muffled sounds of passing cars and buses in the street below, but I couldn't see them. Now and then I could pick out the sound of an individual car churning down the street, its progress marked by the distinctive hum of pavement-destroying tire studs. Here and there across the cityscape, the tops of other high-rise buildings loomed up out of the fog like so many huge tombstones, I thought. Or like islands in the fog.

Wasn't that the name of a book, I wondered. No, it was *Islands in the Stream.* I had never read that particular Hemingway opus.

My familiarity with the title came from working countless crossword puzzles.

That's what happens when you live alone. Your mind fills up with unnecessary mental junk like so much multipath interference on an over-used radio frequency. Just as static on a radio keeps a listener from hearing the words, stream-of-consciousness interference keeps people who live alone from thinking too much. At least it helps. I had brought my grandfather's ashes home with me the night before. Even now, that discreetly labeled metal box was sitting on my entryway table. Sitting there, waiting. Waiting for my grandmother to decide what should be done with it.

I had asked her if there was some particular place where she would like the ashes scattered, or did she want an urn? Her answer was that she didn't know. She'd have to think about it. She'd let me know as soon as she made up her mind.

Chilled by the damp, cool air, I was headed back inside the apartment for another cup of Seattle's Best Coffee when the phone rang. Beverly Piedmont had been so much on my mind that somehow I expected the call to be from her, but it wasn't. It was Sergeant Watty Watkins, the desk sergeant from the Homicide Squad.

"How's it going, Beau? How's your grandmother holding up?"

"Pretty well, under the circumstances."

"Are you working today, or are you taking another bereavement day?"

"I'll be in. Why? What's up?"

"We've got a case that just turned up a few minutes ago, over at Fishermen's Terminal—a fatality boat fire. If it's a problem, I can assign it to someone else."

"Watty, I told you, I'm coming in. I'll take it. Who'll be working the case with me?"

"There'll be an arson investigator from the Seattle Department, of course. As far as Homicide is concerned, pickings are a little thin. Detective Kramer and two of the other guys are off in D.C. for a training seminar this week. I'll probably team you up with Detective Danielson."

I was partnerless at the moment. Both of my last two partners, Ron Peters and Al Lindstrom, had been injured in the line of duty. In the foreseeable future, Ron was stuck in a wheelchair, and Al had just taken a disability retirement. Those two separate incidents had turned me into the Homicide Squad's version of Typhoid Mary. I was beginning to feel like an outcast.

For weeks now, I had been working by myself on the cold trail of a twenty-five-year-old homicide. The bullet-riddled skull had surfaced during the hazardous-waste cleanup of an import/export shipping company that had left Harbor Island in favor of cheaper rent in Tacoma. I had pretty well exhausted all possible leads on that musty old case. Frustrated at being exiled to a dead-end case and tired of getting nowhere, I was bored stiff and ready for some action.

Sue Danielson is one of the newest additions to the Homicide Squad. Not only is she relatively inexperienced, she's also one of the few female detectives on the team. Still, a partner is a partner. Beggars can't be choosers.

"Sue Danielson's fine," I said. "Is she there already? Does she have a car, or should I come down and get one?"

"She's right here," Watty replied. "I'll send her down to Motor Pool as soon as I get off the horn with you. She'll stop by Belltown Terrace to pick you up on her way north."

"Good," I said. "I'll be waiting downstairs."

And I was. Sue pulled up to the curb at Second and Broad in a hot little silver Mustang with a blue flashing light stuck on the roof. Some poor unfortunate drug dealer had been kind enough to equip the Mustang with a 5.0-liter high-output V-8 before unintentionally donating it to the exclusive use of the Seattle P.D. by way of a drug bust. As I crammed my six-three frame into the rider's side, I wished the bad guy had been taller.

Short crooks tend to buy cars that are long on horsepower and short on headroom.

"How's it going?" I asked.

"Great," Sue said brusquely.

I was still closing the door when she gunned the engine and shot into traffic just ahead of an accelerating Metro bus that was lumbering down Second Avenue. Seattle police vehicles are supposedly nonsmoking in these politically correct days, but there was more than a hint of cigarette smoke wafting around in the Mustang when I got inside. Despite the cold, the driver's-side window was rolled all the way down.

I reached behind me for the seat belt as Sue threw the car into a sharp right onto Clay and raced toward First.

"If you don't mind my saying so, from the way you're driving, I'd guess it isn't all that great," I said.

Sue Danielson made a face. "It's my son," she said. "Jared. He got himself suspended from school yesterday afternoon for fighting in the lunch line. He says one of the other kids stole his lunch money during gym. He claims all he wanted to do was get the money back. So the principal handed out a three-day suspension. Great punishment! How do those jerks figure? Since when is letting a teenager stay home by himself for three days a punishment?"

Ah, the joys of parenthood. No wonder the Mustang reeked of cigarette smoke. Sue Danielson was upset, and I couldn't blame her. Being a parent is a generally thankless can of worms. Being a single parent is even more so. But in police work having a partner whose mind isn't totally focused on the job can prove to be downright dangerous. Cops live in a world where even momentary lapses in concentration can be fatal.

"How old is Jared?" I asked.

"Twelve."

"Generally a good kid?"

"More or less," she said grudgingly.

"Let me give you some unsolicited advice, Sue. The only cure for a twelve-year-old male is time. Lots of it. Wait and see. By twenty, Jared will be fine."

"If he lives that long," she added.

"Where is he right now?" I asked. "At home?"

Sue nodded grimly. "Probably in the family room on the couch, watching MTV even as we speak. I dragged his ass out of bed before I left home and told him if he so much as poked his head outside the door, I'd kill him. Personally. And I left him with a list of chores to be done, starting with scrubbing the kitchen cupboards inside and out."

"That's all you can do for the time being, isn't it?"

"I guess so."

"Then forget about it. For right now anyway. Tell me about the case. Who's dead? Do we know?"

By then we were hightailing it down Elliott past the towering but invisible grain-terminal complex that was totally shrouded in its own thick mantle of fog. Sue is still relatively new to Homicide, but she's a good cop. Her jaw tightened momentarily at the implied criticism in my comments, but she took it with good grace. After a moment or two, her face relaxed into a rueful grin.

"I guess I needed that," she said. "Thanks for the friendly reminder."

"The case," I insisted, still trying to change the subject.

She nodded. "The dead guy's on a boat up here at Fishermen's Terminal. Somebody from a neighboring boat saw the fire just after five-thirty this morning. By the time the fire department got there, the cabin was fully engulfed. They didn't know there was a body inside, though, until just a few minutes before Watty called you. I came in early to finish up the paper on yesterday's domestic in West Seattle, but I wasn't getting anywhere. I couldn't concentrate. I was glad the other two guys turned him down."

"Turned who down?"

"Watty. When he asked them if they wanted to work this case."

"Asked them?" I repeated. "I thought Watty's job was to assign detectives to cases. Since when did he start issuing engraved invitations?"

"Don't take it personally, Beau," Sue counseled. "You know how people talk."

"No, I don't. What's the problem? What are they saying?"

Sue Danielson shrugged. "That three's the charm. First Ron Peters and then Big Al."

So that was it. Those jerks. I had wondered, but this was the first time anyone had come right out and called a spade a spade.

"You mean everybody really is scared shitless to work with me."

"Don't worry about it, Beau," Sue said with a laugh. "I told Watty I'm a big girl, and not at all the rabbit's-foot-carrying type."

"Gee, thanks," I grumbled. "I suppose, under the circumstances, I should take that as a vote of supreme confidence."

Sue clicked on the turn signal. We swooped off Fifteenth and tore around the cloverleaf onto Emerson. At the stop sign, she paused, looked at me, and winked. "As a matter of fact, you should," she said. "Besides, now we're even."

"What do you mean 'even'?"

"You give me advice on child rearing, and I help you get along with your peers. Fair enough. Tit for tat."

Enough said.

The official name, the one used by the mapmakers who write the Puget Sound version of the *Thomas Guide,* may be Salmon Bay Terminal, but most Seattleites know the north end of the Interbay area as Fishermen's Terminal. It's the place where Seattle's commercial fishing fleet is berthed during the months when the boats aren't out on the Pacific Ocean, plying the waters between the Oregon Coast and the Bering Sea, trying to beat the foreign-owned, U.S.-registered vessels and each other to whatever remains of the once-plentiful West Coast fishery.

We raced through the parking lot outside Chinook's Restaurant and bounced over a series of killer, tooth-rattling speed bumps. Past two huge buildings marked Net Shed N-4 and Net Shed N-3 we darted up a narrow alley that was crammed full of firefighting equipment. We threaded our way as far as Dock Three where the fire lane out to the boats was full of trucks and a throng of firemen rolling and restoring equipment. Sue pulled over and parked the Mustang, leaving the blue light flashing on top of the vehicle.

It was early in November, and all the boats were in port. On the east side of the pier stood a long line of two-masted wooden fishing schooners. A few were old sailing vessels that had been converted from wind-driven to diesel propulsion. The others had been built with engines but had carried sails as well at one time. These old wooden boats, used by long-line fishermen to harvest halibut and black cod, were berthed down one side of the planked dock. On the other side were the seine-style–pilothouse-forward–long-liners. On Dock 4, next door to the west, were the salmon seiners, recognizable by their raised mainbooms and open afterdecks.

I wouldn't have known the difference if it hadn't been for Aarnie "Button" Knudsen, one of the guys I once played football with for the Ballard High School Beavers. The summer between our junior and senior years in high school, Button invited me to come work on his father's salmon boat. He told me it was a great part-time job, one he'd had every year from the time he was eleven.

I'm sure it would have been a good deal—if I had ever made it to the fishing grounds, that is. Unfortunately, it turned out I was a terrible sailor. I signed on, but by the time we reached Ketchikan in southeastern Alaska, I was so horribly seasick that Aarnie's disgusted dad gave up, put me off the boat, and finagled me a ride home. Who knows? Had things been different—had I actually found my sea legs and followed in Button's family footsteps—I might never have become a homicide detective. I might have spent my life slaughtering fish instead of studying slaughtered people.

Out beyond the buildings, we came to the place where the fire department had set up a perimeter by roping off the wooden pier at the point where it met a wider paved section. A group of old salts in coveralls, men I suspected to be mostly of Norwegian descent, stood talking to one another in subdued tones, all the while uneasily eyeing the charred wreck of a boat halfway down the dock.

I came down to Fishermen's Terminal sometimes, just to walk around. Early on a chill late-fall morning like this one was, it can be a seemingly idyllic place. Noisy gulls wheel overhead, appearing and disappearing, flying in and out of the fog. Water laps against the pilings. Boats shift and creak, occasionally thumping against the pier. But this idyllic setting is only that—a setting, like the flat backdrop painted on a stage.

The foreground holds the action where a troupe of men do the "work" of fishing—repairing boats and nets, cleaning fish-holes, hosing, painting, building bait benches and fishpens. I have utmost respect for these guys who, year in and year out, pit themselves not only against the unforgiving sea but also against the vagaries of international politics and government regulation. Most of them are independent as hell and more than slightly ornery—a little like the mythical cowboys of the Old West. Come to think of it, a little like me.

Rites of Passage: A Memoir

of the Sixties in Seattle

WALT CROWLEY

Walt Crowley (1947–) began his writing career at age nineteen at The Helix, *Seattle's premier underground newspaper from 1967 to 1970, writing political pieces and drawing cartoons and cover art. During the 1980s, he was a writer for the* Seattle Weekly *and a commentator on KIRO and KCTS-TV. Crowley has written histories about such Seattle institutions as the Blue Moon Tavern in the University District, Group Health Medical Co-operative, Seattle University, Metro, and the Rainier Club. Crowley is director of HistoryLink.org, which chronicles Seattle community history.* Rites of Passage: A Memoir of the Sixties in Seattle *(1995) intersperses the political and intellectual currents of the decade with Crowley's personal experiences.*

TROUBLEMAKERS

In a city, as in a world, it

takes all kinds.

—MURRAY MORGAN

If the clay of my personality was still damp at age fourteen, the same could be said of Seattle when I arrived virtually on the city's 110th birthday. I like to think that we grew up together; certainly we both changed during the next ten years.

I was singularly underwhelmed by the city. Having lived much of my life close to three of the nation's largest cities, I found Seattle puny, provincial, and puritanical. I would learn only much later about the richness of its past and the titanic struggles for wealth, labor, and reform which shaped the city's destiny. Stories of old strikes and scandals had no place in the classroom, least of all at Jane Addams Junior High School. Neither, from what I could tell, did education.

I had left Ridgefield High School, consistently rated one of the nation's best, to enter what was regarded as one of the worst in an undistinguished system. It wasn't really a school at all but an asylum for victims of juvenile dementia and hormonal hysteria. On my first day, I walked into the lunch room to discover a full-scale food fight in progress. Sandwiches, cartons of milk, and assorted fruits arced overhead while prowling bullies hijacked the trays of weaker students. Shocked, I marched directly into the administration office to alert officials to this obvious collapse in social discipline. The vice principal listened to my appeal for action and then replied, "You're going to be a little troublemaker, aren't you?"

The Rev. Martin Luther King Jr. had just visited Seattle, and troublemakers were much in the news at that time. Some historians argue that the Sixties really began on February 1, 1960, when four black students refused to give up their seats until they were served at a Woolworth's lunch counter in Greensboro, North Carolina. The tactic galvanized black and white activists alike: here was something new, personal yet powerful, that individuals could do to dramatize injustice and, perhaps, shame the system into action. For young black intellectuals in particular, the "sit-in" offered an independent course of activism free of the more cautious and hierarchical approaches of the black clergy and lawyers who had brought the struggle into the Sixties chiefly via the churches and courts.

. . .

In October 1961, the new Seattle branch of CORE [Congress of Racial Equality] led a "selective buying" campaign to compel the major downtown department stores to hire more black clerks. The campaign, which emulated similar ones in San Francisco and elsewhere, was later expanded to include "shop-ins" at area grocery stores, in which protesters would fill and then abandon their shopping carts. Similar tactics clogged up Nordstrom's during "shoe-ins." Quintard Taylor writes that Seattle yielded

CORE its first employment gains for blacks and adoption of corporate "equal opportunity" policies by Nordstrom and other major retailers.

(The Seattle CORE was first led by Reginald Alleyne Jr. and then Walter Hundley, who came to Seattle in 1951 to head the leftish Church of the People in the University District. He went on to lead the Seattle Model Cities program and to serve in the city government as director of the Seattle Office of Management and Budget and Department of Parks and Recreation. Years later I would find myself variously his employee, ally, and adversary.)

Another measure of social progress came in March 1962 when Wing Luke was elected to the Seattle City Council. He was the first nonwhite ever elected in the city, and his seat on the Council was the highest elective office yet attained by a Chinese American anywhere in the continental U.S. Luke was no mere token; he became a voice for the "other Seattle" and championed causes such as open housing and minority employment.

These signs of local activism and progress were the exception. McCarthyism, de facto segregation, a smug, pro-business press, and relative prosperity had silenced the noisier voices in Seattle following World War II. The boosters of a "Greater Seattle" preferred to repress memories of the town's more raucous and unsavory past (they might have succeeded but for authors like Murray Morgan and Bill Speidel) and projected an image of an "All-American City" soaring into the Jet Age aboard Boeing's shiny new 707s. Their greatest promotional coup was the 1962 world's fair, officially called "Century 21 Exposition"; in an ironic way, it would prove to be their undoing.

The fairgrounds were still under construction when we occupied our new home in Lake City. Soon after, Boeing confessed that there was no air cushion vehicle project and assigned my father to work on hydrofoils, a competing technology which he held in contempt. (Boeing sank millions into these quirky craft, which ride underwater wings and never made a dime.) Not long after, he finagled a transfer to the missile division, working first on the Dyna-Soar, a winged, reusable "space bomber" which is the granddaddy of the Space Shuttle, and later the silo-launched Minuteman ICBM. My mother also went to work for "The Lazy B," as most

Boeing workers called their employer, as a secretary and rose to become a social assistant to president Bill Allen.

The spring of 1962 saw the opening of the world's fair. It was downright dinky compared to Brussels's sprawling exhibition, a fact I delighted in pointing out. Regardless of its deficiencies, the Seattle world's fair wrought a number of subtle but important changes. Foremost, it showcased and elevated a new kind of progressive leadership, epitomized by the late Eddie Carlson, former head of Westin Hotels and United Airlines. He practiced a sincere and effective style of inclusive politics that cut across the old class lines. His vision is suitably memorialized in the Space Needle, a modernistic lingam which, whatever its architectural merit (I happen to like it), banished the spirits of the old from the village and welcomed in the new.

The fair also salved Seattle's chronic inferiority complex as a parade of visitors marched through town: the Shah and Empress of Iran, Prince Philip of the United Kingdom, cosmonaut Gherman Titov (who scandalized the town by announcing that he had not seen god in space), astronaut John Glenn, New York Gov. Nelson Rockefeller, Vice President Lyndon Johnson, Attorney General Robert Kennedy (who would become a frequent visitor and mountain-climbing companion of Jim Whittaker), and entertainers Bob Hope, John Wayne, and Elvis Presley. Elvis had not been in Seattle since performing at Sick's Stadium in 1957, and his return to film *It Happened at the World's Fair* virtually paralyzed the city.

Highbrows used the fair to try to redeem the city's cultural reputation, which had languished since Sir Thomas Beecham, then conductor of the Seattle Symphony, condemned the town as an "aesthetic dustbin" in 1943. Current conductor Milton Katims brought Van Cliburn and Igor Stravinsky to inaugurate the new Opera House (built within the shell of the 1928 Civic Auditorium) and later staged *Aïda*. The production was a financial disaster, but this boomeranged in the arts' favor by prompting the creation of PONCHO (Patrons of Northwest Civic, Charitable and Cultural Organizations) to expand and stabilize private funding.

The state had to bend its notorious "blue laws" to accommodate all of these outsiders in Seattle, and the flamboyant Gracie Hansen provoked blushes and titters with her Las Vegas–style Paradise International Club revue on the fair's "Gay Way." Dr. Athelstan Spilhaus, director of the U.S. Science Pavilion (now the Pacific Science Center), challenged Gracie to visit his exhibit. As reporter-historian Don Duncan relates the story, she found it "terrific, but it will never replace sex and cotton candy." She invited Spilhaus to take in her show, but there is no record that he did.

Sex and science did achieve a temporary fusion in a "Gay Way" revue called "Girls of the Galaxy," until Seattle's censors shut it down. Meanwhile, U.S. Attorney Brock Adams and the FBI led a highly public raid to shut down overt gambling at several downtown restaurants and "amusement centers." Bingo, pinballs, and other games of chance flourished in Seattle at the time, "tolerated" by officials and police under the convenient fiction that it was unclear whether or not the state constitution allowed the city to prohibit gambling.

Seattle progressives tried to exploit the civic momentum of the fair to fuel a long-sought plan for regional mass transit. The current debate over urban sprawl and pollution dated back to 1958 when attorney James Ellis and allies in the Municipal League and League of Women Voters proposed the creation of the "Municipality of Metropolitan Seattle." Metro was envisioned as a super-utility, which would be insulated from the county's notoriously corrupt and partisan politics. As originally presented to voters in March 1958, Metro would build and operate a regional water quality and sewage system, direct comprehensive planning, manage regional parks, and, most important of all, establish a regional mass transit system. Conservative voters in the suburbs defeated the plan by a narrow margin but a scaled-down Metro, limited to water quality, won approval the following fall.

At about this same time, the state began planning a new central freeway for Seattle. The Highway Department ignored Seattle's pleas for a rail transit right-of-way in the future Interstate-5, and a bold plan offered by Paul Thiry, architect of the Seattle Coliseum, to "lid" the freeway through the downtown. The state literally bulldozed its way through Seattle, destroying thousands of homes and leaving a trench that would not begin to close over for two decades.

It was clear to many that I-5 would not solve the city's growing traffic congestion and smog. Hoping to exploit the civic momentum of the fair, as well as Metro's rapid success in cleaning up the putrescent Lake Washington and the popularity of the city's new Monorail, Ellis and his allies decided to ask anew for permission for Metro to create a mass transit system. Conservatives suspected a stalking horse for a socialist dictatorship, and the AAA and other highway interests saw the system as unwelcome competition. Confused and distracted voters turned down the idea in September 1962. But Jim Ellis wasn't done yet.

Century 21 drew millions and it even made a small profit, something very rare in the world of fairs. All of these strangers in Seattle's midst challenged its provincialism and spurred a reexamination of its prudishness and prejudice. The fair opened a window, and the inshore flow refreshed the city at a moment when it might have suffocated on its own stuffiness.

. . .

ON THE AVE

The hippies are acting out what the Beats wrote.

—GREGORY CORSO

By the fall of 1965, the inspiration of the Beatles and other rock stars had made long hair sufficiently popular among teenage boys that the Seattle School Board felt compelled to ban it. Shaggy locks and beards, for those who could grow them, also became more and more common on the UW campus.

A record 2,222 additional students—more than the G.I. Bill surge of 1946—matriculated that quarter at the UW. I was among the first wave of the 20 million Americans who would celebrate their eighteenth birthdays between 1964 and 1970 and commence their "higher education."

Our arrival was announced in the September 22, 1965, edition of the *University District Herald,* which warned of a new menace in the campus community: "beatniks."

Over the next several weeks, *Herald* publisher Lillian Beloine worked herself into a virtual froth over the growing numbers of idle, unkempt, possibly communistic youngsters loitering along University Way NE, the main business street near the UW better known simply as "the Ave."

I remember my first visit to the Ave one hot summer evening in 1963. My best friend John Moehring (later one of Seattle's most prolific psychedelic poster artists) and I stepped off the bus somewhere around 43rd Street. As we started to cross the Ave, two sandal-clad, bearded men strode past us. One had just inserted a crumpled cigarette into his mouth when the other commented, "Shit, man, that looks like a penis after the struggle." Not exactly Saul on the road to Damascus, but for me an epiphany nonetheless. I was home.

John and I became regulars in the District, commuting almost nightly from our north-end homes, he on a Honda 90, I on a Lambretta TV-200 scooter, singing Verdi duets as we cruised the Ave. Our destinations were chiefly the Pamir House, which featured folk singing in an old house at the corner of 41st and the Ave, and the Eigerwand, then a tiny hole in the wall between 42nd and 43rd specializing in rancid coffee and fiery conversation. It had originally been founded by alpinist Eric Bjornstad and his partner Jim Walcott as a hangout for mountain climbers and other outdoor enthusiasts, but the District's small cadre of bohemians and artists soon took it over.

In 1965, the Eiger moved a block south into a larger space formerly occupied by the cabaret Queequeg (which moved across the University Bridge to become the Llahngaelhyn). The clientele expanded correspondingly, and began to get noticeably younger. On warm days and evenings, a large contingent would stretch out along the wall of the adjacent Adams Forkner Funeral Parlor parking lot, strumming guitars, peddling a little weed, and generally just "making the scene."

And we never called ourselves "beatniks." Anyone halfway hip knew that Herb Caen had coined that word as a put-down. If you were "beat," you didn't need a label.

It was really all quite innocent, but not in the eyes of the establishment. The assistant King County prosecutor denounced us as "unbelievable bums" and we began to attract police attention. Weekend nights became circuses as crusaders descended on the Eiger to save us all from Satan, and a growing number of dope dealers offered to save us from the Christians.

The student editors and writers of the *UW Daily* responded quickly to the *Herald*'s alarum. Deb Das wrote a sympathetic column followed by an article headlined, "Beatnik Scare: Lower Ave Draws Beards Like a Magnet." On October 15, *Daily* editor Jerry Liddell urged "coexistence" with the "Fringies." That word was new to us on the Ave, and we liked it. Soon, some clever entrepreneur printed "Fringie" buttons to make it official.

In late October, the U District YMCA/YWCA convened a panel discussion of the Fringie problem. Lillian Beloine participated, sniffing that she couldn't find the word "Fringie" in her dictionary. Also present were Liddell, Eiger co-owner Walcott, a kid who called himself "Tran," attorney and U District business Brahman C. M. "Cal" McCune, and assistant professor of philosophy John Chambless, a relatively recent transplant from Berkeley. . . . Chambless had the best line of the event. "Where do the people come from who give the District a bad name? They come from the newspapers."

They also came from the Narcotics Squad. On November 2, 1965, officers raided a house in the district and arrested thirteen suspects, including Walcott, for possessing and dealing marijuana. Seattle was in the big leagues—it had a "drug problem."

Street

JACK CADY

Jack Cady (1932–) was born in Columbus, Ohio, and graduated from the University of Louisville in 1961. He served in the U.S. Coast Guard from 1952 to 1956, and since then has worked variously as an auctioneer, social-security claims representative, truck driver, landscape foreman, and professor of English, including at Pacific Lutheran University in Tacoma. Cady was also the editor and publisher of the Port Townsend Journal *from 1974 to 1976. He has been awarded the* Atlantic Monthly *"First" Award, the National Council for the Arts Award, the National Literary Award, the Washington Governor's Writers Award, the University of Iowa Press Iowa Award, the World Fantasy Award, and the Nebula Award. His numerous works include horror, ghost, and gothic novels and short story collections. His novel* Street *(1994), from which the following selection is taken, is a vivid and often surreal depiction of life on Seattle's streets during a serial murderer's killing spree.*

A weather system, more gray and ancient than a solitary old Indian, rolls from the Pacific across mountain ranges that have stood ten million years. The weather breeds in the Aleutian Islands, moving south and east as it bumps against the coasts of Alaska and Canada, the weather roiled and turbulent with rain. Wind raises whitecaps across the wide and Indian face of Puget Sound, and rain speckles whitecaps with small pluckings in the susurrant rush of water. Rain plows against the faces of tall buildings in the city, and it runs down the trunks of ancient trees. As darkness closes its jaws on the city, electric lights become brilliant in primary colors. In the parks, burrows of small animals flood. Mice and shrews are forced to take wet cover above ground, and they stand huddled and blinking in the rain.

The city, itself, is long and narrow. It carries a freeway the length of its spine, and is enclosed by lakes. At this time of day helicopters rise from a nearby airport. They chip-chip-chip through low skies, monitoring the freeways. Radio announcers jive with the pilots, and the pilots tell soon-to-be-homeward-bound workers which roads are open. Taillights are like the eyes of demons as they flash in tens of thousands through the mist.

. . .

Thus day ends and night begins. Commuters' taillights brighten like demonic eyes. Rain (that cannot wash sorrows) washes the street. It penetrates the wool blanket mugged around Elgin's shoulders while he sniffs scents of rain, fish, oil, hemp, and gull droppings along a deserted pier. Smells congregate and his nose separates them, finding proper origins for each. Elgin looks into the dark void of Puget Sound, his eyes moist with tears not rain. He will search for Maria in the morning, but this day is no doubt the last set aside, by anyone, exclusively for Teeney. Teeney was a daughter of our tribe. Elgin murmurs, but no college jock is there to hear.

. . .

Freeways extend north and south from Oregon to Canada, carrying overloads of tractor-trailers, buses, camper trucks, and endless streams of autos. Freeways run between great mountain chains, the Olympics to the west, Cascades to the east. Above the chains stand ancient volcanoes, Mount St. Helens, Mount Rainier, Mount Baker. The volcanoes bear permanent glaciers. Freezing mist called whiteouts sail on their peaks. These are sacred mountains above a land now turned profane. Indians used to worship here. Now Indians sometimes hesitate in the hurry and scurry of pedestrian traffic to stand silent and amazed. The mountain ranges are ten million years old, not volcanic but tectonic; folding plates of earth's crust crumpled. The volcanoes stand twelve thousand feet above a city proud of its skyline.

. . .

The city hums. This is not a busy hive. It more resembles schematics for a computer; traffic lights are gates, and cars swing right or left like electronic impulses. Traffic covers the street, as the street leads to the freeway.

On a corner beside a sign pointing to a freeway, a handsome Yankee lady searches her purse. She finds an envelope containing bills she will pay. She places the bills back in her purse. It is the envelope she wants. The lady takes cash from her purse and puts it in the envelope, quite a lot of cash. Then, in an action still possible in the Northwest, she approaches an elderly gentleman who wears a tailored suit. The lady explains what she wants, quietly indicates a young woman and two children who sit on the sidewalk half a block away. The gentleman nods. He takes the envelope, adds money of his own, walks toward the destitute woman. He bends down, picks an origami crane from a small box, and leaves the envelope.

. . .

Traffic pounds. Cars pass parks, wooded ravines, vacant lots, and hillsides too steep for houses. Pockets of wildness still exist in this city. Trees stand everywhere, for, in perpetual rain, trees grow like weeds. Wild roses twine among wild blackberries in every place inaccessible to bulldozers. Even now, as traffic runs the freeways like an iron along its board, deer live in ravines while raccoons pilfer from garbage cans. This is the Western Flyway, thus ducks, geese, scoters, grebes, an occasional sea harrier. Squirrels are not an endangered species here, nor are rabbits. Sea lions congregate before fish ladders. All around, life scurries and breeds, and, beside the boom of traffic, also dies.

Cold Snap

THOM JONES

Thom Jones (1945–) was born in Aurora, Illinois. He earned a B.A. from the University of Washington in 1970 and an M.F.A. from the University of Iowa in 1973. He lives in Olympia, Washington. He received the American Short Stories Award in 1992, 1993, 1994, and 1995, in addition to the O. Henry Award in 1993 for the story "The Pugilist at Rest." He also received a National Book Award nomination in 1993 for his collection of stories The Pugilist at Rest. *From 1994 to 1995 he was a Guggenheim Fellow. His two other collections include* Cold Snap: Stories *(1995) and* Sonny Liston Was a Friend of Mine *(1999). Jones's stories capture the immediacy of stream-of-consciousness prose while retaining the lucidity of traditional objective realism. They capture what the narrator of the short story "Cold Snap" describes as "the Van Gogh effect"—an epiphanic moment when incisive pain meets with clarity of vision, if only temporarily.*

Son of a bitch, there's a cold snap and I do this number where I leave all the faucets running because my house, and most houses out here on the West Coast, aren't "real"—they don't have windows that go up and down, or basements (which protect the pipes in a way that a crawl space can't), or sidewalks out in the front with a nice pair of towering oak trees or a couple of elms, which a real house will have, one of those good old Midwest houses. Out here the windows go side to side. You get no basement. No sidewalk and no real trees, just evergreens, and when it gets cold and snows, nobody knows what to do. An inch of snow and they cancel school and the community is paralyzed. "Help me, I'm helpless." Well, it's cold for a change and I guess that's not so bad, because all the fleas and mosquitoes will freeze, and also because any change is *something,* and maybe it will help snap me out of this bleak post-Africa depression— oh, baby, I'm so depressed—but I wake up at three in the morning and think, Oh, no, a pipe is gonna bust, so I run the water and let the faucets drip and I go outside and turn on the outdoor faucets, which are the most vulnerable. Sure enough, they were caking up, and I got to them just in the nick of time, which was good, since in my condition there was no way I could possibly cope with a broken water pipe. I just got back from Africa, where I was playing doctor to the natives, got hammered with a nasty case of malaria, and lost thirty pounds, but it was a manic episode I had that caused Global Aid to send me home. It was my worst attack to date, and on lithium I get such a bad case of psoriasis that I look like alligator man. You can take Tegretol for mania but it once wiped out my white count and almost killed me, so what I like to do when I get all revved up is skin-pop some morphine, which I had with me by the gallon over there and which will keep you calm and, unlike booze, it's something I can keep under control. Although I must confess I lost my medical license in the States for substance abuse and ended up with Global Aid when the dust settled over that one. God's will, really. Fate. Karma. Whatever. Anyhow, hypo-mania is a good thing in Africa, a real motivator, and you can do any-thing you want over there as long as you keep your feet on the ground and don't parade naked on the president's lawn in Nairobi and get expelled (which I did and which will get you expelled; okay, I lied, you can't do *anything*—so sue me). On lithium, while you don't crash so bad, you never get high, either, and all you can do is sit around sucking on Primus beer bottles, bitching about how hot it is when there's so much work to do.

While I'm outside checking my faucets, I look my Oldsmobile over and wonder was it last year I changed the antifreeze? Back in bed, it strikes me that it's been three years, so I go out and run the engine and sit in the car with my teeth chattering—it's thirteen below, geez! And pretty soon the warm air is defrosting the car and I drive over to the hardware sec-

tion at Safeway and get one of those antifreeze testers with the little balls
in it. At four in the morning I'm sitting in my kitchen trying to get it out
of the plastic jacket, and it comes out in two parts, with the bulb upside
down. No doubt some know-nothing Central American put it in upside
down for twenty cents an hour in some slave factory. I know he's got
problems—fact is, I've been there and could elucidate his problems—
but how about me and my damn antifreeze? I mean, too bad about you,
buddy, how about me? And I'm trying to jury-rig it when I realize there
is a high potential for breaking the glass and cutting my thumb, and just
as that voice that is me, that is always talking to me, my ego, I guess, tells
me, "Be careful, Richard, so you don't cut your thumb"—at that instant,
I slice my thumb down to the bone. So the next thing you know I'm driving to the hospital with a towel on my thumb thinking, A minute ago everything was just fine, and now I'm driving myself to the emergency room!

Some other guy comes in with this awful burn because a pressure cooker
exploded in his face, and he's got this receding hairline, and you can see
the way the skin is peeled back—poached-looking. The guy's going to need
a hair piece for sure. A doctor comes out eating a sandwich, and I hear
him tell the nurse to set up an IV line and start running some Dilaudid
for the guy, which he deserves, considering. I would like some for my
thumb, but all I get is Novocain, and my doctor says, "You aren't going
to get woozy on me, are you?" I tell him no, I'm not like that, but I have
another problem, and he says, "What's that?" and I tell him I can't jack
off left-handed. Everybody laughs, because it's the graveyard shift, when
that kind of joke is appropriate—even in mixed company. Plus, it's true.

After he stitches me up, I'm in no pain, although I say, "I'll bet this is
going to hurt tomorrow," and he says no, he'll give me some pain med-
ication, and I'm thinking, What a great doctor. He's giving me *pain med-
ication.* And while he's in a giving mood I hit him up for some prostate
antibiotics because my left testicle feels very heavy.

"Your left testicle feels *heavy?*" he says skeptically.

Yeah, every guy gets it, shit; I tell him my left nut feels like an anvil. I
mean, I want to cradle it in my hand when I'm out and about, or rest it
on a little silk pillow when I'm stationary. It doesn't really hurt, but I'm
very much conscious of having a left testicle, whereas I have teeth and a

belly button and a right testicle and I don't even know. I tell him I don't want a finger wave, because I've been through this a thousand times. My prostate is backing up into the seminal vesicles, and if you don't jerk off it builds up and gets worse, and the doctor agrees—that does happen, and he doesn't really want to give me a finger wave, especially when I tell him that a urologist checked it out a couple of months back. He puts on a plastic glove and feels my testicle, pronounces it swollen, and writes a script for antibiotics, after which he tells me to quit drinking coffee. I was going to tell him that I don't jerk off because I'm a sex fiend; I have low sex drive, and it's actually not that much fun. I just do it to keep the prostate empty. Or should I tell him I'm a doctor myself, albeit defrocked, that I just got back from Africa and my nut could be infected with elephantiasis? Highly unlikely, but you never know. But he won't know diddle about tropical medicine—that's my department, and I decide I will just shut my mouth, which is a first for me.

The duty nurse is pretty good-looking, and she contradicts the doctor's orders—gives me a cup of coffee anyhow, plus a roll, and we're sitting there quietly, listening to the other doctor and a nurse fixing the guy with the burned forehead. A little human interaction is taking place and my depression is gone as I begin to feel sorry for the guy with the burn, who is explaining that he was up late with insomnia cooking sweet potatoes when the pressure cooker blew. He was going to candy them with brown sugar and eat them at six in the morning and he's laughing, too, because of the Dilaudid drip. After Linda Ronstadt sings "Just One Look" on the radio, the announcer comes on and says that we've set a record for cold—it's thirteen and a half below at the airport—and I notice that the announcer is happy, too; there's a kind of solidarity that occurs when suffering is inflicted on the community by nature.

My own thing is the Vincent van Gogh effect. I read where he "felt like a million" after he cut off his ear. It only lasted for a couple of days. They always show you the series of four self portraits that he painted at different times in his life as his mental condition went progressively downhill. Van Gogh One is a realistic-looking pic, but as life goes on and his madness gets worse he paints Van Gogh Four and it looks as though he's been doing some kind of bad LSD, which is how the world had been look-ing to me until I cut my thumb. It gave me a three-day respite from the blues, and clarity came into my life, and I have to remind myself by writ-ing this down that all the bad stuff does pass if you can wait it out. You forget when you're in the middle of it, so during that three-day break I slapped this note on the refrigerator door: "Richard, you are a good and loving person, and all the bad stuff does pass, so remember that the next time you get down and think that you've always been down and always will be down, since that's paranoia and it gets you nowhere. You're just in one of your Fyodor Dostoyevski moods—do yourself a favor and for-get it!"

I felt so good I actually had the nerve to go out and buy a new set of clothes and see a movie, and then, on the last day before the depression came back, I drove out to Western State and checked my baby sister, Susan, out for a day trip. Susan was always a lot worse than me; she heard voices and pulled I don't know how many suicide attempts until she took my squirrel pistol and put a .22 long-rifle slug through the temple—not really the tem-ple, because at the last minute you always flinch, but forward of the tem-ple, and it was the most perfect lobotomy. I remember hearing the gun pop and how she came into my room (I was home from college for the summer) and said, "Richard, I just shot myself, how come I'm not dead?" Her voice was calm instead of the usual fingernails-on-the-chalkboard voice, the when-she-was-crazy (which was almost always) voice, and I real-ized later that she was instantly cured, the very moment the bullet zipped through her brain. Everyone said it was such a shame because she was so beautiful, but what good are looks if you are in hell? And she let her looks go at the hospital because she really didn't have a care in the world, but she was still probably the most beautiful patient at Western State. I had a fresh occasion to worry about her on this trip when I saw an attendant rough-handling an old man to stop him from whining, which it did. She'd go along with anything, and she had no advocate except me. And then I almost regretted going out there, in spite of my do-good mood, because Susan wanted to go to the Point Defiance Zoo to see Cindy, the elephant that was on the news after they transferred the attendant who took care of her, for defying orders and actually going into the elephant pen on the sly to be her friend.

There are seven hundred elephants in North American zoos, and although Cindy is an Asian elephant and a female and small, she is still considered the most dangerous elephant in America. Last year alone, three people were killed by elephants in the United States, and this is what Susan had seen and heard on the color television in the ward dayroom, and she's like a child—she wants to go out and see an elephant when it's ten below zero. They originally had Cindy clamped up in a pen tighter than the one they've got John Gotti in down in Marion, Illinois, and I don't remember that the catalogue of Cindy's crimes included human murder. She was just a general troublemaker, and they were beating her with a two-by-four when some animal activist reported it and there was a big scandal that ended with Cindy getting shipped down to the San Diego Zoo; I think there was some kind of escape (don't quote me on that) where Cindy was running around on a golf course in between moves, and then a capture involving tranquilizer darts, and when they couldn't control Cindy in San Diego they shipped her back up here to Tacoma and put her in maximum-security confinement. It was pretty awful. I told Susan that over in India Cindy would have a job hauling logs or something, and there would be an elephant boy to scrub her down at night with a big brush while she lay in the river, and the elephant boy would be with her at all times, her constant companion. Actually, the elephant would be more important than the boy, I told her, and that's how you should handle an elephant in America—import an experienced elephant boy for each one, give the kids a green card, pay them a lot of overtime, and have them stay with the elephants around the clock. You know, quality time. How could you blame Cindy for all the shit she pulled? And in the middle of this, Susan has a tear floating off her cheek and I don't know if it's a tear caused by the cold or if she was touched by Cindy's plight. The reason they sent my sister to the nuthouse was that you could light a fire on the floor in front of her and she would just sit there and watch it burn. When our parents died, I took her to my place in Washington state and hired helpers to look after her, but they would always quit—quit while I was over in the Third World, where it's impossible to do anything. It was like, *Meanwhile, back in the jungle/Meanwhile, back in the States.* . . . Apart from her lack of affect, Susan was always logical and made perfect sense. She was kind of like a Mr. Spock who just didn't give a shit anymore except when it came to childish fun and games. All bundled up, with a scarf over her ears, in her innocence she looked like Eva Marie Saint in *On the Waterfront.*

We drove over to Nordstrom's in the University District and I bought Suz some new threads and then took her to a hair salon where she got this chic haircut, and she was looking so good that I almost regretted it, 'cause if those wacked-out freaks at the hospital weren't hitting on her before they would be now. It was starting to get dark and time to head back when Susan spots the Space Needle from I-5—she's never been there, so I took her to the top and she wandered outside to the observation deck, where the wind was a walking razor blade at five hundred and eighteen feet, but Susan is grooving on the lights of Seattle and with her home-made lobotomy doesn't experience pain in quite the way a normal person does, and I want her to have a little fun, but I'm freezing out there, especially my thumb, which ached. I didn't want to pop back inside in the sheltered part and leave her out there, though, because she might want to pitch herself over the side. I mean, they've got safety nets, but what if she's still got some vestige of a death wish? We had dinner in the revolving dining room, and people were looking at us funny because of Susan's eating habits, which deteriorate when you live in an outhouse, but we got through that and went back to my place to watch TV, and after that I was glad to go to sleep—but I couldn't sleep because of my thumb. I was thinking I still hadn't cashed in the script for the pain pills when Susan comes into my bedroom naked and sits down on the edge of the bed.

"Ever since I've been shot, I feel like those animals in the zoo. I want to set them free," she says, in a remarkable display of insight, since that scar in her frontal lobes has got more steel bars than all the prisons of the world, and, as a rule, folks with frontal-lobe damage don't have much insight. I get her to put on her pajamas, and I remember what it used to be like when she stayed at home—you always had to have someone watching her—and I wished I had gotten her back to the hospital that very night, because she was up prowling, and suddenly all my good feelings of the past few days were gone. I felt crappy, but I had to stay vigilant while my baby sister was tripping around the house with this bullet-induced, jocular euphoria.

At one point she went outside barefoot. Later I found her eating a cube of butter. Then she took out all the canned foods in my larder and stacked them up—Progresso black beans *(beaucoup)*, beef barley soup, and canned carrot juice—playing supermarket. I tell her, "Mrs. Ma'am, I'll take one of those, and one of those, and have you got any peachy pie?"

She says, "I'm sorry, Richard, we haven't got any peachy pie."

"But, baby, I would sure like a nice big piece of peachy pie, heated up, and some vanilla ice cream with some rum sauce and maybe something along the lines of a maraschino cherry to put on the top for a little garnish. Nutmeg would do. Or are you telling me this is just a soup, beans, and carrot juice joint? Is that all you got here?"

"Yes, Richard. Just soup and beans. They're very filling, though."

"Ahhm gonna have to call Betty Crocker, 'cause I'm in the mood for some pie, darlin'."

Suzie looks at me sort of worried and says that she thinks Betty Crocker is dead. Fuck. I realized I just had to sit on the couch and watch her, and this goes on and on, and of course I think I hear someone crashing around in the yard, so I get my .357 out from under my pillow and walk around the perimeter of the house, my feet crunching on the frozen snow. There was nobody out there. Back inside I checked on Susan, who was asleep in my bed. When I finally saw the rising of the sun and heard birds chirping to greet the new day, I went to the refrigerator, where I saw my recent affirmation: "Richard, you are a good and loving person," etc. I ripped it off the refrigerator and tore it into a thousand tiny pieces. Only an idiot would write something like that. It was like, I can't hack it in Africa, can't hack it at home—all I can hack is dead. So I took all the bullets out of the .357 except one, spun the chamber, placed the barrel against my right temple, and squeezed the trigger. When I heard the click of the hammer voilà! I instantly felt better. My thumb quit throbbing. My stomach did not burn. The dread of morning and of sunlight had vanished, and I saw the dawn as something good, the birdsong wonderful. Even the obscure, take-it-for-granted objects in my house—the little knickknacks covered in an inch of dust, a simple wooden chair, my morning coffee cup drying upside down on the drainboard—seemed so relevant, so alive and necessary. I was glad for life and glad to be alive, especially when I looked down at the gun and saw that my bullet had rotated to the firing chamber. The Van Gogh effect again. I was back from Van Gogh Four to Van Gogh One.

They're calling from the hospital, because I kept Susan overnight: "Where is Susan?" "She's watching *Days of Our Lives*," I say as I shove the .357 into a top drawer next to the phone book. "Is she taking her Stelazine?" "Yes," I say. "Absolutely. Thanks for your concern. Now, goodbye!"

Just then the doorbell rings, and what I've got is a pair of Jehovah's Witnesses. I've seen enough of them on the Dark Continent to overcome an instinctive dread, since they seem to be genuinely content, proportionately—like, if you measured a bunch of them against the general population they are very happy people, and so pretty soon we're drinking Sanka and Susan comes out and they are talking about Christ's Kingdom on Earth where the lion lies down with the lamb, and Susan buys every word of it, 'cause it's like that line "Unless they come to me as little children. . . ." Susan is totally guileless and the two Witnesses are without much guile, and I, the king of agnostics, listen and think, How's a lion going to eat straw? It's got a GI system designed to consume flesh, bones, and viscera—it's got sharp teeth, claws, and predatory instincts, not twenty-seven stomachs, like some bovine Bossie the Cow or whatever. And while I'm paging through a copy of *Awake!*, I see a little article from the correspondent in Nigeria entitled "The Guinea Worm—Its Final Days." As a doctor of tropical medicine, I probably know more about *Dracunculus medinensis*, the "fiery serpent," or Guinea worm, than anyone in the country. Infection follows ingestion of water containing crustacea *(Cyclops)*. The worms penetrate the gut wall and mature in the retroperitoneal space, where they can grow three feet in length, and then generally migrate to the lower legs, where they form a painful blister. What the Africans do is burst the ulcer and extract the adult worm by hooking a stick under it and ever so gently tugging it out, since if you break it off the dead body can become septic and the leg might have to be removed.

The pain of the Guinea worm is on a par with the pain of gout, and it can take ten days to nudge one out. The bad part is they usually come not in singles but in multiples. I've seen seven come out of an old man's leg.

If and when Global Aid sends me back to Africa, I will help continue the worm-eradication program, and as the Witnesses delight Susan with tales of a Heaven on Earth I'm thinking of the heat and the bugs in the equatorial zone, and the muddy water that the villagers take from rivers— they pour it in jugs and let the sediment settle for an hour and then dip from the top, where it looks sort of clean; it's hard to get through to them that *Cyclops* crustacea may be floating about invisibly and one swallow could get you seven worms, a swallow you took three years ago. You can talk to the villagers until you're blue in the face and they'll drink it anyhow. So you have to poison the *Cyclops* without overpoisoning the water. I mean, it can be done, but, given the way things work over there, you have to do everything yourself if you want it done right, which is why I hate the idea of going back: you have to come on like a one-man band.

On the other hand, Brother Bogue and the other brothers in the home office of Global Aid don't trust me; they don't like it when I come into the office irrepressibly happy, like Maurice Chevalier in his tuxedo and straw hat—"*Jambo jambo, bwana, jambo bonjour!*"—and give every one one of those African soft handshakes, and then maybe do a little turn at seventy-eight revolutions per minute: "Oh, *oui oui*, it's delightful for me, walking my baby back home!" or "Hey, ain't it great, after staying out late? Zangk heffen for leetle gorls." Etc. They hate it when I'm high and they hate it when I'm low, and they hate it most if I'm feeling crazy/paranoid and come in and say, "You won't believe what happened to me now!" To face those humorless brothers every day and stay forever in a job as a medical administrator, to wear a suit and tie and drive I-5 morning and night, to climb under the house and tape those pipes with insulation—you get in the crawl space and the dryer hose vent is busted and there's lint up the ass, a time bomb for spontaneous combustion, funny the house hasn't blown already (and furthermore, no wonder the house is dusty), and, hey, what, carpenter ants, too? When I think of all that: Fair America, I bid you adieu!

But things are basically looking up when I get Suz back to the hospital. As luck has it, I meet an Indian psychiatrist who spent fifteen years in Kampala, Uganda—he was one of the three shrinks in the whole country—and I ask him how Big Daddy Idi Amin is doing. Apparently, he's doing fine, living in Saudi Arabia with paresis or something, and the next thing you know the doc is telling me he's going to review Susan's case file, which means he's going to put her in a better ward and look out for her, and that's a load off my mind. Before I go, Suz and I take a little stroll around the spacious hospital grounds—it's a tranquil place. I can't help thinking that if Brother Bogue fires me—though I'm determined to behave myself after my latest mishap—I could come here and take Haldol and lithium, watch color TV, and drool. Whatever happened to that deal where you just went off to the hospital for a "little rest," with no stigma attached? Maybe all I need is some rest.

Susan still has those Jehovah's Witnesses on her mind. As we sit on a bench, she pulls one of their booklets out of her coat and shows me scenes of cornucopias filled with fruit and bounty, rainbows, and vividly colored vistas of a heaven on earth. Vistas that I've seen in a way, however paradoxically, in these awful Third World places, and I'm thinking, Let them that have eyes see; and let them that have ears hear—that's how it is, and I start telling Suz about Africa, maybe someday I can take her there, and she gets excited and asks me what it's like. Can you see lions?

And I tell her, "Yeah, baby, you'll see lions, giraffes, zebras, monkeys, and parrots, and the Pygmies." And she really wants to see Pygmies. So I tell her about a Pygmy chief who likes to trade monkey meat for tobacco, T-shirts, candy, and trinkets, and about how one time when I went manic and took to the bush I stayed with this tribe, and went on a hunt with them, and we found a honeycomb in the forest; one of the hunters climbed up the tree to knock it down, oblivious of all the bees that were biting him. There were about five of us in the party and maybe ten pounds of honey and we ate all of it on the spot, didn't save an ounce, because we had the munchies from smoking dope. I don't tell Suz how it feels to take an airplane to New York, wait four hours for a flight to London, spend six hours in a transient lounge, and then hop on a nine-hour flight to Nairobi, clear customs, and ride on the back of a feed truck driven by a kamikaze African over potholes, through thick red dust, mosquitoes, black flies, tsetse flies, or about river blindness, bone-break fever, bilharziasis, dumdum fever, tropical ulcers, AIDS, leprosy, etc. To go through all that to save somebody's life and maybe have them spit in your eye for the favor—I don't tell her about it, the way you don't tell a little kid that Santa Claus is a fabrication. And anyhow if I had eyes and could see, and ears and could hear—it very well might *be* the Garden of Eden. I mean, I can fuck up a wet dream with my attitude. I don't tell her that lions don't eat straw, never have, and so she's happy. And it's a nice moment for me, too, in a funny-ass way. I'm beginning to feel that with her I might find another little island of stability.

Another hospital visit: winter has given way to spring and the cherry blossoms are out. In two weeks it's gone from ten below to sixty-five, my Elavil and lithium are kicking in, and I'm feeling fine, calm, feeling pretty good. (I'm ready to go back and rumble in the jungle, yeah! *Sha-lah la-la-la-lah.*) Susan tells me she had a prophetic dream.

She's unusually focused and articulate. She tells me she dreamed the two of us were driving around Heaven in a blue '67 Dodge.

"A '67 Dodge. Baby, what were we, the losers of Heaven?"

"Maybe, but it didn't really matter because we were there and we were happy."

"What were the other people like? Who was there? Was Arthur Schopenhauer there?"

"You silly! We didn't see other people. Just the houses. We drove up this hill and everything was like in a Walt Disney cartoon and we looked at one another and smiled because we were in Heaven, because we made it, because there wasn't any more shit."

"Now, let me get this straight. We were driving around in a beat-up car—"

"Yes, Richard, but it didn't matter."

"Let me finish. You say people lived in houses. That means people have to build houses. Paint them, clean them, and maintain them. Are you telling me that people in Heaven have jobs?"

"Yes, but they like their jobs."

"Oh, God, does it never end? *A job!* What am I going to do? I'm a doctor. If people don't get sick there, they'll probably make me a coal miner or something."

"Yes, but you'll love it." She grabs my arm with both hands, pitches her forehead against my chest, and laughs. It's the first time I've heard Susan laugh, ever—since we were kids, I mean.

"Richard, it's just like Earth but with none of the bad stuff. You were happy, too. So please don't worry. Is Africa like the Garden of Eden, Richard?"

"It's lush all right, but there's lots and lots of dead time," I say. "It's a good place to read *Anna Karenina*. Do you get to read novels in Heaven, hon? Have they got a library? After I pull my shift in the coal mine, do I get to take a nice little shower, hop in the Dodge, and drive over to the library?"

Susan laughs for the second time. "We will travel from glory to glory, Richard, and you won't be asking existential questions all the time. You won't have to anymore. And Mom and Dad will be there. You and me, all of us in perfect health. No coal mining. No wars, no fighting, no discontent. Satan will be in the Big Pit. He's on the earth now tormenting us, but these are his last days. Why do you think we are here?"

"I often ask myself that question."

"Just hold on for a little while longer, Richard. Can you do that? Will you do it for me, Richard? What good would Heaven be if you're not there? Please, Richard, tell me you'll come."

I said, "Okay, baby, anything for you. I repent."

"No more Fyodor Dostoyevski?"

"I'll be non-Dostoyevski. It's just that, in the meantime, we're just sitting around here—waiting for Godot?"

"No, Richard, don't be a smart-ass. In the meantime we eat lunch. What did you bring?"

I opened up a deli bag and laid out chicken-salad sandwich halves on homemade bread wrapped in white butcher paper. The sandwiches were stuffed with alfalfa sprouts and grated cheese, impaled with toothpicks with red, blue, and green cellophane ribbons on them, and there were two large, perfect, crunchy garlic pickles on the side. And a couple of cartons of strawberry Yoplait, two tubs of fruit salad with fresh whipped cream and little wooden spoons, and two large cardboard cups of aromatic, steaming, fresh black coffee.

It begins to rain, and we have to haul ass into the front seat of my Olds, where Suz and I finish the best little lunch of a lifetime and suddenly the Shirelles are singing, "This is dedicated to the one I love," and I'm thinking that I'm gonna be all right, and in the meantime what can be better than a cool, breezy, fragrant day, rain-splatter diamonds on the wraparound windshield of a Ninety-eight Olds with a view of cherry trees blooming in the light spring rain?

American Bullfrog

CHARLES D'AMBROSIO

Charles D'Ambrosio (1958–) grew up in Seattle and graduated in 1991 from the Iowa Writers' Workshop. He has published fiction in the New Yorker, *the* Paris Review, *and numerous other periodicals and anthologies, including* Best American Short Stories. *He is the recipient of the Aga Khan Fiction Prize, the* Transatlantic Review/Henfield Foundation Award, *and a James Michener Fellowship. The following selection comes from his short story "American Bullfrog," which appears in his collection of short stories,* The Point *(1995).*

W e waited outside school for two hours, but Hopper and Riles never showed up. We hustled up Fifteenth to the Safeway and started to nickel-and-dime the food stamps, something Regimbal's dad taught us, sending us to the store after school to break the bills down and bring back the accumulated change, so he could return later and buy beer, cigarettes, toilet paper, and soap. Regimbal's dad was one of many thousands of men laid off at Boeing and worked odd off-the-books carpentry jobs at our church, and for other parishes in the dioceses, and also groomed the baseball fields, raking the basepaths and chalking in the foul lines. He told my dad he aimed to chase work, to move Regimbal and Carol Ann to Grand Junction. Naturally, from listening to Mr. Regimbal, we both learned to hate Boeing. Fuck Boeing, we'd say now. Before, as kids, me and Regimbal had decided that his dad was better than mine, because he built airplanes, Boeing airplanes, which were the most important things in Seattle, and we loved to watch the jets soar, streaks of silver like airborne salmon in the ocean of blue sky. My dad was a schoolteacher, a job we both had a low opinion of. But now I think Regimbal was a little ashamed of his dad's circumstance, which, the way it works, was his too.

We got in the express line over and over and bought crap until we were chased out of the store by the manager, a thin queer shaking his feather duster at us. "Scoot, scoot," he said.

Regimbal got pissy. "Hey, we can shop here the same as anyone else."

"Get out," the guy said.

The pockets of our field jackets bulged with candy, potato chips, fruit pies, grape pop, apples and bananas, a package of lunch meat, the kind with green olives embedded in it.

"How much did you get?" I asked.

"Five-ten, five-twenty, one two three," Regimbal said, clinking coins in his palm. "Five dollars twenty-three cents. You?"

"Four-nineteen," I said.

We ran for Carbone's down Fifteenth, a broad avenue along the borders of which some dreaming developer, years ago, had planted palm trees. Tropical palms in Seattle—you never saw the crows in them. They looked natural enough in the rain, though, and it was soon going to rain hard.

"Do you want any of this food?" Regimbal asked.

"I'll have the pie I got," I said. "Why'd you get that baloney?"

"I just always wondered about it," he said. "It's all right, too."

"I bet Diane's already there."

"I don't see why you had to call her."

"Why not? You jealous?"

"There won't be any other girls there."

"There might be."

Carbone's old house was across the alley from ours. On Sundays after church my dad and Mr. Regimbal would sit on our back porch and argue about the changes in Seattle. Mr. Regimbal said like usual the average guy, meaning him, was going to get screwed in the butt. "Look at what happened to Carbone, for godsakes," he'd say. My dad, who was fairly average himself, was relieved to see the neighborhood improve, after years of neglect and decline, even though he admitted to Mr. Regimbal that, morally speaking, he was against homos. But Seattle was in the dumps. Boeing had by that fall laid off sixty thousand men, and a lot of the run-down houses in our neighborhood, first rented by hippies and then blacks, were now getting bought and fixed up nicely by queers. I'd got so I could identify a homo when I saw one. They seemed neat and clean but quite shy, as a people.

All the houses across the alley, the entire block fronting Fifteenth, had been condemned that fall, and during the day their boarded windows and lopsided porches and yards scrabbled over with blackberry vines gave the neighborhood a mean, blighted, toothless appearance, but at night, reduced to vague silhouettes, they looked cruel and romantic in a manly way, I thought, sort of raggedy and rotten, disheveled and proudly standing on their last legs, despite a serious beating. The houses were slated for demolition in the spring, to be replaced by condos—a word I had never heard before. When the construction sign first went up, it had sounded to me like people would be living inside birds.

. . .

Blue rain beat through the street lamps and the tufted palms.

"You coming?" Regimbal said. He stood beside Hopper, each of them holding a six of Rainier Ale, known to us, and to all boys in Seattle in the seventies, as green death.

About nine of us crossed Fifteenth, passing through the screen of tall black firs bordering Volunteer Park which we called Ball-and-Queer, and headed up the sloping hill toward the art museum. We huddled under cover of the sagging [boughs] of a blue spruce, rain dripping off the tips, outside the circle of packed dirt we sat on, and watched for the queers. A chunk of hash made the rounds in a pipe carved of bone. We all grazed on the junk me and Regimbal had bought with the food stamps. North and west of us a wide field spread out fairly flat until it dropped down a steep hill behind some trees. Beyond those trees the buoyant light of the city rose, warm and yellow. I took a sip of the warm beer and watched the horizon. The fags were like wildlife to me, wary animals that only came out at night, and hunters, too, looking for prey. I had the idea they were fags out of loneliness. That is, they came here to the park, at night, in the dark and the rain, with flashlights, to find something a person should be able to find in an easier place, a warmer and drier and better place.

"I got attacked one night," Riles said.

I addressed his nose. "Where?"

"Down by the reservoir."

"How many?" Regimbal said. He was smoking one of Hopper's cigarettes, letting it bob from his lips. We had stopped shaving at the same time, thinking to have a race. We were like those five-and-dime toys with a magnet and a pile of metal shavings and a picture of Bluto. Regimbal, it turned out, didn't have a mustache. He had a section of goatee.

"I don't know," Riles said. "Six, seven."

We all stared at the horizon. The queers would wander among the trees, using flashlights to signal each other, white beams cutting through grainy, rain-slashed dark. They had a code of their own that was impossible to crack.

"They're taking over," Regimbal said.

"There's a light!" Hopper stood up. "See?"

I'd missed it. And then I saw it, two quick flashes from the right, followed by a long steady answer from the left. Hopper lifted a chunk of log and handed it to Regimbal.

"They're all over there," he said, aiming Regimbal's head. "You see? Who throws better, you or John?"

"Me," Regimbal said, although that wasn't the truth.

"Okay," Hopper said.

Regimbal tucked the log under his arm. The rain cut in a sharp slant against us as we headed out into the open field. Each of us had a beer. Green death was only available at the state liquor store, and was greatly prized for its potency. They sold it from stacked cases, always warm, which made it a decent drink for cold nights outdoors.

"I gotta piss," I said.

I took a leak in the middle of the field. My dink was still wet and sticky from Finklebien. I watched the line of trees. Some summer nights the fags flashed in the dark like fireflies. I had only begun to notice them recently, within the last year, although I assume they existed before that. I zipped up. Where I'd been holding myself, my hand had blood on it.

"Shit," I said. The blood was rust-colored.

"What?" Regimbal said. "Let me see."

"Forget it, man, get away!"

I started walking and noticed that from all the beer I'd drunk the whole world bounced.

"So we're just gonna throw that log at them?" I said.

"I hope I hit one," Regimbal said.

"Don't, man. Just get 'em to chase us."

"You chickenshit?"

I seemed to be seeing everything through water. The rain hummed in my ears. I thought I heard someone calling my name. I looked around.

"What?"

"Did you hear that?" I looked behind us. I suddenly felt awkward beside Regimbal. My body ached with awareness; I felt squeezed by silence.

The field was sloppy, pocked with puddles, and Regimbal stomped in one, spraying me with mud. I tripped him and we fell, we wrestled, rolling in the grass and mud and rain. We were boys, right, and instead of talking about what we were doing, against the silence, we banged into each other an awful lot, and this, in its own way, was a kind of discussion we were having, a debate. Afterward, muddy and wet, with grass in my hair, I felt better, easier, calmed down.

Indian Killer

SHERMAN ALEXIE

Sherman Alexie (1966–), a Spokane/Coeur d'Alene Indian, grew up on the Spokane Indian Reservation in eastern Washington. After attending Reardan High School, where he was "the only Indian . . . except for the school mascot," he enrolled in Gonzaga University in Spokane and eventually transferred to Washington State University, where he began writing poetry. Soon after graduating, he published his first book, The Business of Fancydancing *(1991), which contains poetry and short stories. Sherman Alexie has published nine volumes of poetry, four collections of short stories, including most recently* Ten Little Indians *(2003), and a novel. He has also written two screenplays:* Smoke Signals, *adapted from his book* The Lone Ranger and Tonto Fistfight in Heaven *(1993) and made into a film in 1998, and* The Business of Fancydancing, *made into a film directed by Alexie in 2003. A Seattle resident, Sherman Alexie writes with honesty, compassion, bittersweet humor, biting satire, and a vivid appreciation for the fantastical. The following selection comes from his novel* Indian Killer *(1996), about an Indian man, John Smith, who lives and works in Seattle and wanders the city as a serial killer stalks his next victim. Throughout the novel, Alexie depicts the desolate existence of many American Indians living in large urban areas.*

OWL DANCING AT THE BEGINNING
OF THE END OF THE WORLD

John stepped off the elevator, ignored offers to go for beers, and walked through the downtown Seattle streets. There were so many white men to choose from. Everybody was a white man in downtown Seattle. The heat and noise in his head were loud and painful. He wanted to run. He even started to run. But he stopped. He could not run. Everybody would notice. Everybody would know that he was thinking about killing white men. The police would come. John breathed deeply and started to walk slowly. He was walking in work boots and flannel shirt through Seattle, where men in work boots and flannel shirts were often seen walking. No one even noticed John. That is to say that a few people looked up from their books and a couple drivers looked away from the street long enough to notice John, then turned back to their novels and windshields. "There's an Indian walking," they said to themselves or companions, though Indians were often seen walking in downtown Seattle. John the Indian was walking and his audience was briefly interested, because Indians were briefly interesting. White people no longer feared Indians. Somehow, near the end of the twentieth century, Indians had become invisible, docile. John wanted to change that. He wanted to see fear in every pair of blue eyes. As John walked, his long, black hair was swept back by the same wind that watered his eyes. He walked north along the water, across the University Bridge, then east along the Burke-Gilman Trail until he was standing in a field of grass. He had made it to the wilderness. He was free. He could hunt and trap like a real Indian and grow his hair until it dragged along the ground. No. It was a manicured lawn on the University of Washington campus, and John could hear drums. He had been on the campus a few times before but had never heard drums there. He walked toward the source of the drums. At first, he thought it was Father Duncan. He was not sure why Father Duncan would be playing drums. Then he saw a crowd of Indians gathered outside a large auditorium, Hec Edmundson Pavilion. There were two drums, a few singers and dancers, and dozens of Indians watching the action. So many Indians in one place. There were white people watching, too, but John turned away from their faces. He stepped into the crowd, wanting to disappear into it. A small Indian woman was standing in front of John. She smiled.

"Hey," she said.

"Hey," he said.

"I'm Marie. Are you a new student here?"

"No."

"Oh," she said, disappointed. She was the activities coordinator for the Native American Students Alliance at the University and thought she'd found a recruit. A potential friendship or possible romance.

"What's your name?"

"John."

"What tribe you are?"

He could not, would not, tell her he had been adopted as a newborn by a white couple who could not have children of their own. Along with the clipping about Father Duncan's disappearance, John always carried the photograph of the day his parents had picked him up from the adoption agency. In the photograph, his father's left arm is draped carefully over his mother's shoulders, while she holds John tightly to her dry right breast. Both wear expensive, tasteful clothes. John had no idea who had taken the picture.

His adopted parents had never told him what kind of Indian he was. They did not know. They never told him anything at all about his natural parents, other than his birth mother's age, which was fourteen. John only knew that he was Indian in the most generic sense. Black hair, brown skin and eyes, high cheekbones, the prominent nose. Tall and muscular, he looked like some cinematic warrior, and constantly intimidated people with his presence. When asked by white people, he said he was Sioux, because that was what they wanted him to be. When asked by Indian people, he said he was Navajo, because that was what he wanted to be.

"I'm Navajo," he said to Marie.

"Oh," she said, "I'm Spokane."

"Father Duncan," said John, thinking instantly of the Spokane Indian Jesuit.

"What?"

"Father Duncan was Spokane."

"Father Duncan?" asked Marie, trying to attach significance to the name, then remembering the brief fragment of a story her parents had told her. "Oh, you mean that one who disappeared, right?"

John nodded his head. Marie was the first person he'd met, besides the Jesuits at St. Francis, who knew about Father Duncan. John trembled.

"Did you know him?" asked Marie.

"He baptized me," said John. "He used to visit me. Then he disappeared."

"I'm sorry," said Marie, who was definitely not Christian. With disgust, she remembered when the Spokane Indian Assembly of God Church held a book burning on the reservation and reduced *Catcher in the Rye*, along with dozens of other books, to ash.

"I know a Hopi," said Marie, trying to change the subject. "Guy named Buddy who works at the U. He's a history teacher. Do you know him?"

"No."

"Oh, I thought you might. He hangs around with the Navajo bunch. Jeez, but they tease him something awful, too." John barely made eye contact with Marie. Instead, he watched all of the Indians dancing in circles on the grass. It was an illegal powwow, not approved by the University. John could figure out that much when he noticed how the dancers were trampling on the well-kept lawn. Indians were always protesting something. Marie had organized the powwow as a protest against the University's refusal to allow a powwow. Only a few of the Indians had originally known that, but most everybody knew now, and danced all that much harder.

. . .

THE SANDWICH LADY

John sat on a sidewalk in downtown Seattle beneath the Alaskan Way Viaduct. An ugly, gray monstrosity that would surely fall to pieces during a major earthquake, it served as a noisy barrier between downtown Seattle and the waters of Elliott Bay. However, as an unplanned benefit, the Viaduct also provided shelter for Seattle's homeless.

Beneath the Viaduct, one could find cover from Seattle's rains, with the nearby waterfront and Pike Place Market attracting tourists who were sometimes willing to empty their pockets of loose change.

When he worked downtown, John visited the homeless Indians who congregated beneath the Viaduct and those in Occidental Park in Pioneer Square. But John was more often drawn to the Indians beneath the Viaduct. He'd walk down there during his lunch hours to spend time with them, though he never spoke more than a few words to anyone. Usually, he just walked by those real Indians, who sat in groups of three or four, nodding their heads when John walked past.

"Hey, cousin," the homeless Indians always called out to John. "You got any coins?"

John had come to know a few by their names, King, Agnes, and Joseph, and he recognized a few dozen by sight. Before he'd met them, John had shared the common assumption that all homeless Indians were drunks. But he had soon discovered that many of them didn't drink. John had been surprised by that discovery, and both relieved and saddened. He was relieved that many of the homeless Indians refused to surrender and drink themselves to death. He was saddened that so many Indians were homeless and had no simple reasons to offer for their condition.

On that evening, John sat by himself, apart from a group of Indians who were singing and telling jokes. More laughter. John watched those Indians, in dirty clothes and thirdhand shoes, miles and years from their reservations, estranged from their families and tribes, yet still able to laugh, to sing. John wondered where they found the strength to do such things. They were still joking and singing when Marie Polatkin drove up in a battered white delivery van. John recognized her from the powwow at the University. The Indian woman with crowded teeth. She haphazardly parked the truck and jumped out, talking fast and loud. The dozens of homeless women and men, Indian and otherwise, who lived beneath the Viaduct soon gathered around her.

"What is this?" John asked a white man in an old wheelchair. He wore an army surplus jacket and a dirty pair of blue jeans.

"It's Marie, the Sandwich Lady," said the wheelchair man.

"Sandwich Lady?"

"Yeah, man. You know? Sandwiches? Two pieces of bread with something between? When was the last time you ate?"

John thought about the lunch box he had left at work. Inside, a can of Pepsi, a convenience-store sub sandwich, an apple.

"Well," said the wheelchair man. "You better get in line if you're hungry. Her sandwiches go fast, man. I help her sometimes, you know? Making the sandwiches. Me and her are tight. Yeah, my name is Boo."

Boo offered his hand, but John ignored it. Shrugging his shoulders, Boo took his place in line, behind a woman talking to herself.

"Here's a ham and cheese, Bill," Marie said to the first man in line. She knew their names! "How you doing, Esther? You look good, Charles. Lillian, how's the tooth? Martha, where have you been? I've got a peanut butter and jelly for your son. Where is that boy?"

The wheelchair man and John stepped up next. John was embarrassed. He had nothing to give Marie, no gift, no blanket, no basket. He wanted to run, hoping to run away from everything, hoping he could run into a new skin, a new face, a new kind of music. He wanted to run into the desert. But he wanted to see Marie, wanted to hear her voice.

"Marie," he said.

"Yes," she said, not recognizing John for a brief moment, then visibly surprised when she did. John was homeless, she thought, an explanation for his strange behavior at the protest powwow.

"Marie," John said again.

"John, right?"

John nodded.

"How are you?" she asked.

"I wanted to see you."

"Well, it's good to see you. Are you hungry? Do you want a sandwich?"

John looked down at the sandwich in Marie's hand. He wondered if it was poisoned.

"No," John said. He struggled to speak. He wanted to tell Marie everything. He wanted to tell her about Father Duncan. He opened his mouth, closed it again, and then turned to run. He ran until he could no longer recognize anything around him.

"Who was that?" the wheelchair man asked Marie as John raced away.

"I'm not sure. A guy named John. Navajo."

"I think he likes you."

"Yeah, maybe, Boo. How've you been? How's the poetry coming along?"

"I wrote one for you," said Boo. He reached into his shirt pocket, pulled out a tightly folded wad of paper, and handed it to Marie. She took it, unfolded it, and read the poem.

"Thank you, Boo," she said. "That's very nice. Here's a turkey and Swiss."

"Thank you," he said and rolled himself away. Marie handed sandwiches out until her arms ached. For an hour, two. She talked to her friends, consoled, reprimanded, and touched them, her hand on their shoulders, her hand clasping their hands, fingers touching fingers, in greeting, in conversation, in departure. She ate a sandwich herself, washed it down with a Pepsi, and watched the night grow darker by degrees. She knew there were many men and women who waited for her to deliver those sandwiches. They waited for the food, for the company, for proof they were not invisible. For the mentally disturbed, Marie knew these sandwich visits might be the only dependable moment in their lives. She also knew she delivered the sandwiches for her own sanity. Something would crumble inside of her if she ever walked by a homeless person and pretended not to notice. Or simply didn't care. In a way, she believed that homeless people were treated as Indians had always been treated. Badly. The homeless were like an Indian tribe, nomadic and powerless, just filled with more than any tribe's share of crazy people and cripples. So, a homeless Indian belonged to two tribes, and was the lowest form of life in the city. The powerful white men of Seattle had created a law that made it illegal to sit on the sidewalk. That ordinance was crazier and much more evil than any homeless person. Sometimes Marie wondered if she worked so hard at everything only because she hated powerful white men. She wondered if she went to college and received good grades just because she was looking for revenge. She woke up at four in the morning to study before she went to class. She rushed from the University down to the shelter, to a protest, to the sandwich van. All to get back at white men? A police car rolled by. Officer Randy Peone. Marie knew him. She knew most of the cops who worked downtown. Patrols had been increased because the police knew something bad was happening. The officer waved to Marie. She waved back.

Blurred Vision: How the Eighties Began

in One American Household

NATALIA RACHEL SINGER

*Natalia Rachel Singer (1957–) lived in Seattle in the late 1970s and early
1980s. She currently teaches creative writing at Saint Lawrence University
in Canton, New York. She is the author of* Scraping by in the Big Eighties
*(2004), a collection of essays published in the American Lives Series of the
University of Nebraska Press. She is the editor, with Neal Burdick, of* Living North Country: Essays on Life and Landscapes in Northern New York
(2001). Her fiction and nonfiction have been published in magazines and literary journals such as Harper's, Ms., Creative Nonfiction, Prairie Schooner,
and The North American Review *(where she is a contributing editor), and
has appeared in such anthologies as* Microfiction *and* The Best Writing on
Writing. *She has won several national awards for her writing, including an
award in the World's Best Short-Story contest, and she has been a recipient
of a grant from the New York Foundation for the Arts for nonfiction literature. The following selection, from her essay "Blurred Vision: How the Eighties Began in One American Household" (2000), recounts the author's spirited
and wide-eyed arrival in Seattle on the brink of the Reagan era.*

> Reagan was elected precisely because he couldn't see
> the other side of the postcards, because he wishes to know
> as little as possible about an America in which illiterate children
> commit murder for the price of a secondhand radio.
>
> —LEWIS LAPHAM

Reading Seattle

I never figured out what was going on around me,
even when it was written on the walls in red.

—JO ANN BEARD

Like centuries, decades—or at least the qualities we ascribe to them—
don't begin or end on schedule, the instant we pucker up for the midnight kissing spree. The sixties weren't the *revolutionary* sixties until the
assassination of JFK and didn't end until the massacre at Kent State, while
the greedy eighties, quite fittingly, hogged some time from both ends. I
think the eighties started early—in November of 1979, on a Sunday. Of
course only hindsight lends that kind of mountain-top clarity to our
visions of the past; down in the valley of the day to day, it was hard to see
the signs, especially when, for me, they had to be read through the rosy
lens of a would-be bohemian optimism that only occasionally grew sharp
with the awareness of the possibility of personal and collective doom.

My boyfriend Joe and I were at the Cause Célèbre, a collectively owned
café where multi-earringed young people in berets scooped up homemade
mocha chip ice cream for the aging hippies, environmental activists, punk
rockers, and artists who would linger for hours embroiled in passionate
conversation, savoring the aromas of cinnamon and socialism in the air.
The Cause, as it was commonly called, was my favorite of Seattle's coffee-
houses within walking distance. Back in Evanston, Illinois, where I'd arrived
for college too late for the revolution but just in time for disco, I'd loi-
tered in vinyl booths of fluourescent-lit diners penning my first poetry
on grease-stained napkins always with the sense that life was elsewhere,
some place with hard wood tables and vanguard attitudes. I had been
brought up reading the *Daily Worker,* had relatives who'd been blacklisted
in the fifties, a second cousin who worked for Cesar Chavez, but at Northwestern, post-Vietnam, the only thing that got people to stand up to The
Man was bad grades. In Seattle, I hoped, I would find my true tribe. At
the moment I had an uncool day job as a technical writer, but I often
stopped in for lunch in my ill-fitting suit, daydreaming an alternative life
for myself in which I donned a beret and joined the collective.

While we waited for our giant sundaes to get built, Joe went to the news-
stand out front and bought a paper. That autumn we were in the rush of

new love, so mutually enthralled that we'd temporarily forgotten the rest of the world. We hardly even watched television—my housemates Claudia and Philip had one but disapproved of it—and when we did, it was just to check on the progress of Joe's home team, the Pittsburgh Pirates, who'd made it to the World Series that year.

Somewhere near the door, a good-looking black man in his thirties, bare-armed under a black leather vest, one bicep held taut in a black leather band, was lecturing his young blond girlfriend about Carter's mistakes. I distinctly heard the word "hostages," and looked at them curiously for a minute, but let it go when Joe returned with our hot fudge sundaes and the *Seattle Post-Intelligencer*. I wasn't very interested in listening in on some chat about Jimmy Carter. He was far too centrist and hawkish and boring for my tastes. I liked Rosalyn because she was pro-E.R.A., but so, I assumed, was every other American woman with a brain. I took a lot for granted in those days.

Because the weekend paper came out on Friday, the sixty-six Americans who had become the captives of some young Shiite Muslims in Iran had not yet made it into print; perhaps the couple near the corner had picked it up on their car radio, but I'm not certain if I haven't imagined them in the first place. While Joe browsed the sports page, I went directly to Arts and Leisure to see what plays were opening that week. Occasionally I gazed out the window, making what I hoped were astute, writerly observations about the brown leaves blowing through the streets like crumpled up paper bags beneath a sky the color of an aged dime. I was twenty-two years old. I didn't know what I didn't know and didn't miss it.

"We should bring Claudia and Philip back some double mocha chip," I said. "Or do you think they would like rocky road?" This was a decision of paramount importance and if I made the wrong choice, I would hear about it.

"Maybe a pint of each?" Joe said. Joe didn't live with us, but he was over so often that he wanted to stay on their good side. He was a guy who knew how to live it up, which was partially why I'd fallen in love with him and partially why I'd been afraid to, why I'd written him off as just a summer-after-college fling until he arrived that October with the boxed books I'd left in his basement and his intention of going for something "real" with me if I was half-receptive.

I plucked off my maraschino cherry and set it on my napkin so as not to ingest any Red Dye Number Two, and started eating.

November 4, 1979. The day began for me and my housemates, and, I would imagine, for most Americans, like any other Sunday of that era. I can recount it in detail not because it seemed auspicious in any collective sense, but because I had just turned an important corner of my youth and was trying to live the examined life, so it seemed like a good idea to keep a journal. Flash back a few years, and this is the scene I recorded from our living room as I sat on Claudia's director chair with my feet propped up on a stool near the wood stove.

Noon. While, unknown to us, fundamentalist Muslims of the Middle East were extracting their vengeance on Christians and Jews in the West, Philip and Joe were creating their own new world order in our small house. Hunched over a card table propped level by Philip's well-worn copy of Heidegger's *Being and Time,* they were engrossed in a game of Risk. Both of them were stoned, their eyes rivered with pink.

"Ah, there go the last of your armies," Philip said, pushing his phalanx of red tokens across what would be Texas, down through the mountains and jungles of Mexico, and into Central America. With his long, narrow face and sun-colored hair which hung to his shoulders in greasy clumps, his mustache and goatee, he resembled the early Lenin. Joe was more like Che Guevara, his full beard flecked red, his shoulder-length hair the rich brown of coffee. If someone had told us that clean-shaven men would soon revive the tight-cropped look of the fifties, none of us would have believed it.

In between, Philip did his eye exercises. When he'd moved to Seattle that September he'd come across a book called *Visionetics,* a how-to primer for the visually impaired inspired by the works of Aldous Huxley. Since then he'd hidden his glasses from himself in a drawer, taken to shifting his eyes in Tricky Dick–like circles, and acquired a ferocious squint. My private name for him was Mr. Magoo. Occasionally he got up uncertainly to get himself a beer or to stir the pinto beans he'd left simmering in a giant pot on the stove. With his slow, dreamy, myopic moves, the mere act of making lunch could be drawn out for hours.

"You'll regret this," Joe said half-heartedly, removing his men from the region. Philip was teaching Joe the game and Joe wasn't very good at it. Although he liked the intellectual sport of military strategy, Joe was far more interested in getting high and listening to the Grateful Dead and talking about the works of Jack Kerouac or Hunter S. Thompson than he was in playing a war game. Philip was just as gentle in daily life, yet Risk brought out strange reservoirs of dormant aggression. The rest of the time he let Claudia run the show.

Claudia's own nickname for herself was "the brick lady." She believed in being honest and firm with people, and claimed to have a strong bullshit antenna for humans who failed to live by their principles. Up since seven that morning (on a Sunday!) putting her slothful housemates to shame, she was downstairs in her studio painting a series of gray squares for a collage she was assembling to illustrate her favorite Pythagorean theorem. The Wagner opera she was blasting gave Philip and Joe's military maneuvers a Germanic air, and even though I felt assaulted by images of giant-breasted Brunhildas and horn-helmeted warriors, I wouldn't have dreamed of complaining. I assumed my distaste for opera pointed to yet another deficiency in me, more evidence of my need for Claudia's instruction. Just that day I was savoring the dense prose of *One Hundred Years of Solitude,* by Gabriel García Márquez, on Claudia's recommendation, and although I was not yet familiar with the term "magic realism," I felt that I'd finally found a sensibility—warm, comic, mythic, lush, yet still in control—that gave me a blueprint for all I hoped to fertilize out of the wild flowers and weeds of my own imagination. I was honored that she took me seriously and introduced me to her new friends not as an aspiring writer but a writer plain and simple, just as she referred to her boyfriend as a philosopher. I looked up to her because not only had she plucked herself out of a tough, blue-collar childhood to become an artist without any help from family, but she was enough older than me to have been a bona-fide hippie radical, and later, had made a study of holistic health and the occult, topics that excited me in their unorthodoxy. I was in the market for a mentor that year and I hoped, under the spell of Claudia's forceful personality, that I could become not only a totally cultured person, but an evolved being. She exuded both an otherworldly wisdom and an earth-bound self-sufficiency, and I just had to know what she knew.

I had first been exposed to the mystical realms through a college friend, Bill Grossman, but I found his spiritual practice, Zen Buddhism, a bit severe. Bill had abandoned a career in classical tuba to join a monastery, a sacrifice that had scared me since I wanted, as I wrote earnestly in my journal, both to "find my voice" as a writer, and "grow a soul." Now, when he rose daily for a 5 A.M. *zazen*, his only contact with music was to strike the gong. Claudia believed that you didn't have to sacrifice your art to feed your spirit, or even your good taste—flash back to those purple paintings of unicorns and rainbows that were all the rage among certain seekers back then—and I found solace in this.

Claudia came upstairs for a glass of water and frowned. "Philip!" she shouted. When she wasn't deferring to him respectfully on some fine point about Wagner's Ring Cycle or German romanticism or the history of Western metaphysical thought, she always spoke to Philip as though he were her young son, not her lover. "Philip, these glasses you put in the clean rack are filthy! They're disgusting!"

Philip rose wearily to stir his beans, and nodded vaguely. "Cleanliness is not an absolute," he said. "The assumptions of the observer influence the observed."

"Isn't that a twentieth-century concept?" I asked. "I thought you hated the twentieth century."

"The moderns are okay," Philip said. "They were reacting against all that was sordid about the new century. It's what happened after them that gives me pause." At the word "pause," Philip froze, his spoon still in his hand by the flame, and I thought of my favorite game from childhood. Statues. I worried that the wooden spoon would catch fire.

Claudia sighed and winked at me. I took this as my cue to get up and help her rewash every single dish, glass, bowl and fork that Philip had scrubbed after breakfast. Philip, determinedly oblivious to our efforts, stirred more beer into the beans and began grating the cheddar cheese. He could barely see the cheese chunks, let alone the sharp holes in the grater, and I was afraid he'd nick his fingers and leak blood into our food, but what could we do? He believed, like so many others in those mostly apolitical late seventies and eighties, that curing any ill—from dim vision to cancer to poverty to despair—was simply a matter of mind over matter. There were no historical/economic/societal reasons for our failings and triumphs, or if there were, they could be overcome by self-discipline. Sociological analysis was simply pontification of the obvious; socialism, my old friend, was now an old shoe the dogs of history and empire had chewed full of holes. You got a good life if you had self esteem, good karma, and could manufacture your own white light. The simplicity of this formula was almost irresistible.

What an amazing paradigm shift for a wretch like me, the fatherless product of Johnson's Great Society who had found a surrogate daddy in Uncle Sam. I'd been a ward of the public hospitals and the welfare rolls, the kid with the biggest financial aid package in my dorm, yet it was flattering to think I'd raised myself up by my rain boot buckles to make this life journey to Seattle on my own.

The four of us sat down to eat Philip's tasty burritos feeling that all was right in the world. "Smells delicious," Joe said mildly. The room was redolent with garlic. "Yum."

Afterward, Joe and I waddled up the hill to The Cause for ice cream and just missed getting the big news bulletin of the day. I guess the rest is history.

November 4, 1979. A day spent mostly stuffing my face and reading. No wonder I was so chubby in my twenties.

In 1979, Seattle was—as it is now, I think—the perfect, moist setting to give succor to a young, romantic heart. The town was drenched in sensuality and possibility if you had the time to explore it. A shopping expedition downtown through the endless stalls of produce and crafts at the Pike Place Market could take all day if you indulged yourself, letting your nose lead you from fresh crab to wild blueberries; to avenues of cheese pungent with pepper or chives; to herb stands aromatic with lavender, sage, rose, myrrh. You could feel like the adventurer you supposed yourself to be by reliving the Gold Rush era in Pioneer Square, whose dark, wrought iron benches and handsome old saloons and shops had barely escaped the flames that demolished the city in the great fire of 1890. When your feet were tired you could stop to sip lattés in the cozy café of Elliott Bay Books or browse through the shiny new hardbacks upstairs feeling happily anxious—so much to read, and so little time. You could leap back to the future and feel all that giddy optimism of the space race by riding the Monorail through a sky-scrapered cityscape to Seattle Center, the home of the 1962 World's Fair, and stare up incredulously at the Space Needle which reminded us so much of the apartment complex from our baby-boom childhoods, *The Jetsons.*

Newcomers in their twenties were arriving every day, all with their big backpacks and their clunky hiking boots and their chewed-up poetry volumes and their journals and their big dreams. There was still a pioneer mentality at work, the belief that you could start over, live cheaply and well, and become a completely superior being to the anxious striver you may have been in your previous incarnation in whatever dying, industrial wasteland of a city you had fled. If you wanted to be a writer, there were several reading series like the one at Elliott Bay that brought in the famous but seemed to welcome all comers; if you wanted to be a painter, there were new galleries springing up everywhere and openings almost every night. There were so many plays and foreign films and art happenings and readings to choose from that even though Joe and I went out several times a week, we were always pining for the amazing cultural moment we had missed.

For nature lovers, there were countless mountains in the vicinity—the Cascades, the Olympic Range, Mt. Rainier, Mt. Hood, Mt. Baker, and more—national parks galore, the only rain forest in North America, and so many beautifully maintained city parks that you could never tromp through all of them. The natural world featured heavily in my make-over plans. All that previous summer in Chicago, where I'd worked in a cubicle at Greyhound giving people the schedules for trips across America, I'd escaped by reading about the elk in the Hoh River Rain Forest, the white-capped waves at Kalaloch. I liked the picture I held of myself, a twenty-pounds leaner version bounding over mountains with wind-blown hair.

Because Seattle's infrastructure was in flux, we felt that the city was ours for the taking. During the Boeing plant closings of the early and mid-seventies, residents fled in droves with bumper stickers saying WILL THE LAST PERSON LEAVING SEATTLE PLEASE TURN OUT THE LIGHT? And abandoning attractive middle-class houses that could be rented now for a song. The counterculture influence was strong, the result being lots of collectively-owned businesses, co-ops, women's health care cooperatives, and a burgeoning alternative spiritual community—all this before the New Age was a cultural cliché, before the first Windham Hill record was even cut, let alone used as mood music for pitching luxury cars to yuppies on TV. As a Midwesterner who had grown up in a whitebread district without so much as a health food store, these new alternatives to mainstream life seemed revolutionary. The *real* revolution of the baby boom—young people uniting to end an unpopular war, to bring down a villainous president, to declare equality among men, women, blacks, gays, spotted owls— was over, whether I liked it or not. It seemed now in the mild Carter era that the next stage was more about fine-tuning, that the best way to help the planet was simply to lead a thoughtful, balanced life in a beautiful place. I could live with that world view, in a pinch, and so could my housemates. Claudia, Philip, Joe, and I saw ourselves as pilgrims in a strange and wonderful land.

Claudia, her thick, Worcester, Mass., accent still intact, had met Philip in hippie-colonized Boulder where they'd gotten their master's degrees— hers in art and his in philosophy. They had been in a study group that pored over the metaphysical teachings of the nineteenth-century anthroposophist Rudolph Steiner. Philip hailed from Illinois by way of the New School in New York, that major center of toxicity and crime and sellouts that they both intended to avoid forever after. Boulder, once pristine, had been ruined by development, Claudia lamented, and she hoped Seattle's rain would deter rich builders from destroying it as well.

Joe was from a small factory town on the outskirts of Pittsburgh. We'd met as seniors at Northwestern. He was the first person in his family to attend a private college, or to move outside of Pennsylvania, or to contemplate living in sin. Weary of the orange sulfuric clouds that hung over his childhood landscape, he had come to Washington State for the fresh air, the national parks, and, as it turned out, to my astonishment and delight, to be with me.

I had done time in Cleveland in the years it was nicknamed The Mistake by The Lake, when the humid air was so awash with chemicals that it stank like a dead, wet animal. My mother had a near-genius I.Q. but whenever the voices told her that bad people were controlling the thoughts of her two young daughters, she kept us up all night, and couldn't wake up to go to a job. I escaped by climbing trees and reading literature, including the one novel produced by my on-the-road deadbeat dad, and by planning a future life in a future world filled with beauty and nice people who were also smart.

My mother's vision of the world was informed by World War Two, the time of her first breakdown, the year America liberated the camps. She slept with a butcher knife under her pillow, believing everyone outside the family was a potential Nazi. In my mind, she was the Nazi. Sometimes she used the same knife to hold us hostage for our "own good" (so I already knew a little about life under captivity when those unlucky Americans in Iran made the news). To reject my mother, I had only to escape out the window, both literally and symbolically, to believe that the world outside held no treachery. I was so vocal in my belief in the essential goodness of people that friends in junior high nicknamed me Pollyanna. Sometimes I made fun of my own prissy romanticism by quoting Blanche Dubois with a bad Southern belle accent—"I don't want reality, I want magic"— but I secretly admired her rebellious romanticism, her beautiful dreams.

I'd always believed in my visions and dreams, literally. In college, leery of the drive for professional advancement at the expense of personal fulfillment I saw gripping my peers, I began to keep a dream journal. A month before I graduated, while all my friends were waiting to hear about placements in elite graduate school programs or high-flyer jobs in New York or Boston or Washington, D.C., I dreamed I was flying over a map of America until I stopped above the vast green oasis that was Washington State. Taking the dream as a sign, I made plans to move to Seattle at once. I didn't know a soul there, which was partially why I came. Seattle was the kind of place where you could tell people this story and they wouldn't call you a flake.

Dark Blue Suit

PETER BACHO

Peter Bacho (1950–) grew up in Seattle's Central District. A trained attorney, he currently works as an editorial writer for Tacoma's News Tribune *and as a professor in the Liberal Studies Program at the University of Washington–Tacoma. He has published three works of fiction, including* Cebu *(1991),* Dark Blue Suit and Other Stories *(1997), and* Nelson's Run *(2002). He has also published* Boxing in Black and White *(1999), a consideration of the role of boxing in Seattle's Filipino community when the author was growing up. He has received the American Book Award of the Before Columbus Foundation and a San Francisco Bay Area Book Festival honor. This selection from the story "Dark Blue Suit" depicts Filipino life in Seattle circa the 1950s.*

First there were the men, Filipino men. And though they came from different Philippine islands, when they got here, they called themselves *Pinoys.* Most were front-line immigrants, but not newcomers, not for years now. Some had come in the 1930s, many even earlier. As young men— little more than boys, really—they'd left their homes, pushed out by poverty and pulled to this land by adventure and the promise of a new start. And through the years they'd told a wanderer's unchanging lie— yes, we'll be back—to thousands of parents and lovers, sisters and brothers. Most never went back, and you can find their bones in every West Coast town from Juneau, Alaska, to El Centro, California.

Forty years ago, in the 1950s, they filled the Victory Bathhouse and other low-rent venues, their numbers spilling onto King Street, the heart of Seattle's Chinatown. At the Victory, a joint famous among Pinoys, a patron could clean himself in a private bath, or clean out his wallet at the green felt card tables in the rear.

They were *Alaskeros,* men who went each spring to the salmon canneries of Alaska and returned each fall. "Salmon season," they called it, sounding the "l."

Seattle was their assembly point, the headquarters of their Union, a militant and powerful one that dispatched its members to the canneries. Filipino immigrants, many just out of their teens, built the Union in the 1930s; it was a source of pride, not just for them but for all Pinoys.

For more than twenty years, the Union had faced down racism and the hostility of the canning industry and had survived its own destructive cycles of criminal control and purgative reform. But in the 1950s, it took on a foe more dogged and dangerous than its own tendency to implode. The federal government, prodded by Senator Joe McCarthy, was taking dead aim at the Union, recently reformed by a dedicated core of left-wing labor leaders.

The government missed and the Union made it through the decade, dying years later but in its own time. That time came without drama or government interference, with the slow, quiet footfalls of seasons passing. The Alaskeros, who built the Union and founded a Community, are gone now, leaving King Street and the rest of Chinatown to the care of others. But forty years ago Chinatown was much different, particularly King Street, particularly in the spring . . .

From places as different as San Francisco and Walla Walla they came to Seattle, just as they had for twenty or more earlier springs, laying down their dishrags and field knives—the tools of dead-end jobs—for a chance to go north and make Union scale. It also meant a chance to see old friends who, at season's end, vanished with pockets full of cash and mental lists of places to spend it. Or to see once more the pristine Alaskan landscape, a universe removed from hot-plate rooms in Frisco or the dust of Eastern Washington fields. Not everyone went—there were always more workers than work, greater supply than demand—but everyone hoped, at least every spring.

From a distance I can see them still . . . then closer, as my father and I approached. Despite their poverty, most dressed well, wearing suits that Filipino writer Carlos Bulosan called "magnificent." Their splendid clothes and, more impressively, the easy sense of elegance with which they wore them, stood out against the drab backdrop of cheap hotels, pool halls, card rooms, and the dull apparel of Chinatown's year-round residents.

That day, like most days, Dad was also wearing a suit. This one, though, was especially sharp—a somber, dark blue suit, pressed and perfect, fit for a mayor, a movie star, or an Alaskero. "Like Bogart," I heard him mumble earlier as we left the house for Chinatown. "Got to look good," he said. "Show the boys."

At almost five years old, I didn't know much about my father. He didn't talk much, at least not to me. Maybe it was the language. Mine was native English—fluid, made in America. His was borrowed and broken, a chore just to speak; Dad preferred Cebuano. The English I did hear from him I imagined he saved, hoarding words that twisted his tongue. To me, they came mostly in the form of monosyllabic blasts, barked commands to "do dis, Buddy . . . now." And of course, "dis" got done—now, never later.

A man of mystery, my dad. I did know that every summer he would leave us for three months to work in a salmon cannery, only to reappear every September, loaded with money and a level of generosity that would disappear by the end of the month. Other than that, I knew little about him. On the ride over, I decided to find out more.

"Dad, what are you?"

"Wha' you mean?" he replied without looking at me.

"What's your job in Alaska?"

"Foreman."

"Dad, what's a . . ."

"Big shot," he said, and laughed.

"Dad . . ."

"We're here," he said, as he pulled the car into an empty space. "Come on. We got three blocks to go, and I'm gonna see my crew."

We walked briskly to our destination, lower King Street near the train depot, where hundreds of Filipino men, maybe more, were gathered. For two blocks they crowded both sides of the street like a holiday and leaned against women, mostly white. Well dressed and taller than their male companions, the women looked genuinely pleased that the Pinoys had picked this spot.

I recognized two of them—a tall, pretty blonde and a tiny redhead—from other trips to Chinatown with my folks. One day Mom, Dad, and I were walking in one direction while the redhead was going the other way. Just as we passed, she glanced at my father and smiled a quick little upturned twitch. Mom didn't notice, but Dad did. And just as he did with me, he looked straight ahead. At the time I wondered how a person so small could smell like a garden.

But it was the men who mattered, at least to me. From a block away I heard their voices, and as we approached, the noise grew louder. Through the din, I could make out some words. English words, and I heard songs and long peals of laughter to stories or jokes spoken in languages we didn't speak at home.

I'd been to Chinatown many times before, but I'd never seen it this way. Chinatown had somehow shed its drabness to become an outdoor cabaret, with samba the music of choice even without a band.

We paused at the edge of the crowd while Dad carefully straightened his hat, a flawless Borsalino of finely woven white straw. He turned to look at me and must have sensed my apprehension.

"Don' be scared," he said, and grabbed my hand. "I'll tell you who's good and who's not."

His strong grip erased my fear. It said I was Vince's boy, which, even then, I knew wasn't a bad thing to be.

"Psst!" someone hissed nearby as we cut through the crowd. My father didn't turn to look, but I did.

"Psst!" There it was again. I traced it to the old hotel two doors up from the Victory. A stylishly dressed Filipino—I didn't know him—was standing in the doorway. He started walking toward us, fast.

My father turned to see who it was. Dad's face showed faint recognition but no sign of warmth. Then, as the man kept coming, Dad shot him the Look. I knew the Look, having had it recently applied to me at the dinner table when I balked at having to eat my mother's latest fare, boiled chicken over rice with a side of pork and beans. I ate it, but only after my mother's pleas had failed and she'd invoked my father to employ the Look.

As I stood there, I was pleased at having my father's stern gaze directed elsewhere. I knew it worked on me but I wanted to find out if it had universal application. I didn't have to wait long.

"Hello, Johnny," Dad said. His tone was flat, almost lifeless, and his greeting, if it could be called that, came from between clenched teeth and lips that didn't move. As he spoke, he released my hand, folded his arms across his chest, and created a barrier that said *stay back.*

Johnny pretended not to notice. "Vince! Vince!" he said enthusiastically. Real or feigned, I couldn't tell. "Jus' got in. Long time no see."

"Yeah," my father replied. "Long time."

"Me and you," Johnny said. "I go with you this year." Dad said nothing.

Johnny, sensing a wall and hoping to avoid it, swerved sharply and turned his attention to me. "Good-lookin' boy," he said, with a smile that I knew took great effort to maintain. "Wasn' here las' time I was up. Big for four."

"Almost five," I corrected him.

Johnny bent low toward me. He was so close I could see small beads of sweat on the round tip of his nose. He reached into his pocket and pulled out a handful of one-dollar bills.

"For candy, Sonny," he said as he pushed the loot toward me.

I didn't like this man much—he was pushing too hard—and I knew Dad didn't like him at all. I'd never before taken money from someone I knew I disliked. Nonetheless, my judgment was blinded by the vision of scores of Hershey Bars, purchased by the box; I wasn't sure how many, but I knew it would be more than I was then able to count. The candy was as good as mine—I could already see several boxes stashed safely under my bed—but only if I moved before caution stayed my hand.

"Thank you," I said as I shot my right out, quicker than a jab, palm extended, fingers curled like talons about to close.

For Filipino children of my age and generation, it was almost an instinctive reaction. Bachelor "uncles," friends of my parents, old Pinoys with no wives or kids, doted on us like we were their own, and for a few days each spring and fall, we were. But of course, we weren't, which meant that we, the recipients, were always on our best behavior, as were they, our transient benefactors.

"Ah, Vince, you really dunnit," they'd say after visiting our too-humble frame house. Their wistful tone said they could have "dunnit" too, given a break here or there, and that maybe they still would. But then again, after twenty years in the new land, maybe not.

Filipino American kids and our legion of bachelor uncles—a case of old gold-toothed smiles meeting young gap-toothed ones. They gave us gifts and small wads of greenbacks plus stacked columns of coins, and, like public television, we accepted donations gladly.

But I knew that this welcome tradition might not be honored because of my father's ill-concealed dislike for Johnny, my newest potential donor. I figured I'd just close my eyes, grit my teeth, and grab the cash, all in a smooth, circular motion that would end with the money in my pocket—a deal hopefully done before Dad could say *Don't take money from jerks like Johnny.* Speed was the key, but this time I didn't have enough.

"No," said the voice, stopping my hawklike swoop just short of its target. I didn't have to look to know I was too slow, or to know that Dad's audio had a visual that could clot my blood. Defeated, my hand fluttered then fell, a useless, guilty appendage that hid in my front pants pocket. I wished my pocket could hide the rest of me.

I summoned the nerve to look at Dad, not directly—I wasn't that brave and kept my view to the ground—but rather through a darting series of eye movements, from the centers of both sockets to their peripheries and back. These visual contortions provided safety but also produced a headache, forcing my return to center focus—I'd seen, though, that the Look was focused not on me, but on Johnny, my discouraged patron.

"Ah, Vince," I heard Johnny say in a whiney voice that could have been mine. "It's jus' money." I knew then that Dad's gaze frightened everyone, not just me.

"No money," my father said. There was no whine in his voice. "At least not from you."

"Ah, Vince," Johnny pleaded. "I . . ." he said, and paused. "Never mind," he said softly. "Never mind."

I knew without looking that Johnny was moving away, retreating beyond the range of Dad's evil stare. I felt a tug on my arm and instinctively followed my father.

"Come on," he said.

We continued our walk along King Street. I looked back and saw Johnny. He'd resumed his post in front of the old hotel, staring after us dejectedly. To my quick look, he shrugged a reply. Neither of us knew what he'd done to earn my father's wrath.

"Dad," I asked meekly, "how come you don't like him?"

"Thief," he said, then paused, as if "thief" were just the first of a full deck of bad names. This confused me; my father had friends, close ones, who were hard men. Some were thieves; others, even worse.

"Thief!" he said again, in lieu of an explanation. I didn't expect further elaboration and was surprised when it came. "Card shark," he added. Confusion again. Uncle Pete was a card shark and also my father's good friend. There had to be more.

"Johnny work with Leo five years ago," my father explained after we'd walked a few more steps. "Not my cannery, I wasn' there. He take advantage on Leo. Almost three months' hard work, Leo come back. Broke. No, worse than broke. He borrow money from the boys but can't pay back. Of course they're mad. I give him money when he get to Seattle. Tell him to pay them and go home."

My father then looked at me. He stared until I turned toward him. "If you not here," he said evenly, "I make that Johnny bleed." I was amazed that his dull monotone could carry violent, angry words so far, so powerfully. Dad could've been at a service station, using the same voice to order "four bucks regular, check the oil."

"Just remember, Buddy," he continued. "You got family, you got friends—back home in Cebu, but 'specially here, where you got nothin'."

Part 3. Unto Itself (1990s–Early 2000s)

A Fair Trade

MICHAEL BYERS

Michael Byers (1969–) was born in San Francisco, California, and gradu-ated from Oberlin College and the University of Michigan with an M.F.A. in creative writing. He has published short stories in the country's best liter-ary periodicals. Recognitions and awards for his writing include the Editors' Prize from Missouri Review, *the* Transatlantic Review/Henfield Founda-tion Award, *and the Whiting Foundation Writers Award in addition to a Stegner Fellowship from Stanford University. His collection of short stories,* The Coast of Good Intentions *(1998), received the Sue Kauffman Prize for First Fiction from the American Academy of Arts and Letters in 1999. His first novel,* Long for This World, *was published in 2003. This selection from the story "A Fair Trade," which appears in* The Coast of Good Intentions, *depicts a young girl's arrival in Seattle right after World War II and, after leaving the city as a young woman, her subsequent return later in life.*

On the morning of the third day the train slowed and entered the city. Andie, at the window, saw a harbor full of ships. A series of hills ran down to the water. The old woman next to her, Bella, sat up and sighed. "Well, at last," she said, her cheek quivering under a coat of pow-der. "The fright of it. I know I'll be a dead woman before I do this sort of thing again."

Andie gathered her things, pulled her enormous suitcase upright.

"I wonder if you would help me for a moment," said Bella. "I wonder if you would take my hand and squeeze, rather, like this." She demonstrated. "I have an awful time with that particular hand."

Andie took the old woman's hand, soft and pliant, and flattened it gently between her palms.

"Oh, my. Oh, dear, do," Bella said. "Precisely. Now this one. Oh, yes, exactly. Oh, exactly. Oh." She closed her eyes, put her head back against the seat. "My goodness," she said at last, and reached into her purse. "And here are three dollars for your trouble."

"I don't need any money."

"Of course you do."

Andie took it and stood with her suitcase. "Anything else?"

"No. I have to meet my sister," said Bella, "and I think I'll just sit and put that off for a while."

Andie made her way to the door. The soldier with the long nose noticed her and touched his hat. "Finally here," he said.

"So we are."

"Meeting someone?"

"Yes. My aunt," said Andie. "Thank you very much."

"Relax," said the soldier. "You're too small to keep."

Andie stepped onto the sunny platform. Immediately she saw her aunt Maggie, standing like a ladder under the iron awning. She was taller than Andie remembered, with sharp elbows, and already she was stepping, high and deliberate, like a stork, through the crowd. She wore brown pants and sandals, and her hair was piled on her head and fixed with a tortoiseshell clip. "Well," she said. "You look a little woozy. My God, what a suitcase. You can live in that, I suppose."

"Sorry. It's all we had."

"Sorry? Forget sorry." Grunting, her aunt took the suitcase and led her away, into the depths of the yellow-tiled station and out the other side, back into daylight. The smell of seawater hung in the air, and a tall white building stood shining in the sun. "I haven't got a car, all right," said Maggie, leading her to a taxi, "so we're taking a cab, and I don't want you to think anything of the expense. There are buses, however, and we don't have to worry about being stuck out in the sticks by ourselves. I myself like to come into town and see a movie now and then, and I'm happy to do whatever you'd like to do, Andie, within reason, of course, though I think you'll find everything to your liking. And so," she said, tending to a stray strand of hair, "I think that's that. You're very tall, you know. You're going to be tall like your grandfather— that's where *I* get my height. You don't remember him, I'm sure."

"Not really."

Maggie sighed, opened the taxi door for her. "No, and more's the pity. Everyone else, you excluded, I haven't much use for."

They rode through downtown, up a hill and down the other side, out to the very northern edge of the city, where the houses, less frequent, finally petered out into farmland and forest. The road narrowed, grew sinuous, and at last they left the pavement entirely and rattled a mile along a dirt road to Maggie's house. It was a small white house set down in a meadow, the porch sagging, the chimney pot perched slightly askew, the driveway a rut in the grass; the house was surrounded by the dark green moat of the garden: flowers in front, vegetables behind, rhododendrons clustered on the sides.

The front hall was dim and smelled peculiar, like burned meat, with a flattish damp smell like old newspapers, and Andie felt a clutch of apprehension. But the house grew brighter as they went through it, and in the kitchen, yellow curtains shaded the windows. She followed her aunt onto a sunny back porch and across the porch to a small white door.

"So, dear," her aunt said, showing her in. "This used to be the storeroom, but I've fixed it up for you. Sorry about that smell, by the way. I found a leg of lamb for us to have tonight but it went up in flames, and then I had to clean the oven, which is not something I usually do. This should be all right for you? You don't need much furniture, I hope."

"No, I love it," Andie said, not altogether insincerely. There was a cot and a white wooden desk, a white chest of drawers, and three windows: one over the bed, two over the desk. Beneath her shoes she felt grit on the floor. A nice room, nicer than she'd had in San Diego. "I absolutely love it."

"Well, you don't have to act like that. It's the only thing I have. I guess you'd like a bath."

"I must look terrible."

Her aunt licked her teeth—in the top row they overlapped one another, left to right—and regarded Andie. "No, you don't. I thought you would, but you don't. You're a little pale, I guess. But, no, you look presentable."

"I would like a bath."

"Well, then, darling, I'll get you some towels," said Maggie, and went off into the hallway.

Andie opened her suitcase on the floor. Inside were her ratty underwear, her hairbrushes and combs, her piles of sweaters—all of them smelling of cooking grease—and her shoes. Like a bird, she lifted one arm, then the other, sniffing her armpits. Through the windows she could see the garden: tomatoes and beans on their poles. The walls of her room were white, and so was the ceiling; only the doorknob, solid black enamel, stood out in the whiteness, like a single period on a page without text.

Later, in the back yard, her aunt knelt on a towel, weeding the flowerbeds, her hair in a bandanna. "So, I was thinking, Andie," she said, "I might warn you of a few things around here."

"Shoot." Birds dashed above her, singing.

"Well, first, I work a good deal, and I don't know how *you* are with people, but I, Andie, am *not* very sociable, unlike, say, your mother, so you shouldn't expect to see anyone out at the house. I don't know very many people, and all our relatives keep to themselves, which is fine by me. Oh, look at this. This is botrytis," she said, holding out a leaf. "Mold." It was soft and wet, like bad soap.

"For example," she said, wiping it off, "take the MacEwins across the road, to whom I've spoken exactly three times in the seven years of my life here. You'll want to leave them alone, I think. They're old and sick, and by now they must depend on their man to do just about everything. And there's a nephew out here whom we all try to more or less ignore— Dale's his name—and I haven't seen *him* since Christmas, a young man who makes his own *marmalade* in his spare time, if you know what I mean. He wants in the army but they keep refusing him and then he goes home to make his marmalade. Disgusting stuff, and I've got *closets* full of it, hidden away, and I guess I should just throw it all out but I haven't got the heart. That's not a weed."

"Sorry."

"Dale's your *cousin,* now, he's your uncle's son. Your uncle Bernard, who's in the navy. But not like your poor father. Bernard's on a supply ship or something. Out of harm's way." She shook her head, yanking at the ground. "Of course you've never heard of these people."

"No," she said.

"Well, they're hardly worth the bother." Maggie stood and stretched, her knees cracking, reached into her apron, and pulled out a small pair of silver scissors. "These, Andie, are for flowers. Pick what you want, but these and only these are what you use. Otherwise you'll leave a mark."

So it was with a sense of orderly pleasure that Andie went to bed early, with light still showing through the tops of her three windows. She loved her room, she decided, all her own. She tried to sleep, but the rush of wind through the trees kept her softly awake. Her cot, unsettlingly narrow at first, became quickly the perfect slip of bed, floating above the white floor, where, later, moonlight played its watery patterns through the trees. She could smell the sea. Outside, an animal was scratching, occupied with something. Alone, alone, Andie thought, the world opened. Between waking and sleep she remembered the three dollars in her pocket, and she dreamed, briefly, of the long unpopulated passages of the darkened train.

The next evening they rode into town, to the Neptune Theater, near the university. "I was sorry to hear about your father," Maggie said on the bus, "though he didn't treat you in any overly generous way, in my opinion. Certainly he stepped into harm's way."

"Yes," Andie said; "he wanted to." She felt the leather seats, tough and worn, with little horny patches where they'd been repaired.

"I've been wondering, also, about your feelings toward your mother. If you don't mind my asking."

"Not really."

"I guess I just wonder if you're happier now, away from her. I know I would be, if I were you. She's not the ideal guardian, I mean to say."

"I'm not that sorry to be gone."

"Well," Maggie said, considering, and clicking her shoes together in the aisle. "But, also, you should understand what compels her. She is irresponsible, but given her upbringing it's a little hard to hold it against her."

"She made me do everything," Andie said. And this was true: her mother had done essentially nothing for months, lying in bed for weeks on end, long before her father was killed. It had not been a glamorous life, her mother creeping out to the porch by noon, usually venturing no farther, tucking her clothes around her and sitting to watch the traffic, always dangerously prone to self-dramatization, crying against the shelves in the PX. "She hardly went outside except to go to parties."

"Well, she's done that all her life. All her life, I tell you. She was very upset when your father went out to sea and left her alone. My sister has never been any good at being on her own, Andie. Your father in the navy knew that before he went in, but off he went anyway, leaving the two of you to fend for yourselves."

"He volunteered," Andie said.

"Well, yes. Growing up, your mother just couldn't stand to be unaccompanied. She is terribly lonely without you, but I convinced her it's the best thing for her now, as I believe it is. We may," she said, "telephone her sometime, if you want to. Though there is the expense to consider."

Andie clasped her hands in her lap. She felt obscurely obligated to defend her mother and her father, but in fact she was unsure whose side she should be on. Everyone had acted poorly, as she saw it, and she seemed to have no one left. Her father, a small, often timid man, had talked his way from a desk job onto a battleship, an idiotic posturing for which Andie would never forgive him. "At least I didn't lie around in bed for months and months," she said at last. "I didn't have a crackup even before he died."

"Yes. Though as far as that goes," said her aunt, calmly, patting Andie's hand, "it's good training for being a wife, should you ever care to embark on that particular enterprise."

They reached the top of a hill, where the bus paused, taking on passengers. Andie smelled her armpits again, quickly; then, sitting up straight in her seat, looked ahead and behind, at the long bright city avenues stretching away from them in both directions, the streetlights sparkling in the rain. Despite everything, this filled her with a mild delight, a feeling that they might tip either way. And then they were off again, downhill.

The Neptune, green-walled like a grotto, was full and bustling. Student voices echoed off the tiled walls. The dark lobby was wet and speckled with bootprints, and Andie clung to her aunt. They sat between two long rows of college boys in white sweaters, Andie with her elbows in her lap. She had been to the movies only rarely, and she'd found them excessive, all the noise and bluster once the lights went down. The college boys in their boots cheered the newsreels: Germany retreating, tanks disappearing in puffs of dust. The boys punched each other, raised their heavy arms like clubs, and then, somewhat worriedly, watched the pictures from the Pacific. The room shook and exploded. Soldiers marched, dark and gaunt in their netcovered helmets. "After this," said her aunt, patting her hand, "we'll have some real entertainment."

Halfway through the news Andie began to cry, thinking of her father. She missed him, but more than that, she felt sorry for his last, bad minutes, drowned or maybe burned alive; she didn't know. His little blue shirts hung in her closet in San Diego, almost too small for her. The music in the newsreels didn't help: the slow marches, the flags half-masted over the endless graveyards. Little white fountains sprang up where pilots fell into the sea. Her aunt clasped her arm in the dark and whispered, "It's soon over, dear," and Andie averted her eyes. Above an exit door stood a lit-up clock, and she watched the minute hand creep thoughtfully around. During the movie the long slope of people around her munched and stirred, and it was mildly discomforting, as it had been on the train, to be among them. Imprisoned in San Diego she'd been obliged to keep one eye on her mother—she'd shopped and cleaned; she'd cooked and emptied the garbage. It was Andie who had opened the telegram, read its three or four formalisms out loud in their yellow, fly-buzzing kitchen, and helped her mother back to bed. Only a month ago, she realized, with some surprise.

On the long ride home, houses gave way to stretches of weeds and brambles. They were the last to leave the bus, and they walked the open road home. A wind had begun, sliding downhill past them to the lake, bringing with it the smell of summer grass. "Well, I feel bad about what I said earlier, so I should add," said her aunt, "that your father, whatever his faults, had a very nice way about him, I remember, a pleasant smile, and he was always kind to your mother, despite everything. He was a gallant man and a good sport, and had no shortage of friends, because he was a good man, and everyone liked him. You have nothing to be ashamed of concerning your father." They were approaching the house, dark in its green cloak. "Yes, I always did like your father," her aunt said, and opened the gate. "But more's the pity, I guess."

Her aunt, an accountant at the Sand Point Naval Station, walked to work in the mornings, and Andie walked most of the way with her, down the dirt road, past farms and gardens, up a little hill and down the other side. The base, on Lake Washington, was a set of low brown buildings, and from the top of a rise they could see a runway where potbellied airplanes sat awaiting repair. "They don't do an awful lot of things at this place," said her aunt, swinging her arms. "We watch expenses, you know—gasoline and coffee and what-not. It's a pretty dull job, I have to admit, though I do like the airplanes."

Andie asked whether she had met any pilots.

"Oh, well, they're a sorry crew, most of them, incapable of writing their own names. Farm boys. My humble and contrary opinion is that if you want a real man, you should look in the civilian population. If I were to look for someone, that's certainly where I'd go. Not that they don't ask me, of course. The pilots. Thank you very much. I am not unbeautiful, I believe."

"You're very pretty," Andie said. It was more true than not. "Men ought to be falling all over you."

"Oh, don't think you have to say that sort of thing, Andie. I'm perfectly capable of judging things myself. My awful teeth, for example. Like a poker hand. But it's *very* sweet of you to say."

After these walks Andie liked coming back to her aunt's orderly house in the grass; it was still July, and she had little to do. She spent the mornings on a blanket in the sunny garden, with the radio through the kitchen window for company, and when after a few weeks she became bored with the garden—and by then she was as brown as a glove—she began exploring; first, beyond the hedges, where the yard opened into a field; then farther, into a black wall of pine trees, where the air was cool and the earth soft under her shoes. Deep within these trees she found a clearing, and in the middle of the clearing was an old tree on its side, stripped of its branches and bark, now silvering in the open, smooth and good to sit on. Around her the woods receded into their mild dimness, and above her hung a ragged circle of sky. Now and then an airplane crossed over, low, on its landing course toward Sand Point, its propellers feathering the air and its metal seams visible from below. Grasshoppers leaped from the weeds and she let the insects crawl on her arms, spitting their juices and swiveling their pea heads, intricate creatures. It was all marvelous to her, really; this, she thought, was what she had missed: these long days, with nothing to do, and no one around.

So her days were empty by design.

Sometimes she wrote a letter to her mother, though she hadn't much to say. Her white room baked dry in the afternoon sun and smelled lightly of paint. She thought occasionally of the soldier with the long nose and the old gaseous woman, both now perhaps dead, a strange and exciting idea. What she believed for weeks to be a train whistle was, according to her aunt, the horn of a ferry on the lake, the midday run to Juanita. Her aunt's bedroom was uninteresting: familiar photographs, her aunt's underwear in the top drawer, old and fragile but otherwise run-of-the-mill. The closets held the usual things and smelled benignly of cedar, though one closet was filled entirely with hats and hatboxes. On a hot day the dim hallways were cool, and little black flies traced ovals in the air, from the hall window around to the screen door, where they threw themselves with what seemed unusual vigor toward the bright, unreachable yard. A fan in the living room whirred all day, tilting the lampshades. Now and then a car went by on the road, kicking up gravel.

All these things Andie loved.

. . .

When Andie was fifty-five she moved back to Seattle, as many others were
doing. Her aunt, she learned, was still alive, now seventy-eight.

The city had changed entirely. Even from the air—perhaps especially—
the changes were obvious: the new denser sprawl of things, many of the
old empty places filled in. Downtown, once squat and marine, was now
as glassy and enterprising as Houston or Charlotte, and it saddened her to
see that so much of what she had known was gone for good. Her work—
after her divorce, she had worked in computers—was bringing her here,
and soon she bought a house, revived what had been an elaborate garden
in the fenced back yard, and settled down to what she expected would be
the last, longest chapter of her life. She did not call Maggie, though she
meant to; she lived much as her aunt had lived, and there were days when
she would look at the telephone guiltily and chide herself for not calling.
But eventually this passed and she could gaze out at her yard or through
her wooded window at work and feel she had taken care of everything.
Now that she had money, she found it a pleasure to eat well and some nights
to drink too much and sit in her bathtub among the green tiles and listen
to the radio. Her daughter, in Dallas, was married and rarely visited, and
Andie was by far the oldest woman at work in a business populated by men
not yet thirty. Her husband, she thought with some satisfaction, would be
useless here. Goaded by the youth around her, she ran regularly around
Greenlake and bought a fancy bicycle, and she whirred happily through
the streets, though her knees hurt and the seat was hard and too narrow.

Then one night, watching television with the lights out, she saw Har-
rison Beam, an old man, interviewed from his wheelchair. The round nut
of his head was pale, he had lost his hair, and his smooth voice was broken and uncertain. He had gone on, she learned, to design parks in the
city, parks that were now in danger of being built up. It was a terrible thing,
he said, and Andie, curled comfortably under a blanket, agreed with him.
He was sweet, harmless. He put her in mind of her aunt, whom she called
the next morning, a Saturday. When she offered to take her aunt to lunch,
Maggie, speechless for a moment, said, "Oh, it's *Andie*. Well, I wondered
when you'd be back."

Seattle Now: A Letter

EMILY BAILLARGEON RUSSIN

Emily Baillargeon Russin (1969–) is a fourth-generation Seattleite. She attended Lakeside School in Seattle and graduated from Bryn Mawr College. She received an M.F.A. in creative writing from Emerson College. She has worked in the past as a managing editor for the Seattle Weekly. *Currently she lives in Seattle and works as a freelance writer and editor. Her articles and essays have appeared in* The Seattle Times, Seattle Weekly, New England Review, *and* Comstock Review. *In 1998, she received first-place honors in arts writing from the Washington Press Association. In the following selection from her essay "Seattle Now: A Letter" (1999), Russin recounts her return to Seattle after a sojourn on the East Coast and then profiles the Microsoft campus and culture.*

A Seattle native, I returned here in 1996 after nearly a decade of pretending to be an easterner. Before I went off to college in Pennsylvania, I couldn't wait to leave the provincial Northwest behind, a region whose remote time zone seemed a solar system away from places like New York and Washington, D.C., places that made an impact on the rest of the world from minute to minute. Then, in the early 1990s, it happened: Seattle became all the rage; only I wasn't around to rage in it. My parents, in their quiet neighborhood on the shores of Lake Washington, ended up with Nirvana lead singer Kurt Cobain and his equally headline-grabbing wife, Courtney Love, as next-door neighbors. When the media descended on my childhood street following Cobain's 1994 suicide, I watched it on "Hard Copy" from the other side of the country. Phone calls from home began to include reports of Courtney sightings from our backyard, and grunge music, not symphonies, accompanied meals when I came back for visits. My parents, the whole city, everyone I knew, it seemed, reveled in the eye of Seattle's popularity storm—while I was missing out. Back in Boston, my post-college home, I drove Interstate 90 (the Massachusetts Turnpike) blaring Seattle bands on my car stereo. I lived for two years in a rickety old house alongside the Pike, where I took comfort in knowing that I could walk out my front door, take a left, and head west on the same road for three thousand miles. Seattle, in effect, lay down the street.

Now that I'm back, I'm still trying to catch up with everything that's already happened. Everyone has heard the hype, heard the garage bands on the radio, and every day millions of people wake up and head to their nearest Seattle's Best Coffee or Starbucks (Seattle's other best coffee). It's 1999, and the city's still warm after being red-hot. The place is livable, literate, and energized, offering successions of mountain views, water views, evergreen views—an array of picture postcards. In the last decade, Seattle has moved away from being a two-industry town, known only for its Weyerhaeuser Lumber and Boeing 747s, to an internationally recognized center for Pacific Rim trade, computer software, on-line bookselling, and coffee, as well as a booming market for outdoor outfitters. Northwest cuisine has also grown out of these success stories, incorporating local seafood, produce, and pan-Asian accents. In the last year downtown has made room for a world-class symphony hall, an outdoor baseball stadium, waterfront condos, the Nordstrom flagship store, and an upscale shopping mall that connects to Nordstrom by means of a skybridge. More construction is anticipated: voters recently approved initiatives to pay for a new outdoor football stadium (and the subsequent demolition of the Kingdome), a new main branch public library, and a much-anticipated light-rail system.

It wasn't always this way, nor in all likelihood will the status associated with such developments, once it has been bestowed, remain. The fervor surrounding Seattle's designation as "most livable city" by *Fortune* magazine in 1996 has dwindled, and in fact Seattle recently showed up in a national poll as ranking sixth or seventh as one of the metropolitan areas with the worst traffic. As you might expect, Seattleites don't take too kindly to all the growth, all the newcomers. Washington State increased in population by ten percent in the four years previous to Seattle's title, making this the seventh fastest growing state in the country. All of this seemed to start sometime after droves of Southern Californians sought refuge from their smog pits and headed north in the late 1970s and early 1980s. Quick to deride these migrating hordes, a local newspaper columnist coined a term for the infiltration: Californication. Seattle spilled over the half-million mark four years ago, and is now purported to be at the center of a three-million-person sprawl spreading out from the city limits in all directions. Even the islands across the bay, Bainbridge and Vashon, are trading in their weekend retreat reputations for inclusion on the ever-expanding roster of Seattle's bedroom communities. In its ongoing mission to make a group of incompatible individuals live together so they'll be able to create on-camera discord, MTV's "Real World" crew spent eight months here in 1998 with their seven twenty-something experimental subjects, setting out to prove just how cool this place still is. Or was. For the "Real World"-ers, that didn't much matter. They lived, free of charge, in a refurbished warehouse on a pier, complete with pool table, fish tanks, and hot tub.

Those who venture here—much like the party that landed in November 1851 on West Seattle's Alki Point (which they originally named New York–Alki, in optimistic homage to their home town, and which translated from the Chinook language means "New York, By and By")—come with the sense that they're pioneers. After arriving here, Seattle founding father Arthur Denny, along with his twenty-two companions, built four cabins on the inhospitable site and the following February, 1852, plumbed the bay for its deepest point and moved across to what is now Seattle. The incoming waves of transplants to the area stand at the edge of a continent, their backs to places they left behind, and there's no easy next move. Seattle attracts these people, present-day explorers who go as far as they can—until they can't go any more. Like the gold-seekers who stopped in

Seattle in the 1840s on their way to or from the Yukon, newcomers to this city have heeded, but revised, the age-old migratory call: "Go West, young man" has become "Go to Seattle, where the streets are paved with stock options."

I don't work for Microsoft, myself, but plenty of people do—upwards of 30,000 worldwide and 15,000 in Washington State alone. This company has managed, in a matter of two decades, to woo the best and the brightest in nearly every field and put them to work for a greater cause: "a computer on every desk in every home." Therein lies the vision of Bill Gates, the richest man in the world, a man who graduated from my high school long before I got there, and who, with Microsoft co-founder and high school pal Paul Allen, began a quest for world dominance in the computer software industry that has resulted in last fiscal year's revenues of $14.48 billion and an anti-trust suit that could forever alter the company's business practices. A lot of my friends work for Bill, and for those of us on the outside, it seems like one of those career tracks that occupies the space between paychecks and an endless conveyor belt of top-secret, patented products. I have only the vaguest idea of what my friends at Microsoft actually do, or what their job titles are—that they work for Microsoft seems to suffice in dinner-party conversation. "Stock options" is the catch phrase that gets passed around, though not so much these days; when I count on both hands and feet the years some of my acquaintances have been working away in the Seattle suburb of Redmond, some even before they graduated from college, I start to feel the pangs produced by my newspaper editor's salary. But part of why Microsoft succeeds is that, for all its highly motivated drones, it's really like being in college all over again.

When I was in high school, Redmond was barely a blip on anyone's radar. It consisted of a tiny grid of pizza joints, a few gas stations, and a collection of even tinier strip malls; the rest was open farmland. But today the cookie-cutter condos and housing developments form a patchwork of modernity that shows no signs of stopping where it is. Today Redmond boasts a new "Town Center," an open-air shopping mall hedged in by office parks, the school district headquarters, a cineplex, and a series of chain

restaurants. The countryside has given way to an edge city, one that is
thriving with a new, younger population of Microsoft couples. (Even if
only one of the couple works at Microsoft, this moniker extends to both
people, keeping in mind, however, that even Bill met Melinda, his wife,
on the job.)

Back on the Seattle side of Lake Washington, I work for a weekly newspaper that frequently reports on what's up with Microsoft. As recently as
early March we added a Technology section to our pages. Still, I had not
personally set foot on any of the Microsoft campuses, and, tired of recycling the same old legendary accounts about the place for nearly three
years, I decided to see for myself what all the fuss was about. A friend of
a friend, who commutes from Seattle every day, agreed to lead me on "the
corporate pee-on tour." Would everyone, I thought uneasily as I parked
in the visitors' parking lot, drive Hummers and speak in computer languages only they could understand? The main plaza, punctuated by two
foaming fountains, gave the suggestion of a college campus, an intentional
and successful effect for an insulated, workaholic environment. The
buildings themselves were pleasantly unremarkable, spare with green glass
windows and marked with numbers, not names—like an updated version of MIT. The lobby of my guide's building, number eighteen, offered
puffy leather couches the color of ripe mushrooms, and a painted Indian
mask protruded from the balcony over the reception desk. A huge white
banner hung from the balcony railing, proclaiming "Works better. Plays
better. Windows 98." Wearing jeans and smiling, lots of people walked
past me. Needless to say, Microsoft has succeeded in taking the "collar"
out of white-collar; you won't find ties here, or power suits, or, for the
most part, miniskirts. But I couldn't help but equate the whole scene to
a college admission's office prospectus come to life. A stack of my weekly
papers on the granite coffee table reassured me, though, that I hadn't just
stepped into a universe where everyone is still plugging away at an honors thesis. Then, too, there's the small matter of Big Brother: Before my
guide emerged, I typed my name, my guide's name, and my company
affiliation into a laptop at the receptionist's desk, and hit "print." From
under the desk, a grinding sound produced my very own visitor's badge—

which stated, in bold letters, that I was to be escorted at all times while I was on the premises.

Part-time contract workers, temps, and any other category of less-than-full-time worker at Microsoft (and that could be as many as a third of the daily work force at one time, I have heard) are, in the end, another species of visitor unto themselves. According to Washtech, the Washington Alliance of Technology Workers and the self-proclaimed "voice of the digital workforce": "Microsoft employs more than 6,000 workers— including approximately 35 percent of its total Seattle-area work force— through employment agencies. Many of these people work as 'permatemps,' or workers who are employed indefinitely through temp agencies." Perks? How about benefits, for starters? Such words indicate possibilities as faraway and magical as "stock options." An editor friend of mine spent five months of the last year at Redwest, the newest and most visually attractive of all the Redmond campuses, and the home of most of the editorial content departments, including MSN. My friend knew, upon accepting her temporary position, that she could expect one thing: She would be making well over the usual hourly wage paid an editor. She also came to realize that "there are subtle ways in which you know you're fodder." Her orange photo ID badge, instead of signifying her being one of the gang, separated her from the Blue Badges (the full-timers). "I liked the people," she admitted, after her stint ended. "They were really professional." Her enthusiasm was kept in perspective when, during a meal in the cafeteria modeled after a ski lodge, right before the anti-trust trial began, a huge screen unfurled from the ceiling. Bill Gates and company president Steve Ballmer addressed the troops, live, via closed-circuit projection, about the impending court case. "I was making $14 an hour, and I didn't exist," she recalled. "I wasn't even a mote in Bill Gates's eye. [I was] a speck of dust—which was kind of a profound realization."

During my visit, when my guide ushered me into his office, I wasn't terribly impressed until the word "perks" came up. It turns out that besides getting their own ten-foot-by-ten-foot offices, working their own hours, and wearing whatever they want, Microsofties are each visited by an ergonomic specialist to assure that their work environment doesn't exacerbate any physical problems—or, more likely, cause such problems in the first place. My guide, who has a history of back ailments, was able to get tall desks so he can alternatively sit and stand whenever he needs to. His chairs and computer keyboards were also personalized for his maximum benefit. After our talk, I was walked over to the Soda Room, where a wall of refrigerators housed hundreds of cans of soft drinks— all for free, for anyone in need of a sugar jolt or a thirst-quencher. The network of identical hallways reminded me of dorm life, and of that camaraderie that comes with close quarters and a gradual depletion of brain power. When the tank hits empty, a series of old arcade games in every building awaits you. We walked outside, past the fitness trails (separated by levels of difficulty), a basketball court, soccer fields, volleyball net, and arrived at a cafeteria. "Is this what you really want to see?" my guide asked as my eyes grew wide at the subsidized prices (a giant salad with meat, $4.25; pizza by the slice, $1.25), and the easygoing, all-you-can eat atmosphere. From the other side of the room, an espresso machine whirred. I wasn't sure how to answer his question; I was simply looking for something typical in what I had already concluded was an atypical place.

In a courtyard across campus, we stopped and read the tiles arranged in a checkered pattern at our feet. For each new product the company ships out, a new tile marks the occasion. "It gives us something to point to," my guide said. At the entrance to the courtyard, a timeline of tiles reads like a manual of office products. Beginning in 1975, Microsoft began with a program called BASIC, and forged ahead from there. Suddenly, it dawned on me that some of the people I had seen milling around could have been the very same ones who had invented these programs. And here I was, at the source of it all. I had a similar rush when I first set foot on Harvard's campus, a feeling of unworthiness brought on by standing where many important people had stood before.

The Microsoft Company Store sells every component of the typical Microsoft wardrobe, which makes working through the night, as lots of employees are rumored to do regularly, less of a problem. Just go to the store and buy a clean shirt—preferably one with MSN emblazoned on the breast. Or, to hide that all-nighter, I-fell-asleep-on-my-desk hair, a

Slate baseball cap. They even sell Microsoft boxer shorts (plaid, of course), along with every style of computer carrying case imaginable. Wandering the aisles to the strains of Green Day, customers (mostly men) perused the shelves of CD-ROMs available to them for a huge discount. My guide pointed out Age of Empires, a build-your-own-society game that seems to be all the rage on campus (a thinly disguised master plot for techies to wreak havoc on the outside world, an ultimate revenge-of-the-nerds fantasy). This is the Microsoft U store, a one-stop-shopping student union where you can buy a school mug, pen, stationery, a birthday card, and a team T-shirt at the same time. The campus plan, which Microsoft has steadfastly applied to all its buildings, has resulted in a comfortable, though rather closed-off, world, but the sense of focus and energy that it seems to generate are as palpable as anything displayed by a cheering squad. Why would anyone be unhappy or cynical here? Everywhere you turn there are intelligent people, free futuristic gadgets, and subliminal messages congratulating you on your newest patent, product, and advancement. The cafeterias are open all night long; you can join intramural sports (even crew); and you're paid what you're worth. Life is good—if you are a full-time employee. Graduation, that bittersweet event, comes only when your earnings permit you to leave the million-dollar mark behind, but by then you'll be ready to get a real job: as a parent.

. . .

Some post-graduates of Microsoft U find themselves worth a few million dollars or more and ready to put it to use for a communal benefit, though not in the usual philanthropic sense. The years of being encouraged to produce and succeed have left them with a can-do, can-oversee attitude—which means that they're not much attracted to the prospect of being just so many faceless board members, for the most part, and they're certainly not up for envelope licking. Seattle City Council member Tina Podlodowski is a former Microsoftie who decided to run for office following her "retirement." Just in time for Christmas 1998, two ex-Microsofties developed a new board game, Cranium, and made that their "retirement" option. Brewster cites Habitat Espresso, a nonprofit coffeehouse, as an example of another characteristic post-Microsoft project.

Microsoft co-founder Paul Allen is perhaps the most visible personality to emerge from these golden trenches. No longer with the company, Allen has immersed himself in numerous projects that read like a checklist recording the fulfillment of many an adolescent dream. Besides starting his own tech company, Starwave, and his umbrella group, Vulcan Northwest (which includes his investments), Allen, an amateur guitarist and well-known Jimi Hendrix fan, is the driving force behind a $100 million structure that hugs the monorail at the foot of the Space Needle. A tribute to his rock idol that will open sometime in 2000, the Experience Music Project will be a temple in honor of the Seattle-born Hendrix. Los Angeles architect Frank Gehry, together with the crew that made the special effects from the movie *Titanic,* are collaborating to make a multisensory experience unlike anything in existence. The fragmented, globular masses, which refer to Hendrix's smashed Stratocasters, will contain 140,000 square feet and, according to Allen's Web site, ". . . will help visitors discover this process and their own creative potential with traditional and interactive exhibits that borrow elements from museums, schools, research centers, and theme parks. The philosophical basis for EMP can be traced back to Jimi Hendrix's idea of Sky Church, a place where artists could exchange ideas, write and make music without the constraints of the music business."

Allen's gestures don't stop there: In 1997 he formed Football Northwest in order to facilitate the purchase of the Seattle Seahawks, and essentially paid for an election that would secure public funding for a new football stadium—a controversial use of moneyed muscle. He owns the Portland Trailblazers basketball team, and is funding the renovation of the grand old railroad depot, Union Station, as well as the Cinerama, the big-screen movie theater that is supposed to feature the *Star Wars* prequel when it arrives. So what does Allen signify for the future of a get-rich-quick city like Seattle? It seems that his exuberance, his longtime passions, are assuming permanent visible form here as monuments, temples to leisure and the good life. And while we needn't be reminded yet again that this is all due to the folks who brought us Windows and Word, and that, hey, it's his money to play with, there's an emerging sense of the city as a vast personal playground that has become increasingly unsettling.

Allan Stein

MATTHEW STADLER

Matthew Stadler (1959–) grew up in Seattle and has published four novels: Landscape Memory *(1990),* The Dissolution of Nicholas Dee *(1993),* The Sex Offender *(1994), and* Allan Stein *(1999). He has received the Richard and Hinda Rosenthal Award for Fiction from the American Academy of Arts and Letters, the Whiting Foundation Writers Award, the Ingram–Merrill Foundation Award for Fiction Writing, and a Guggenheim Fellowship. Stadler's writing has been anthologized in* Best Gay Fiction of 1996; In A Different Light: Visual Culture, Sexual Identity, Queer Practice; *and* Men On Men 4. *He has written for Seattle's* The Stranger, *the* New York Times Book Review, *the* Seattle Weekly, *and the* Village Voice. *He is literary editor of* Nest: A Magazine of Architecture and Design. *He is also the editor and co-founder of Clear Cut Press. In this selection from* Allan Stein, *the narrator recounts a Proustian moment of semiconsciousness upon waking in his city apartment in the predawn dark and goes on to describe the café where he and his friend Herbert like to meet.*

My story began properly in the perpetual darkness of last winter (almost spring, it was March) in the city where I used to live. Typically I woke up in the dark, 6 A.M. on most days, delivered from sleep by the icy stream of air spilling in my open window. The lighted clock of the railroad tower said six exactly. This round clock of black iron and creamy glass was the first thing I saw in the mornings. No one was ever on the way to work yet, nor had the lumbering buses and trucks started with their tentative, practice engine roars. (Later, in clouds suffused with the bright yellow and opium-poppy-orange of the risen sun, they would billow in every district of the city like grim flowers and release their belched gray emissions, which gave a pleasant taste to the winter air.) I am a teacher, or had been, which explains the early hour.

Opening the window from bed, only my head and one arm untucked, was my first habit of the morning. It was independent of me, like shifting the buried, cool pillows to the top in the deep middle of the night, neither conscious nor strictly unconscious—something between a dream and the address of a friend, which I had scribbled while dragging the phone as near to the table as it would go before absently tossing the newspaper on which I had written it into the garbage, along with the bones of a fish, so that it was lost both there and in my mind until, when the brisk air of morning rushed in the open window, the whole address, neatly printed, leapt to view, bright and clear as the pinpoint stars, noisy as a child, and my mind's eye, conscious, grasped it again, though only for a moment. Minutes later, in the chaos of morning, it was gone, but so was any memory of having lost it.

All my thoughts were thin and brittle when I woke. My expansive dreams, ideas that multiplied like the crystalline spread of urine released into space (which I have heard is a beautiful sight, witnessed only by astronauts, the discharge turning golden and immense in the black void), became whole great cities of geometrical fantasy, complex and beautiful as hoarfrost, before shattering suddenly into unreadable shards at the slightest touch of fact or feeling (a crease in the pillow bothering my cheek, for example, or the sour taste scraped from my teeth by a dull, swollen tongue). The scrim of night outside was fragile. Its thin black mask could not hide the sheer abundance of the day ahead, nor the fact that it was morning already elsewhere, evening again elsewhere still, and a bright summer afternoon somewhere so distant one passed through two accelerated days in the metal shell of a jet airplane just to get there. My mother, Louise, once asked me what separates one place from another. I was only a child, and of course I had no idea. Other places, I guessed, which begged the question.

252

The oatmeal I ate before bed and left too close to the coiled heater was covered by a film of dry skin, which burst under the slightest pressure, my thumb for example, if it strayed too deeply gripping the bowl. I always licked this thumb, after its plunge, and the cold sweet paste it unearthed from beneath the film was enjoyable. I could hear my friend Herbert, in the adjacent apartment, bellowing fragments of popular songs, which he only ever partly remembered. Herbert and I were always awake early, even while the rest of the city slept. He is the curator at the city's art museum, and they let him keep whatever hours he likes. I had no reason to be awake. The school where I taught resolved some misgivings that arose over Christmas by granting me a paid leave of absence.

. . .

Herbert was the only friend I discussed this with. Others, especially my colleagues from school, were so moved by the weight of the "tragic accusations" that I could feel myself *becoming* tragic simply with the approach of their cloying, caring glances. Their eyes had the gleam and submerged instability of glaciers, vast sheets of luminous ice beneath which chasms creaked and yawned. One of them would appear uninvited before my table at a café, fat Mr. Stack the math teacher, for example, and shuffle toward me as if compelled by this hollowness behind his eyes, as slow and devouring as the ice that once crawled down the face of the continent. (My mother described a boyfriend of hers this way, one evening while she and I sat in a diner eating turkey sandwiches with gravy, a special treat she gave me far more often than I deserved. I was eleven years old. It wasn't five minutes before this very boyfriend appeared at the window with his face pressed to the glass, miming hello and making a fool of himself. She winked at me, then looked right past him, blowing smoke from her cigarette, saying nothing. Finally he went away.) I have none of my mother's cool reserve, so I avoided my colleagues when I could or, if forced by good manners to accept a repeated invitation to lunch, tried to speak cheerfully about my "new career" at Herbert's museum, a fiction I had devised, which, like most lies, eventually became true. I learned a great deal about art from Herbert during the few weeks that he helped me perpetrate this lie.

It first occurred to me one cold March afternoon while we sat at a café drinking. Herbert likes to drink and so do I. We are compatible in many ways, and being neighbors a great deal of our lives became shared; watering plants, checking the mail, and chitchat soon became socializing, shared travel, and a natural intimacy that has made me more comfortable with him than with anyone. This particular café (that cold March afternoon) was called Shackles, under which name it masqueraded as a pre-Victorian public house. Nothing in our city is pre-Victorian, except perhaps the famous lakes and the view out.

Dark wood, patterned velvet, newsprint advertisements for nineteenth-century ales (enlarged, scarred, and varnished for display), wall sconces fashioned from gas fixtures, and poor lighting made up Shackles's costume. Windows, curtained on brass rods at eye level, let us watch the street while easily hiding ourselves, if need be, by a simple crouch or slouch nearer the table. The unfortunate waiters were disguised as croupiers from Gold Rush–era Nevada (preposterous puffy sleeves, frilly red armbands frayed to the elastic, tidy vests with fake watch pockets and chains, plus anomalous cummerbunds), none of which kept the young students who took these jobs from supplementing the costume with beautiful earrings of silver or brass, chrome-pierced nostrils, ersatz-Maori cheek tattoos, braids and bangles twined about their elegant thin wrists or tied in colorful cloth cascading from their heads—the result being much more like science fiction than the vague nostalgia the owners must have been aiming for. One of the waiters was a lanky blond angel named Tristan, and Herbert adored him. Tristan was also a student at the university, and Herbert kept offering him an "internship" at the museum, to which the boy always replied, "It sounds completely fascinating," before shuffling off with our drink orders, and then nothing would come of it. We drank there whenever Tristan was working. When he wasn't working, Shackles became, to Herbert, "that hideous dive" and we went to a much nicer café near to our apartment house.

Our city is a virtual monument to indiscriminate nostalgia, sometimes (particularly when I look out my window at the nighttime buildings smartly lit by floods and spots) appearing like a grand, jumbled stage set for all the dramas of Western history. Muscular towers of concrete and glass, paid for by young stock wizards and software geniuses, offer a heady compote of modern forms and ornaments, collapsing three hundred years of the Enlightenment—vaulting skylights, vast glass cathedrals, forests of tall columns appended by apses (in which vendors sell coffee, magazines, and snacks), death-defying elevated wings of stone, granite monstrances balanced on steel pins, and sprawling webs of metal and tinted glass suffused with natural light (for the enjoyment of employees taking their sack lunch in the firm's "winter garden") into singular monuments, so that one can review an entire history without straying out-of-doors. Lighted in the manner of Rome's Campidoglio, these generous knick-knacks dominate the city at night.

Their grand theatricality is sadly compromised, for me, by the awk-ward, insistent fact that I grew up here. My childhood lurks behind these bright scrims and screens, unruly and constant, threatening to overturn the whole facade and reveal the actual place to me.

Sleep Dummy

MATT BRIGGS

Matt Briggs (1970–)was born in Seattle and grew up in the Snoqualmie Valley. He received a B.A. from the University of Washington and an M.A. from the Writing Seminars at Johns Hopkins University. He has published stories in the North Atlantic Review, The Raven Chronicles, Northwest Review, *and* ZYZZYVA. The Remains of the River Names *(2000) is a collection of eleven stories set in the Seattle area. In 2002, he published* Misplaced Alice, *a collection of seventeen short stories. The following short story,* "Sleep Dummy," *which comes from* The Remains of the River Names, *begins with a chance encounter at the Seattle Art Museum.*

I ran into Nathan Anderson, an old friend, at the Seattle Art Museum at a travelling exhibition of an artist I had never heard of, Edward Hopper, but judging from the reaction of the people walking through the rooms I guess he was pretty famous. I came on these paintings that terrified me. In one painting there was a woman—she looked like a needle freak with yellow skin, except she had too much meat on her bones—who was gazing out the window beyond the frame. Light from the portrait's window fell on her haggard face. She sat on the bed looking out the window. For me that picture portrayed every morning after.

A man stood in front of the painting like a child looking into the Christmas window display at the Frederick & Nelson department store. He was short and skinny. I could tell he had muscles under his tight black T-shirt and his faded Levis. He wore a huge belt buckle of a snake eating its own tail that I think was a vintage artifact from the early seventies. His face, lined and flat, had a healthy color, even though he was thin as a knife.

I remembered a man who had worn a belt buckle like the one this guy was wearing, and I realized then that this was Nathan, who I knew years ago, when I first moved to Seattle. He and I had once hit it off. I don't know whether it was because we were drinking rum and smoking reefer or because there was a physical attraction—I was a little too gone to recall— but we lost track of whose drink was whose after I accidentally drank from his glass and left a red lipstick smear on the rim. After that, we drank from both glasses. After we were toasted he said, "Janice baby, let's get drunk together," which frankly meant, "let's get roaring obnoxious and fuck." After a joint and another glass of rum chased with a couple of beers, we made it back to my apartment. We stumbled into my soft bed, we pulled the warm sheets over our heads and, well, we weren't in the position to say "no," or much of anything else. We woke at sunrise and drank coffee in the indistinct gray light that came out of the mid-winter Seattle sky.

As we sat on my couch with the rancid coffee I had prepared with three scoops of tinned grounds, Nathan wrapped his arm around me and held me so tight that I had difficulty raising the cup to my lips. "Quit it," I said, happy to have some one to be grumpy with.

It had been a rough six or seven weeks the winter I dropped out of college; actually I dropped out of attempting to save money for college. Things like rent and groceries took everything I earned running around the tables of the Red Diner downtown. I stayed up late partying, and found a million men, with their deep belly buttons under black curled hair, their fatty muscles, and the deep salty smell of their arm pits attractive enough that they would find their way back to my place. In all of these cases they would wake before dawn and dress in the dark. Leaning down, they kissed me and lied to me at the same time; smacking their lips as they left, they said the mantra that would start another day for me, "I'll call you." And sometimes they would. But they never lay in bed with me and waited long enough for me to make some coffee and lay with me on the sofa and sort out the time of the day like Nathan had done.

I suppose that I wouldn't remember all of these things—the long winter, the succession of guys, and the few times with Nathan—if I had never missed my period. When it finally stopped, I bought a bottle of red wine and a urine test at Fred Meyer, aware as I paid the old woman behind the counter—a woman who was much older than Mom when Mom finally died—that the cashier knew it wasn't good news that I had to buy something like this. A man who buys a urine test is a good thing, but a woman who does it, that is just bad news. At home I took the test and drank the red wine to celebrate the positive. I didn't even know when the last time I had a period was, so I found a friend who had a friend who knew a doctor and got it cleaned out before I started thinking about pink or blue pajamas with the special vinyl foot pads.

Nathan stopped by an oil painting of what from the other side of the room looked like a watchtower overlooking a blood red battlefield, but when I came close I saw that it was really just a railway station at the edge of a sunset. "Nathan?" I said. I tried for a friendly, *Hello it's been years* tone of voice. But who can control these things? My voice cracked, and then in an effort to cover it up, I said, "It's been some time." Which came out in clear, slow syllables.

He turned around and I thought, "Oh fuck, I've never seen this man in my life." His face was so thin that I could see the arc of his skull in his forehead. But he smiled and said, "Janice?"

I don't know, but recognition from someone who hasn't seen me in almost twenty years—this was a gift. If he had suddenly reached into his pocket and wrapped a twisty wire from the grocery store around my finger and proposed, I would have married him even though I know what all of that is about.

We went to coffee and I realized then that Nathan had not aged as well as I had thought. We talked about my job. We talked about some of the people we knew in common. We hit it off decently enough. But I could tell something was bugging him. He was so skinny and he ate so little. He ordered a hamburger with two slices of cheese, and he ordered an extra side of fries, and then he ate all of his fries and he ate the cheese off his hamburger. He drank the Coke, and he drank six cups of coffee. Bathroom city. We talked about the people we had known all those years ago. When I maneuvered the conversation to the present, talking about the fall of the Soviet Union, or the new Museum downtown, or whatever, his interest would tail off. He would watch someone on the street and say something about her hair. When we talked about what we would do next, he said, "Actually, I have an appointment."

He did ask for my number. But that was only the polite thing to do.

I, however, was getting too old to be polite, and I was attracted to him. One of the things that attracted me to him were the stories I had heard from our mutual friend, Paul Lane, of the abuse Nathan had put himself through, drinking until the bars collapsed behind him, pushing his endurance with whatever powder or capsule or paste was available. He had lived high on the hog, like most people these days just don't. I think, maybe, they look at the wrecks of the seventies, the multitude of vomit-drowned celebrities and the old hippies hanging out in backwoods bars, still wearing love beads even though they have no one to love, and they are afraid. They are afraid of becoming a cultural backwater, of letting things just slip along while they remain in a time and place no one remembers properly, resurrected only in momentary retro styles and spoofy parties. Finding Nathan was like finding a genuine jeans jacket with vintage bead work in a thrift store.

Beyond this, though, I just had the basic motive of wanting to get a real, warm human body into my bed, male and my age preferably.

I still use a body pillow I bought from a flea market the sixth year of my marriage to Art. I call this thing my sleep dummy because it helps me sleep, and with its thick, overstuffed sections it makes me believe I'm sleeping with someone. When I lived with Art, the overstuffed torso usually lay at the foot of our bed. But there were nights when I had to pull it out and lay it in the hollow Art's body usually filled. I had to have the bulk of something there or I just couldn't sleep. Just before I left him I realized that I had been living with the sleep dummy. After work, I'd pull it into Art's spot and then read through my murder mystery and magazines. Finally I would fall asleep. When I woke up in the morning, its head would be resting on my chest; I don't know where Art was, because he wasn't in my bed.

Now I live in an apartment by myself, close to work, and I'm still sleeping with the dummy. Over the years, I've spilled coffee on it. I've dropped ashes on it. It has acquired its own character in the stains and wrinkles and worn patches. I think of my sleep dummy as the character, Mr. Paterson, from *Tea and Nightshade Murders*. He's the short, squat, male sleuth who drinks himself to oblivion while pondering the questions of the murder over his bottle of sherry. I always say, "Good night, Mr. Paterson," before I turn out my light.

I showed up at Nathan's apartment a couple of nights later with a bottle of wine, spaghetti in a plastic Tupperware container, and fresh bread. Nathan answered the door, wearing a bathrobe draped over his thin limbs, the pale fabric worn and stretched in places his body wasn't. He was clean-shaven and smelled like lavender bath crystals, so I assumed there must have been a woman in his apartment because I couldn't picture him in the bath tub, floating alone among the white bubbles. I said to him, "I thought I might drop by, but if you have company. . . ." I was looking past him at the freshly vacuumed carpet; at the geometric order in the alignment of the sofa, coffee table, TV; at any sign of a woman, like a compact left on the coffee table, or even something as conspicuous as two mugs on the table. I didn't see anything. I didn't even hear water running or any other activity by someone other than Nathan.

"It's nice to see you," he said, something I was not expecting to hear after his ambivalence at the diner. He stepped back like he wanted me to come in. The carpet in his apartment was plush compared to the worn astro-turf carpet of the hallway. The warm air from the lamp-lit rooms of Nathan's apartment washed over him, carrying the lavender smell of his bath and the faint odor of cough drops or Vick's Vaporub into the bright hallway. I stepped in. "There is enough for three," I said, as I set the round Tupperware down in his dark kitchen.

"Three? Did you invite someone?" he said.

"Isn't there someone here?"

"Who would visit me?" and when he said that, at first I was relieved and I almost felt a giddy twitch along my hips. Then I wondered why he felt it was necessary to say something so pathetic.

He turned on the lights in the kitchen to show plain tile counters, empty of the standard appliances, like a toaster or microwave or espresso machine.

The only standard thing was a Mr. Coffee. "I need to change, but I'll be right back. There's coffee. Please, sit down." I watched him walk down his hallway, turn into what I assumed was his bedroom and close the door.

Nathan returned wearing a white sweater and slacks. They hung on him. He smiled at me and held out his arms. We hugged and I could feel the ridge of his backbone under the sweater. He groaned and pulled back from me. "You will have to catch me up on everything, including the sordid details of your marriage to what's his name."

"Art."

He stopped and looked at me. "I'm sorry. I can tell that we're getting off to a bad start. First we met like a couple of characters in a bad short story at that Edward Hopper exhibit. I already feel like a manifestation of a cliché. We can get beyond all that after we eat. It's very kind of you to drop by."

"A cliché, what do you mean?"

"I don't know. I just think I've seen that movie too; you know, I've already read that story."

"I'd never seen Hopper's painting before. I liked them."

"They're great," Nathan said. "But you can buy his coffee table book at Costco. I think anything you can buy from a warehouse immediately enters some phase of clichéhood."

"I made my spaghetti from scratch."

"And your sauce?"

"Prego," I said. "From Costco."

"Let me get the wine," he said. "Immediately."

I sat in a square stuffed chair in the living room. The TV was on, but turned to a blue screen. He poured the wine. It gugged and the sharp odor filled the room. "Do we need to heat up the food?"

"It should still be warm."

He placed the wine bottle in the center of the coffee table, and the plate in front of me with an exact motion, like the place was marked with tape. He set the napkin, the fork and knife. "Do you use a knife with noodles?"

"I don't know; do you? You don't use chopsticks," I said. I put one of the couch pillows into my lap, propped my elbows on it and quickly drank the bitter wine.

He set the Tupperware container next to the wine and opened the lid, wafting smells of hamburger and tomato sauce and the pasty Mission noodle odor.

He dumped a mess of noodles and meat sauce on my plate, splattering the table. He took the knife, and gave me his fork. He sat and put half as much as I had on his plate. He wrapped noodles around his knife. Shoving the food into his mouth, he freed his hands to pour more wine. He filled my glass.

I drank the acidic wine. The glass was too full and I slopped some onto the table, where it mixed with the splattered spaghetti.

"Great," he said. "This is just great." He wiped his mouth clean, setting his knife flat on his plate. "This is really good."

I drank my wine in huge gulps. "You don't have to like it," I said. "To be honest, I'm a really bad cook, and the fact that this spaghetti isn't making you puke on impact is amazing to me."

"No," he said, he raised his eyebrows. "This *is* good."

"You like it then?" I asked.

"Excellent," he said. He made the okay sign with his thumb and forefinger.

I cleaned my fork by sticking it down my mouth, up to the widest point of the handle. I made sure I had Nathan's eye contact. Then I handed him the clean fork. He dropped it on the table. "That's just too sexy," he said.

I pretended for a second to be interested in wiping up the mess of spilled wine and sauce, and then looked up quickly. I caught Nathan spitting out a little of the food. I didn't know what to do. I said, "Are we really going to eat all this? Or are you going to make a pass at me?" I stood up to leave for the bathroom. When I stood, the two glasses of wine entered my head, and I momentarily felt my feet slip into space; then the vertical lines of the doors and windows twisted straight.

When I came back to the room, the drapes were open to a view of the apartment across the street and the downtown skyline above the roofs and the pale shapes of clouds in the sky. A few planes moved under the bellies of the clouds, like artificial stars or massive glowbugs. Nathan had cleared the table, except for the wine. He sat in the square stuffed chair. He fit in half, and his arms were pale and skeletal. His skull stood black in the halo of his thin hair, glowing in the lamplight. The tumbleweeds of his hands clawed the arm rests. I didn't want to make a pass at him.

"What's wrong?" I asked.

"I'm tired, that's all."

"Don't you like me?"

"Yes. It's not that."

"What are we not saying?" I asked him. But I had turned around and I didn't want him to answer. I just wanted to get all of the crap, him spitting out my spaghetti and his skull-like cheekbones, not necessarily on the table, but at least up toward the surface where we could look at it. I examined our reflection in the window, Nathan sitting on the chair and my hips a little too wide and a little too healthy. I didn't want to go home drunk to Mr. Paterson. "Won't you at least let me sleep in bed with you?"

He looked out the window. His head nodded into a clenched fist. It doubled like a knot in a thick rope. "Okay. But that's my limit."

"I'll accept that," I said.

"I mean it," he said.

We lay in his bed, small enough that my side, soft and fleshy, pressed into the hard, sharp angles of his body. But his skin was hot and still smelled like lavender. I listened to the sick rise of his breath. It rose into the cavity of his mouth, and hissed in the chambers of his lungs. I pulled the smooth shape of his head against my breasts, until the hiss settled, and his breath smoothed. I fell asleep to the quiet rhythm, looking forward to the gray light of the morning, when I could wake, me in bed with him and he in bed with me.

Breaking In

PAISLEY REKDAL

Paisley Rekdal (1970–) was born and raised in Seattle and is of half-Chinese, half-Norwegian descent. A graduate of the University of Washington, she is currently an assistant professor of English at the University of Utah. Rekdal has published an essay collection, The Night My Mother Met Bruce Lee: Observations on Not Fitting In *(2000); and two poetry collections,* A Crash of Rhinos *(2000), which won the Contemporary Poetry Series Competition, and* Six Girls Without Pants *(2002). She has been awarded an NEA Fellowship in Literature and is a past winner of the* Michigan Quarterly Review's Lawrence Goldstein Poetry Award. *Her essays address questions of ethnic identity and assimilation, while her poetry often elaborates on related issues of the interrelationship between the public and private. The dynamic between social and personal boundaries, as played out in her Ravenna neighborhood home and on the streets of Seattle, is further explored in the personal essay* "Breaking In," *which appears below.*

The second time my family's house was burglarized my father and I were asleep. It was summer; my mother had left on business while I, a sophomore at Roosevelt, and my father remained at home. That night the two of us went to bed early; we heard nothing else until morning.

It was most likely around midnight that the burglar, according to police reports, wrenched open the sturdy cedar door that opened onto our porch. The door was only a year old, a replacement for our last one—itself a

Adapted from "Breaking In," by Paisley Rekdal, originally published in *The Chattahoochee Review*. Reprinted by permission of the author.

flimsier pine version with chipped paint—that had similarly been destroyed by another burglar in pursuit of our VCR.

It was a common repeat crime that summer in Ravenna: police had warned my parents he would certainly return once the insurance replaced our VCR, and so my mother sent the new recorder to our uncle's house. I imagine that the burglar must have run room to room, snapping his flashlight at promising shadows, dragging fingers along desk edges for change, forgotten jewelry. And he must have been terrified when, stopping at our stairwell to listen, he caught the faint rumble of a man's snores, the tossing of a teenage girl in bed at the room by the top of the staircase.

What amazed my mother and amazes me still is that we slept through it: the crack of wood tearing from wood, the whisper of a stranger's footsteps on our wood floor. "How *could* you?" my mother demanded, shaking her head at the splintered door, the icy web of shattered glass. Then turned to me. "This has got to be one of your boyfriends."

Her angry and repeated insistence that the break-in was my fault didn't surprise me. For months my mother had monitored the boys I infrequently dated, cutting off phone or outing privileges at the slightest provocation. My habits she observed sometimes so prohibitively that one year I was grounded for three months for going to a boy's home without a chaperone. Her punishments I found extreme but predictable; she knew, though could never prove it, that I snuck out of the house nights, sometimes even bringing the boy I met back home with me. It was a habit as compulsive as it was dangerous, and for my last years in high school I never once thought about stopping.

My route outside the house was simple: I waited till my parents slept then left by slipping out my bedroom window. This was risky; my bedroom faced my parents' room and at all times their door was open. Still, as soon as they turned off their lights I undid the mesh screen and slid open the window. Then I pushed myself onto the roof of my father's study, swinging down the wood fence before dropping to the graveled garden. On these nights I did anything: joined friends in the University District two miles away, hid in the ravine with the neighborhood boys, or simply walked between my house and school, sometimes wearing a cotton men's bathrobe over my clothes. Often I went alone. I do not recall that I had fears for myself during those years that went beyond social humiliation; today, I am almost proud of this indifferent, self-obsessed rebellion.

But I am aware how easily I could have paid for it. I have a memory of standing with a girlfriend, Dara, on Montlake Bridge at two in the morning when a yellow Pontiac stopped beside us and two blonde men offered us rides. Dara quickly accepted for us both, flirting with the man in the passenger seat who called himself Sid. Sid moved to the backseat with Dara, motioning for me to slide into the passenger seat next to the driver, Shane. Reluctantly, I got in the car. As I moved to maneuver the seat, my right hand touched something sharp and I drew out a small knife from beneath the seat. Shane explained that the knife was for cutting away the trim from his new wiper blades. "They stick," he said, pointing.

By the end of the night we had parked near Discovery Park to watch the sun rise over the Sound. Sid and Dara held hands as they walked further and further away from Shane and me down a wooded path tangled with blackberry vines. After they disappeared, Shane began shyly conversing with me about his two current passions: John Steinbeck and A.A. "I'm off alcohol now," he said. "I go to meetings every Friday." I thought of Dara's father then, how he once tried to kill Dara's mother in a cocaine-induced rage. "That's good," I told Shane. "That's really great."

Minutes later Sid and Dara trudged back up the hill, Dara slightly disheveled. Shane looked at me with great embarrassment as we walked back to the car. He didn't say anything as Sid and Dara exchanged numbers, Sid sliding his hand under Dara's shirt. "You shouldn't ride with strangers," Shane warned as he let me out. He blushed as he spoke, touching my arm. "You got lucky," he said, "but don't do it again." He looked back in the mirror at Sid as he spoke, his mouth twisting. I thought of the knife as I stumbled out of the car, waving as Shane pulled away. I never saw the men again.

The nights I snuck out of my parents' house, all of Seattle became possible, gorgeous and exciting. The warehouses along Lake Union gleamed under the powdery yellow streetlights, their chrome viscera of tubes and pipes glittery and slick. By day Seattle seemed unbearably drab: too industrial or hippie or glum, the paint on all the houses flaking in the rain. Even the people seemed boring, washed-out in their blue jeans and sweatshirts. But at night the city's features changed. The University District emptied of students, filling with the sullen thumping from the Underground Dance Club, young men in black leather and spiked hair standing at its entrance, their faces arsenic-colored.

Everywhere we went, there were boys. Dara greeted them eagerly, going off with the most insistent, bumming rides for us up to Greenlake where we would sit on the Aurora bridge, throwing empty beer cans at passing cars or walking around the unlit lake, scaring ourselves with the sight of shadows suddenly lengthening out of other shadows. She liked to explain men's lovemaking techniques in painful detail, numbering each boyfriend according to eye color and ability. She talked endlessly about the bodies of boys we met as we traveled place to place, so that the city became an erogenous map of someone else's pleasure: a catalogue of vicarious titillation so linked to place and time that even years later when I drive around the city I feel a distant, envious shiver passing each landmark.

Meanwhile, I was saving it for college. "That's *years* away," Dara groaned, but I shrugged. It didn't matter how much I might want sex or how Dara snickered. Something wouldn't let me give in.

Sometimes, wrestling with a boy in a stranger's car, I'd find things beside me: a tire iron, a heavy flashlight. *How much will this hurt?* I wondered. It was an intimacy that I knew depended on pain for consummation, a violence making me an object to be worked upon, broken into, protected. Virginity showed me a weaker self, and it was the surrendering of that self—the notion that only someone else could take it away—that frightened me. Losing my virginity would be a kind of theft.

Beside this, however, the damp or stained surfaces of other people's couches only brought the memory of my parents' house into closer view. What was lurking there right now? I didn't worry about my parents waking up to find me missing so much as them discovering an intruder in the house. If I left doors and windows open so that I could get out, surely someone else could use them to get in. Images of my parents shot or stabbed terrified me, but I couldn't stop myself. My only hope was that no one had watched me, marking which places I made vulnerable in my desire to escape.

"You do whatever anyone tells you," my mother accused me once, exasperated. She didn't understand that I didn't listen to anybody; if I had, I might never have left the house. I loved our home with its shaggy wood exterior. I loved the rhododendrons with their sticky heads blooming in our backyard. I loved my parents too, reading the books they read, watching the movies they watched. But being another adult with them, I was also invited to see the vulnerability that surrounded us, the jeopardy of our lives.

I would never be like Dara, I thought. And yet it didn't bother me, sheltering in this half-world of adulthood I could explore like a city. It didn't matter what other people thought or saw. There was the boy, there was the pain, there was the door that was my body and the choice that kept it closed.

So "It's not my fault!" I heatedly cried when my parents agonized over the cost of another door. My mother only cocked an eyebrow and looked at me.

How could my parents not see what I did: that sex was avoidable, strangely safe? Because I could not see myself as a victim, I refused to understand how others could. My parents, I thought, didn't understand how *little* sex meant.

"You're growing up," my father told me jokingly once. "I can't believe such a good-looking child sprang from my loins."

Inwardly I cringed hearing that word "loins" spoken by my father. I didn't want to hear this word from him. I didn't want to know I could spring like that from anybody.

After the carpenters installed our new double doors, thicker than the last with two sets of deadbolts, my mother bought a string of bells and hung them over the handles.

"Now at least one of you will hear something," she said. But what would we do if we did hear a man sneak into our house? My mother talked about sending me to self-defense courses and gave me pamphlets on rape. Was she arming me to protect the house, I wondered, or myself?

I know that my parents were aware I snuck out. Once or twice they even tried to catch me, walking into my room suddenly before going to bed, replacing the screen doors to my window. But each time I would outwit them, slip back minutes before they decided to surprise me in my room.

My sneaking out had become a game between us: my parents trying to wake before I left, me sliding like another shadow into the house before my father went to his study.

"You have to understand," my mother told me recently about this summer. "Your father and I grew up in a generation that just didn't tolerate that kind of behavior. Your generation is different, though. Everything has changed. The whole city has changed. We just have to accept that."

But they didn't really accept it and they still don't. Only recently my parents have agreed to let my fiancé stay with me in the same room when we come home to visit. "But don't tell anyone we're doing this," she warns. "I don't want anyone to think we're condoning this."

"The world condones this," I sigh. "No one cares. Why should you?"

"Because this is our house," my mother explains. "And in our house, we do what we think is best."

She does not say that I am in her house, thus subject to its rules. Nor does she say, though it is implied, that as a family we are intimates in ways that make the vulnerability of one destructive to the others. She doesn't have to. I understand already that it is my body's unfaithfulness which reinforces our eventual and necessary differences. It is my desire that takes me away, my body that has become the door that opens onto our future: a separated family.

In the end my mother was right to worry: I did become known as a slut, though I graduated high school with my virginity intact. I didn't even know about my lost reputation until a friend confessed it to me.

For a long while I was mortified by this, not believing that strangers in school had watched me. *What did they see?* I found myself repeatedly wondering, just as my mother would occasionally ask, "Do you think they ever caught him? Do you think he'll come again?"

After awhile, my ruined reputation amused me. I even reveled in it senior year. Appearing untouchable kept me from any intimacy that might wrench me away from my family. I wore my sex like a rope of bells, let it clash and shiver with each step.

In retrospect I am amazed by what could have happened to me or Dara and didn't, just as I'm amazed my father and I didn't wake during the burglary. But my parents and I believed in the possibility of disaster, we mapped out its various trajectories, baited each other with the appropriate insults. Perhaps because we believed so strongly in the things that could happen, it was eventually as if they did, and so the arguments between my mother and me over my kept but lost virginity, over the assumption my father and I could have protected our house, had been necessary, natural. "What do you remember about my childhood?" I ask my mother occasionally, to which she always replies, "You were a good kid."

"And in high school?" I prod, knowing her answer. But she never gives it to me.

"Still a good kid," she says. "A little difficult, but still a very good kid."

Then I smile and shrug. My mother's hair is thick and gray now, my father's beard entirely white. And me? I live several states away and am not a virgin. But whenever I visit I drive through Seattle at night at least once, surprising myself with the changes. The new and glamorous stores in the Village, pale as bricks of ice cream. The Eastlake warehouses buffed and gleaming, remodeled into condominiums. And I always go to the solid back door of my parents' house, untouched by intruders since its installment, and to the upstairs windows I once prised open so cautiously. And I will sometimes linger in the basement by the door with its spiders' nests to listen to the sounds of the house, its creaks and sudden, almost sexual groans. Sometimes as I sleep I hear steps outside in our gravel and wake swiftly, cleanly, sure that it is our intruder back again to steal from us. But it never is—it is always the wind or a cat—and so I fall back again to sleep.

Cruddy

LYNDA BARRY

Lynda Barry (1956–) was born and reared in Seattle. She studied fine arts at the Evergreen State College in Olympia, Washington, and is best known for her biting cartoons about adolescence, which appear in syndication throughout the United States. She has published a dozen books of comics. She has acknowledged, in addition to the influence of cartoonists such as R. Crumb, the strong influence of literary writers, including Raymond Carver. In her illustrated novel Cruddy *(1999), Barry depicts an emotionally disturbed family life reminiscent of the type found in many of her cartoons. In this selection, she also draws a stark picture of the city's downtown and waterfront.*

I decided my direction by that cool-air smell, fresh and weirdish and coming strong from down the street. I headed into the downtown of Dentsville.

It wasn't such a happy city. People were mainly hunched and staring downward and the buildings were tall but empty looking, like whatever was happening had already passed and wasn't coming back.

A guy with teeny eyes and huge eyebrows was blasting aggressive music on a crooked trumpet and kicking a coffee can at his feet that had rocks and change in it. He got pissed when no one dropped money in and blowgunned notes at the back of their heads. I watched for a while and then I crossed the street. There were some ladies in pastel chiffon scarves who peered at me with too much curiosity at a corner where I waited for the light, so I bolted and jumped in the way of a bus. It wasn't anywhere near hitting me, but the driver blasted his horn and mouthed furious words anyway. Dodging a bus is nothing. Not after you get good at dodging trains. And I was very good at that.

The air smell was more powerful, it wasn't a good smell, not like flowers or food, and it wasn't a rotting smell either. It was complicated, it had many parts, and one of the parts was a core of coldness, if coldness has a smell. To me it does.

At the next corner the smell was knocked to the side by a different smell, doughnuts, slightly rancid but plentiful. The doughnut shop was on a corner of a street that turned very bummy and skruddy with trash and there were little movie houses with faded pictures that displayed ladies bending and squatting with black tape across their eyes and naked boobs. The pictures were warped and greenish and of course there were the dried-out dead flies laying below them. Flies die in so many lonely places. Across the street from the doughnut shop was a two-story neon clown holding a sign that said AMUSEMENTS! but the windows on that building had the boob ladies also.

There were sailors everywhere. Tons of them dressed in white with little caps and black hanging ties, going in and out of the shops and walking close together and laughing. And I was a little bit dazzled by their actualness, their pure Navyness, their handsomeness, and I was thinking it would be a Navy man I married. Only a Navy man. Navy all the way.

And then two of them came up to me. One said, "You got a friend? Will you do two-sies?" The other said, "Shit, Quiver, he ain't even ten!" Horrible waves of nasty booze smells came off of them and one had blood on his teeth. I turned and went into the doughnut shop.

If in your mind a doughnut shop is a clean place with a clean paper-hatted man behind the counter and displays of innocent doughnuts and pots of coffee and good cold milk, well, this place was not like that. Not anything like it. There were people on gummy stools slumping and freaking in slow motion over the sticky counters. No-teeth people smoking, and scary teenagers also smoking, some girls with too much makeup and some boys with scars on their faces and hanging hair. And behind the counter the man was little and harassed looking and his apron was filthy with something that could not come from doughnuts and when he saw me he said "What?" and his voice was harsh. It was hot in the doughnut shop. Super-heated rancid grease air blasting out of vents with dust tentacles waving. "What?" he said again, and rapped on the counter when I looked away.

. . .

I figured out where the cool smell was coming from. It was coming from a thing called The Sound. The Dentsville Sound. Along one side of Dentsville was a body of water, an inlet of salt water coming in from the ocean. There was land on both sides, so it wasn't the ocean, but I was thinking that must be what the ocean would smell like. It had a tide like the ocean and the tide was low and I saw exposed barnacles and clusters of pinched-looking shells, deep blue-black in color. And varieties of seaweed hanging off of things and floating in the water with cigarette butts and pieces of Styrofoam and striped drinking straws. There were dark shapes moving especially deep, I couldn't tell what they were. Possibly fish. But I was thinking of the movie *The Creature,* and I was thinking how now that I saw the kind of water he hung around in, I understood him better. And then I saw a jellyfish. Whitish, nearly transparent, the first one of my life. I marked it in my brain. *Today I saw a jellyfish. Today I saw a jellyfish.*

I stood near a ferry dock and kept breathing the air in, I could not get enough of that kind of air. The smell of french fries made me look up. There was an outdoor stand where people were buying paper baskets of fish and chips and cups of clam chowder. I had heard of clam chowder. Sometimes people ate it in books. But I didn't know what it was and it did not sound good to me. I got in line and watched the two worker guys, teenagers. The one who waited on me had brown skin and full lips and tilted-up black eyes. He wore his paper hat pushed so far forward the point came down to between his eyebrows.

He said, "What you want?"

I said, "French fries."

He picked up the tongs. "What size?"

"Large."

He lifted a paper basket off a stack. "What to drink?"

"Milk."

"No milk."

I said, "No milk?"

He pointed at the board behind him. "We got Coke, Sprite, Root beer, Orange—HEY, DONITA! HEY!" He started waving frantically and cupping his hands around his mouth. "DONITA! HEY! YOU DON'T SEE ME?"

A girl with dark piled-up hair and a lime green minidress was getting into a car. She waved back and called, "I see you, Romel."

The other worker guy nudged him. He said, "Maybe she see you, but what do she see?"

Romel said, "A stud."

"Shit," said the other worker guy. "You ain't going to get none of that. In your dreams maybe."

I said, "Orange, please. And that girl should go out with you."

"Awwww," said Romel, and he was smiling big. "See there?" He tap-slapped the other guy. "You hear what little man say? Say it again."

"That girl should go out with you."

"Haaaa!" said Romel, and the other worker guy laughed. "Because I'm a stud, ain't it? She look at me and see a stud! Put some extra fries up for little man. Little man, you all right. Who beat you in the face like that? I'll kick the shit out of him if you tell me to. You want me to? Where he at?"

I took my fries to some picnic tables near the water. Seagulls swooped around and I threw a fry, wanting to see how a bird would get it out of the water, but a seagull caught it in midair. I threw a couple more and the birds came swarming. I noticed I was feeling decent. Very decent. I walked to a place with a lot of tall totem poles in front of it. And that's where I found it. YE OLDE CURIOSITY SHOPPE. GIFTS. ODDITIES. SOUVENIRS.

Beside the front door was the bone with the sign underneath it that said WHALE PENIS.

I said the words very softly. I pushed open the door and a bell above me rang.

Green Lake

EDWIN WEIHE

Edwin Weihe (1940–) teaches modern literature and directs the Creative Writing Program at Seattle University. A graduate of Brown University and the Iowa Writers' Workshop, he is the author of Another Life and Other Stories *(2000), which includes stories set in Seattle and Paris. In speaking of "Green Lake," the selection here, the author has observed that "if a story is not necessarily about a place, it is, necessarily,* placed, *here in this sensible world we experience too intimately and unnervingly, as through a hand-held camera."*

A new girl in the café, she's called Emily like my sister, brings my cappuccino holding the white saucer in the silver-ringed fingers of both hands as if she might snap it in half. She believes I am reading, she doesn't speak, she slides the coffee to the edge of my book. The dark aroma commingles with the light, rose-watered scent of the freshly scrubbed skin, then the bluejeans, frayed and unwashed, *obligatoire* in this café, and cinched by the red-beaded belt. She smells seventeen. Still, she has done the beast with two backs, if I can trust my nose at this handy elevation, and likely within the hour, though of course this is none of my business.

My business is to drink coffee and read. It allows me to hang my head all day long without arousing suspicion or curiosity. As a child, I had a child's sort of accident, a sudden blow to the upper vertebrae, so that my spine, at the base of the skull, where my kneeling father held it, under this camouflage of bohemian locks, curls now like a shepherd's staff, and keeps my chin more or less glued to my chest, like a good middleweight's. So it's my position in life to be a reader. My little destiny. I'm sure, in fact, that if I were to sit here only a moment or two over a blank table, the first Good Samaritan would stop and quickly shove a book or newspaper or menu, something printed, for chrissakes, under my nose. Only Rosanna, as I recall, ever thought to push the book away, and put in its place, between us, a small mirror, oval and teak-framed, like the artisans sell at Pike Street Market. First she leaned over it to do her mouth with a kind of vermilion, then held a dark point to her eye, then blushed her cheek like sunrise on water. I saw her like that, the parts of her in little, oval worlds of their own.

And so I wait awhile here at this window table. It is my spot, Nancy tells me, if I arrive early enough to claim it. Several years ago, in a different frame of mind, on a Saturday evening as a guitarist improvised on the corner platform, I carved by candlelight my initials in the hard wood, and I can feel them still vaguely here, mine among the others. On winter days when outside the pavement is ice against my face, I may dig in here, reading and sipping, from morning until well into the night. In summer, I'm out by eleven. It's the glare that bothers me, uproots me from my spot—window light that knifes across the page and lifts the words, as though onto a glass slide, separating black from white, and lets them hang there suspended, anxious, like loose souls, so before long you discover your eyes caged and pacing the way they do when you're dreaming. You expect the next breeze from the door to whirl them out into the street.

"You should be out in this," Nancy said. "This gorgeous Sunday. Take your book, why don't you?"

"So that's a new girl," I said. "Emily Claire."

"Just Emily, from Portland. She's seventeen."

"Where's Rosanna? I was supposed to meet her."

"Were you? Well. They're playing her demo on the radio. I've heard it twice already this morning. You know—her demo?"

"Yes."

"Well, they're playing it *ad nauseam* on the radio."

"Is she coming in or not?"

"She is and she isn't," Nancy said. "You know Rosanna. You can never tell where she is exactly."

"I don't care where she is," I said.

"You're a sweet fellow."

"As long as she's here when she said she might be."

She stood silent, playing with the beads of cotton from the frayed border of her apron. It was a short apron, coffee stained, and protruding a little over a generous abdomen, the check pad staring out of its pocket.

"Who am I to talk," she began. "When I was seventeen I had no worries. When somebody wanted to ground me with worries, I'd just hold my fingers up like this, crossed, and fly away. Into the blue. I had my own life. Freedom! Now I'm exactly thirty-six and I have Frank. You've seen Frank. Frank is exactly what I've been trying to avoid my whole life. When I ran into him three years ago, he was crazy with little ticky worries. He'd sit all day biting the hair on his arm. Now he's bloated with them, like a black cloud hanging over me, about to burst. And all he thinks about is doing it. You know? I'm talking morning, noon, and night. Getting loose of his worries. Making little worry deposits, in me, on me, on anybody else who'll sing along. Forgive me."

"What for?"

"It's really not your business."

"And Rosanna? Will she perform here evenings or not?"

"The Demo Queen? Ask her when she comes in," Nancy said.

"Is she coming in this morning?"

"I'm the last to know anything."

It is contrary to my condition, my head hopelessly hung, but just once I would like to look straight into a woman's eyes—you know, into those lakes of longing.

Blood on the pavement will concentrate the mind. I hadn't noticed it coming in, perhaps Rosanna had blinded me, but there it was at the door, and inside the door, dry blood, but fresh too, bright as nail polish. Do not be surprised by this. There's more blood around than you think.

Book in hand, I followed it to the crosswalk where it seemed to pause a moment and collected, as I did, while waiting for the light. Listen, I know what people think when they see a fellow with his face hanging over the pavement, that he's some filthy scumbag scrounging for cigarettes and money. That's why I wear a decent pair of Oxfords, shining up at me, so anybody'll think, Hey, he's only deformed, poor man! And why not a fine pair of shoes since I spend a good part of my waking day, upright or horizontal, looking at them? Still, there's blood on the curb, too. And in the street, despite the laws and condemnations, the refuse: the sales slips and gum wrappers, cigarette filters, fliers for poetry readings, bottle caps and can tabs, chain links, a nail file, a postage stamp, sometimes a photograph or just a bit of a photograph so that all you have is a foot or knee or hand in a pocket. Only a week ago, in fact, I found a letter. All the *i*'s had little circles over them, like halos. What she wanted was her key back. The guy had her key. "Don't touch me! . . . All your promises! . . . Just put it in an envelope," she said. Now she had a post box. She wasn't going back until he gave it to her. Oh, if the key wasn't returned she was going to run him over in the parking lot or on the street when he was crossing and had his head in the clouds, and back up over him and then spin out, burning rubber over his thick skull, and she didn't care if she got consecutive sentences or what. It was a two-page job compressed into a ball the size of a left testicle. In the crosswalk equidistant between curbs.

Now this condom in the gutter. What people will throw off, like skins, into perfectly public places. Well, I come across quite a few right out in the open, in the middle of sidewalks, and hanging limp over the curb, or on a bush like an ornament. How do they get to such places? Thrown from speeding cars, I suppose. Parachuted from windows so high up I can't imagine them. Perhaps there's great merriment in the clouds and all the condoms and nail files and wadded letters are just raining down.

It might explain the blood. Going with the light, I followed it across, then picked up another drop on the sidewalk, and took a left, veering off like an errant atom into the thick grass.

Sunday explained the bells. I suppose they come from St. Matt's, though that's some distance, and thankfully down wind. Sometimes in a wave of quiet, on a day like this, or an evening before the lights come on and the brown shades go down along the sidewalk, I hear somebody's whistling, a chord or two, and next thing I know I'm humming along.

The bright, thick grass gently slopes toward Green Lake. I could smell the water. Now there were real voices and the confusion of radios and dogs barking, close.

Soon I was down among the girls in their shorts and tops. Nymphs on the lawn. Nausikaa and her maids. Hurray! Then a shadow raced at me across the grass, a whoosh of wind over my head. I dropped in self-defense. Dark birds attacking? How many? Two red dogs came bounding after, and leapt, their long red tails whipping my shoulder.

"Are you hit?" cried the first voice coming toward me.

Then her legs—sunlotioned, reeking of coconut, shimmering with fine, grain-golden hair stretching up into bunched white shorts, a sailor's rope for belt.

From behind, another girl approached. "They almost took his crown off!" she exclaimed. Her voice crackled like static.

"Oh, did they hurt you?"

"Safe," I said, waving my book.

"Well, what's the matter with him anyway?" demanded the other girl, hanging back. "Is the guy hung over or what?"

"I'm afraid he may be hurt. It's all right to say so."

My thumb shot up to the back of my neck.

"Jesus," the other said. "They hit him, all right."

"Poor sweetie."

"Somebody's going to get sued around here!" she yelled, moving off toward the faraway guys. Their answer waited, coiled, then whirled through the air, close enough to uncurl my hair. In a second the dogs were snarling and barking, fighting over the Frisbee.

"He can't look up, is all," said the golden girl. "That's right, isn't it? You can't look up?"

"I'm hooked on this," I said, jabbing the ground.

"He's hilarious," giggled the other.

"Poor man," she said, drawing closer. "My name is Dolores. She's Candy."

"Give him our phone numbers while you're at it."

"Shut up, will you? He's so sweet. Like he's proposing or something."

"Get a dog, Dolores."

Dolores leaned over me and whispered. A rabbit ear of her bandeau brushed my nose.

"Can you smell me, mister?"

"Yes," I said.

"What do I smell like?"

"Like flowers on a mountainside."

"Honestly?"

"Jesus, Dolores. What's going on?"

"He wants to see me if you don't mind," she said sharply over her shoulder.

"Is this really necessary?" Candy said, her voice breaking. Then she shouted back to the boys: "The guy wants to see Dolores!"

"Dolores?" one of them shot back. "What's she up to now?"

"It's true, isn't it?" Dolores said, pushing my book aside. "You do want to?"

"What?"

"Want to look at me."

My downed knee slid back, and my body arched achingly at the waist, my curious eyes straining heavenward.

"They don't know a thing about me," she said.

Now Candy is laughing so hard I have to hope she'll choke to death. I stood up and searched the ground for the best way free, then took off way around them, and headed out across the hill.

"Duck!" shouted one of the guys.

Duck? The Frisbee had already struck the small of my back. The sting raced up my spine. Then the snarling dogs were close. In only a few steps and one small leap over the languid limb of another nubile, I was clear and running in my fashion, peeping around my shoulder for the galloping mob.

It's good to run, normally. There's the rub. I stopped, turned slowly like a divining rod, found the scent of the lake. The breeze picks it up, carries it ashore, through the evergreens. My nostrils flared. But with my first step waterward, I fell—book flying—hard into the grass.

This fellow had tripped me up. He lay beside me with thin arms out-stretched, palms up, eyes closed, as if he were counting to ten thousand. *All-e all-e in free!* The sun was pouring into him.

He slept an unshackled sleep, like he owned the whole park. I lay a moment beside him, still as a corpse in the warm grass, and stared at shoes smudged with green across both toes. Only peace I wanted. A soft bed.

I closed my eyes like my friend's. At first the noon light was enough to shine through and make the dance of shadows. Soon I found the dark. My mother came in. Yes, my own mother, like she is. Her face, in a cave of thick brown hair, looked up, yearning. *Up.* Father too, his head like a brown eraser atop a long blue tie. And Emily, her mouth agape. Then others appeared: Nancy, her face ablaze with sunlight, and girls dancing on the lawn, and three small children, their faces waiting like dinner plates, every blessed head raised and raiseable!

Quickly I opened my eyes. Yes. Blazing sunlight. Money in the bank. Stretching a little, I nudged my neighbor's hand.

I searched through my parted shoes for the lake. Looming there, in the way, were three round boys, their shaved heads showing through, like boulders. A Great Mother swooped down behind them.

"You don't need to see this, hear me?" she said. And then: "Is this your book, sir? You should be ashamed of yourself!"

She yanked them away. The view opened wide to the parade of joggers, skaters, bikers on the marked path which lined the lake, and the crescent beach just beyond, and the crouching bodies, still more heads bowed. Then the shimmering water. I could see far out, the red rowboats with their gold oars in the air, and hear the hum of a radio.

I rose, gathered up my book, and headed down to it.

At the shore, the three boys were skipping stones. Behind us, the woman squawked at them to stop. Far out on the lake someone's radio was playing Rosanna's demo. I sat down, put aside my book, took off my shoes and socks, rolled up my trousers. I waded out. The warm water rose up my leg. When I was waist high in it, soaked through to the groin, my feet in the icy bottom, I stopped, stood still, listened. I could hear it, all right. No doubt the station was playing it all day long. The song came over the water and all around me the surface went mirror still. I could see myself reflected in it, my face framed in its riot of dark curls, floating in a white sky, my head cut off, suspended. Myself, it seems, sprung free. *Where?* Then the water wrinkled wildly and I went as quickly as I had come.

"Walter! Billy! Did you hit that man? You, Eddie Beale!"

I listened awhile, then turned back. The beach, in the glare, seemed as blinding as a blank page. Then the three boys appeared, squatting, their round, heavy heads bowed, scrounging for flat stones.

Never Mind Nirvana

MARK LINDQUIST

Mark Lindquist (1959–) was born in Seattle and attended the University of Washington from 1977 to 1979. He graduated from the University of Southern California in 1982. He works as a deputy prosecutor for the Pierce County Special Assault Unit. He has published three novels: Sad Movies *(1987),* Carnival Desires *(1990), and* Never Mind Nirvana *(2000). In the following selection from* Never Mind Nirvana, *Lindquist's protagonist bounces around Seattle's nightclubs in the wake of the city's early-to-mid-1990s alternative music scene.*

I SAW U

Pete makes his first stop at the Alibi Room, a well hidden bar in Post Alley just across from the Pike Place Cinema. He does not like the showy food, the screenplays on the shelves in lieu of books, or the frantic manager who scampers around in Nikes asking people to not use their cell phones. Pete comes here because of Carol.

"Hey," she says when he sidles up to the bar.

"Hey."

A Blur rip-off of a Pavement song plays on the house stereo as Carol shakes a martini. She wears hiphugger flares and a paint-spattered tank top that exposes the butterfly-and-roses tattoo on her chest. She's an artist.

Three months ago she invited him to a show at the Upchurch Gallery.

Her paintings were black and abstract, indicative of a seriously disturbed personality. This intrigued Pete. He was unable to act on his interest, however, as she was busy pawing a boyfriend who resembled a young Elvis Costello. Pete could see they were in the initial infatuation stage.

"So what have you been up to?" Carol says as she brings him a shot of Johnnie Walker Black and a Pike Place Ale.

"Oh, just been worrying about the future."

She nods. "Did you hear about that poll where female White House staffers were asked if they would sleep with President Clinton? Ninety percent said 'Not again.'"

Pete smiles, nods. "Still seeing that guitarist?"

"When he's in town. He's touring now."

So he's probably picking up an STD as we speak.

"They're going through B.C.," she explains. "And then on to Toronto. They're very popular in Canada."

"When's he coming back?"

"Twenty-three days."

He cringes at the fact she's counting, downs the shot.

"He's been sending me these postcards and letters and cassette tapes," she continues, "and I'm making this collage for him and . . ."

Pete is willing to take on an incumbent if necessary, but he knows this can be expensive and time consuming, so he is waiting for an open seat.

On First Avenue he stops at Seattle's Best Coffee, which has replaced Fantasy Unlimited at the corner of Pike. Fantasy Unlimited sold dildos, cool postcards, and specialty clothing, including black leather bodysuits like the one worn by the Gimp in *Pulp Fiction*. Another local treasure lost to downtown development.

As he continues north, past the Champ Arcade—LIVE NUDE GIRLS!—he holds the double espresso with two hands and sips as he walks and the caffeine quickly kicks in with the alcohol and this low-grade speedball warms him.

The wind swirls into his face as he passes Market Place Tower. He considers a detour to the Pink Door in Post Alley, but decides he cannot deal with the color scheme, which is, unironically enough, primarily pink.

So he continues straight on and the Space Needle comes into view—the saucer-shaped restaurant on the top glowing blue and orange over the buildings ahead—and the sight gives him inexplicable comfort, his north star.

An unfamiliar bouncer guards the door of the Frontier Room and will not allow entry of the coffee cup. He also asks for I.D. Pete looks young for his age, but not that young. He sometimes worries that maybe he looks like some kind of law-enforcement agent.

Donna, the buff bartender, brings him a scotch before he asks.

He tips her well.

"How come you haven't brought in any of those sweet young things lately?" she says.

"Because you'll steal them."

"A girl knows what a girl likes."

"I'm glad somebody does."

The obligatory banter accomplished, he sips the house scotch, which hits him like lighter fluid.

He makes a cursory scan for talent. Hardcore drinkers, once the exclusive occupants, have yielded the space to the music scene. Pete zeroes in on a striking waiflike girl, light skin, dark hair, nose stud. She is, however, already with a guy, and he looks vaguely like Chris Cornell from Soundgarden, but is actually Cornell's younger brother from Grace.

"Margaritas" by Love As Laughter plays on the jukebox.

Though Pete appreciates the provincial emphasis on regional music of late, it reminds him that in the eighties you had to put a gun to the bartender's head if you wanted to hear a local band.

He shifts his reconnaissance into the pool-table room. Options appear limited, but he spots a possibility: pale Seattle skin with dark red lipstick, black bob, glasses. Five people sit at her table, two other women, two guys, not coupled up. Next to her beer is an empty shot glass, and she is draining a pint of what appears to be Heffeweizen in long gulps. Two good signs. He sets up a stakeout.

Picking up a copy of *The Stranger*—"Free Every Thursday!"—from a table in the hallway within eyesight of his target, he opens to the "I Saw U" section.

EROTIC DAY GIRL @ CHA CHA 3/10
U: "Have an Erotic Day" T-shirt. Me: blond hair, blackly clothed. Eyes kept meeting. But you left with poser. Single? Coffee? Heroin?

HARVEY DANGER @ SIT AND SPIN
Valentine's Day. U: green/pink/black hair. I said, "Nice hair." Trying to flirt. Failed. Let me try again? "I'm not sick but I'm not well."

He skims ads with headlines such as ART GIRL, NANNIES ON DENNY, BILL'S ON BROADWAY, and KISS ME ON THE BUS. He religiously reads this section of *The Stranger*. He is moved by these screams into the void.

Meanwhile, Drinking Girl With Glasses finishes her beer. As she glances around for a waitress, she sees him looking her way. Eyes meet. Hers dart away. He looks back down at the paper.

She stands. He keeps his nose in *The Stranger* until he senses her approaching. He looks up, feigns surprise at the sight of her, smiles.

She returns the smile, and walks on by.

He waits a couple beats, then follows her to the bar. She is wearing a black skirt and her legs are bare, a bold choice for the schizophrenic season between winter and spring. He cuts around her, catches Donna's eye.

Donna responds with a quick scotch on the rocks.

"What are you drinking?" he asks Drinking Girl as he pulls out his wallet.

She hesitates, then says, "Heffeweizen."

"And a Heffeweizen," he repeats to Donna as he pays.

"Thanks," Drinking Girl says.

"You're welcome."

"So," she says, "are you from around here?"

"Born and raised."

"I just moved here. Got a job at Amazon.com. Figured it was time to get a real job since it's the last year of the millennium and all."

"Actually next year is the last year of the millennium."

"Huh?"

"Two thousand is the last year of the millennium." Blank stare in response.

"Because the first year of the millennium was 1901," he explains. "So 2000 is the last year. Two thousand and one is the first year of the next millennium. That's why Kubrick called his movie *2001*, instead of *2000*."

She still stares blankly at him and he realizes he is totally losing her.

"Where are you from?" he tries.

"Vancouver."

"B.C.?"

"Washington."

"Well, welcome to Seattle."

The beer arrives and they touch glasses in a toast.

"My friends and I are thinking of going to the Crocodile," she says. "You know that place?"

He nods, decides not to mention that he has spent approximately forty-two percent of his adult life there.

"Maybe I'll see you later then?"

He smiles, nods.

Outside, the drizzling rain has let up and a nearly full moon is rising between light cirrus clouds over the Bank of America Building. The sidewalks are filling with nightlife. Pete notices every couple, wonders what the guy has done to get the girl.

He passes the Bethel Church on Lenora and Second. The ever changing marquee reads: LET JESUS BE YOUR RHYTHM SECTION. Further evidence in Pete's mind that too many musicians are still moving here.

Outside the Crocodile Cafe, Pete steps in line behind two guys, one in a suit and the other in a leather jacket. A scan of the flyers on the glass door indicates that the Murder City Devils and Tight Bros From Way Back When play tonight, good news. Kevin, the doorman, spots Pete and waves him past, a small courtesy Pete appreciates.

He strolls through the dining area and doesn't see anyone he knows, so he follows a guy with a black and green Crocodile BEHAVIOR MONITOR T-shirt who clears a trail down the hallway.

In the back bar the haphazardly arranged tables and booths are full. Among the junk that passes for decor are chandeliers, neon bars, papier-mache crocodiles, and sheep with wings hanging from the ceiling. Pete is, as always, disturbed by the winged sheep. If they were pigs, he would understand.

He locates an empty bar stool and thereby avoids the drink line. Jennifer, the bartender, brings him a Johnnie Walker Black. She is cool and pretty and too many people hit on her so Pete does not.

"Did you hear Beth's back in town?" Jennifer says.

"What?"

"Beth Keller. She's apparently back in town."

Pete spent three months living with Beth in a motel thirteen years ago and has not seen her since. He calls those the best weeks of his life, at least when he is drunk.

Stephanie, the owner, steps out from the EMPLOYEES ONLY passage and gives Pete a quick wave. She is tall and stunning and wearing red lipstick, but unavailable, married to a rock star from Georgia who recently moved to Seattle. They have children, which impresses Pete.

"Jennifer," he calls out as she pours a draft for another customer.

"Yeah?"

"Did you see her?"

"Who?"

"Beth."

"No, I just heard she was around."

Pete lights a Camel, drinks his scotch. Estimated blood alcohol: .05 and rising fast. A guy pulls up next to him wearing a SEATTLE THINKS THE REAL WORLD SUCKS T-shirt. Pete thinks this ought to go without saying.

Recognizing the noise of a band taking the stage, Pete dismounts from his stool. He enters the employees' GO door, passes through a narrow room that always puts him in mind of Bobby Kennedy's assassination, and emerges in the live music area. He finds space by the sound booth and leans back against the wall.

The sound mix is muddy—the air is moist with breath and sweat and smoke and so the high ends are muted. The sound tech has not compensated for this. He is probably on drugs, and not the right ones.

The crowd, however, does not mind. Spencer steps up to the edge of the stage and grabs the mike stand—*"I never want you to be a sailor's girl"*—and he leans over the gals in front and their hands flail up at him and his sweat and spit shine in the white spotlight.

Though Pete cannot understand half of the lyrics, Spencer acts like he means it, and the band looks like they're enjoying it, and this taps into a mix of emotions for Pete—he misses the stage, misses those moments, but would rather not, does not, will not, think about this.

He spots a possibility leaning against a wall: tall, hyperthin, no makeup. Most of the young crowd has pushed up front toward the mosh pit and so it is not too jammed in the back near the bar. Pete edges in her direction, acting as if he is trying to find a good sight line to the stage.

When the Devils take a tuning break, Pete decides to make a move. He is not quite drunk enough to say "Come home with me and the material world will melt and it won't matter if God is dead," so he just says, "Hi."

"Hi."

"What do you think?"

"I've seen them when they were too fucked up to stand, so I'd say they're doing great tonight."

Pete takes this abundance of information as meaning she is amenable to conversation. He glances at the half-empty glass in his hand. "Want to go get a drink?" he asks.

"Thanks. But I'm waiting to hear this new song Derek said they would play for me."

Derek would be Derek Fudesco, the bass guitarist.

Back in the dining area, Pete spots a girl eating a veggie Reuben sandwich by herself, reading *The Stranger.* She wears an abundance of rings, but nothing matrimonial.

Pete boozily stares. Girl With Rings remains oblivious. He sips at his beer without taking his eyes off her. Eventually she senses something, looks over, gives him absolutely nothing, returns to *The Stranger.* He looks away, then checks back to see if she does a double take.

Nope.

Pete generally looks for some sign of encouragement, as this, he believes, is among the subtle qualities that distinguish him from a stalker. Seeing none, he moves on.

At the bar he orders another scotch from Jennifer. Kurt Cobain, wearing rose-colored glasses, stares at Pete from a framed photograph above the cash register.

"Who told you Beth was in town?" Pete asks when his drink arrives.

"Hadley, I think. I'm not sure."

He feels the doom of two A.M. upon him and knows all the misery flesh is heir to awaits him at home.

Lying in bed alone and thinking of Beth and all the accompanying regret is one of the worst ends to a night he can imagine, but he knows a lost cause when he is one.

As he's about to step out the south side exit, he spots Drinking Girl—she's weaving down the narrow hall that separates the bar from the dining area and she smiles and waves at him like he's a long-lost friend.

"Are you leaving?" she asks.

"Well . . ."

"Let's have a drink." She tugs him away from the door.

At the bar he turns to her, "Heffeweizen?"

"Guinness."

"Weren't you drinking Heffeweizen earlier?"

"Oh," she says, "and a shot of Jägermeister."

They sit at bar stools and form an alcohol-soaked bond discussing movies and music and the too many people moving to Seattle. In the course of this he learns her name is Rose, born in Renton, biological father left when she was twelve, hates her stepfather—hints of domestic violence—she went to public schools, dropped out of the University of Washington, tried heroin, liked it so tried to avoid it, has stock options at Amazon.com.

Rose does not seem to be conscious of how high her black skirt rides up her thighs. She does seem to be conscious of how she flicks her tongue stud on her teeth, which, Pete notes, are good. She actually looks better than Pete remembers from the Frontier Room and he does not attribute this to alcohol.

"Last call," Jennifer announces.

Time just keeps ticking away.

Rose turns to Pete, "Last call? *Already?*" She sounds heartbroken.

"There's plenty more booze at my place," Pete says. "And some good CDs." He tries not to sound like she is his last likely hope of getting laid tonight. "Just a few blocks from here. Bar never closes."

She appears to be considering, just needs a push.

"The Oceanic Building," he adds, as though this might make a difference.

"I should probably check with my friends."

"Where are they?"

"I don't know." She laughs.

"I have Jägermeister in the freezer."

They walk south on Second Avenue, slurring their feet, hips bumping into each other. Pete hails a Yellow Cab at Pine as rain starts falling.

"You're not an ax-murderer or anything," Rose says as the taxi pulls over, "are you?"

"Not as far as you know."

Pearl's Secret: A Black Man's Search

for His White Family

NEIL HENRY

Neil Henry (1954–) was born and grew up in Seattle. He graduated from Princeton and from the Columbia School of Journalism. He worked as a metro reporter, investigative reporter, national correspondent, assistant foreign editor, and Africa bureau chief for the Washington Post *from 1977 to 1992. Currently Henry is an associate professor of journalism at the University of California, Berkeley. This selection is taken from the memoir* Pearl's Secret: A Black Man's Search for His White Family *(2001), the product of the author's efforts to uncover his family's past in the South while also reconciling that past with his years growing up in Seattle.*

Up until the 1960s all generations of my family lived in a racially segregated America—in St. Louis, Winston-Salem, and Nashville. Even in Seattle, where my parents migrated in 1956, after my father finished his surgical training in the Deep South, the neighborhoods and schools were segregated by local custom if not by Jim Crow law. The city's black residents were largely confined to a several-mile-square patch of real estate in the inner city called the Central Area, where the public schools were predominantly black and abysmally staffed and supported, compared with schools in white areas.

Infused by the ideals of equal rights and opportunity that galvanized their generation of black professionals, and buttressed by legal advances of the civil rights movement elsewhere in America, my mother and father decided in 1960 to test Seattle's de facto system of racial segregation. Unable to buy a house outside the Central Area because of their race—and thereby unable to gain access to premium public schools for their children—my parents secretly commissioned a white middleman named Franz Brodine to purchase a piece of property for them in the city's south end, in a middle-class subdivision called the Uplands, where the public schools were good. For many years, under a 1920s-era racial covenant governing the subdivision, blacks and Asians—unless they were working as domestics— had been barred from residence in this pleasant neighborhood on the shore of Lake Washington.

Although such racial covenants governing neighborhoods and housing were ruled unconstitutional by the U.S. Supreme Court in 1948, the restrictions were still observed in practice in many American cities. My parents' clandestine method of purchasing property in a white neighborhood was typical of the sleight-of-hand upwardly mobile black people in northern cities had to resort to in order to better themselves, to secure equal educational opportunities for their children, and to force the nation to honor its constitutional guarantees. It was one thing for the courts to decide that racial segregation was illegal, as they did throughout the 1950s and 1960s, but it was up to individual black people like my parents to test those decrees, to force the change, and to deal with the personal consequences.

It was on a beautiful street lined with lush, vase-shaped elm trees and tall, elegant pines, amid rows of stately homes overlooking the lake, that my mother and father decided to build a house. After Brodine signed the property deed over to my parents, they commissioned the city's only black architect, Benjamin McAdoo, to design and build the house. A relatively new arrival in Seattle, with a growing reputation for his work, McAdoo took special care with our house, in part because he wanted to make sure our historic move went smoothly. He had already designed and built several other houses for white families in the neighborhood and was well aware that he couldn't live in any of them because he was black. Our victory would be his as well.

For months, as our house was being constructed, the white neighbors were unaware of who owned it. Then, shortly before we moved in that

December, they found out the new arrivals were a black family. Terrified of us and distressed over an assumed deflation of their property values, our prospective white neighbors convened emergency block meetings to cobble together strategies to thwart us. When the city's mayor, Gordon Clinton, got wind of the controversy, he urged civic mediators to quell it somehow. But the white neighbors persisted. They sent petitions from house to house throughout Seattle's south end to gain wider support for their efforts and pooled their money to offer my father a buyout at 200 percent of his purchase price. Anything to stop us.

But my parents were determined. We moved into our new house at 6261 Lake Shore Drive South a few weeks before Christmas 1960, the first black family in Seattle's Uplands subdivision. From that day, my life changed forever. I was six years old, the product of a proud and loving black world, embarking on a new childhood in a world where my family and I were clearly alien and unwanted.

My closest friends, my teachers, my neighbors, the first kid I ever fought with my fists, the first girl I ever kissed on the lips—practically everyone who populated the universe of my school-age childhood was white. I was the quintessential poster child of the era of racial integration, a drop of color on a field of snow. I was the first and only black kid in my class from first to seventh grades. I was the only black kid on my Little League teams, in my Cub Scout troop, and at swimming school. I learned to read, write, and enunciate English with perfect diction and grammar, to use a protractor and slide rule expertly, and to sing first tenor in classical ensembles in the school choir.

Indeed, I outdid most of my white classmates in practically every school subject and was popular enough to be elected president of the student body in junior high school by a landslide. At the height of the Vietnam War in 1968, when I was fourteen, I was awarded a prestigious American Legion medal by local war veterans for civic leadership and academic achievement. I was, in their eyes, the ideal young citizen, a model American.

But I was also hopelessly mixed up.

For the incongruities that defined my childhood were profound and difficult to comprehend. From early on, I felt a weight attached to my childhood on Lake Shore Drive. I knew that, as a black kid, I was in some way carrying a flag for my race and must never let it touch the ground in disgrace. My mother especially taught me to be proud of being black, repeatedly explaining that living amid the white middle class in Seattle was a pioneering and noble venture.

. . .

Frustrated by the discrimination he kept encountering at midwestern hospitals, my father decided to look farther west. My parents had heard wonderful things about the Far West from a white army colleague, a warrant officer from Minnesota, whom they had met in Germany in 1951. The white officer and his wife used to rhapsodize especially about the beauty of the Pacific Northwest, describing the rivers, the mountains, the fishing. It sounded so clean, fresh, and different that the images stuck in my parents' minds when they returned to the States.

That summer, in 1956, my parents dropped my brothers and me off at our grandparents' house in the Ville in St. Louis and, following the path of Lewis and Clark, headed across the Mississippi River and the Great Plains states on a long expedition west, with plans to visit Denver, San Francisco, Los Angeles, Portland, and Seattle. It was Seattle that my mother and father visited first, and they never went any farther. My father drove our old cream- and orange-colored Oldsmobile up and over the Cascade Mountains, across the Lake Washington Floating Bridge to the sparkling city by Puget Sound, and they were astonished by what they saw. The scene that spread before them was so idyllic, so blessed with clear air, freshwater lakes, tall pines, Douglas firs, and majestic snow-capped horizons, that it reminded them of Stockholm, of Salzburg, and especially of Heidelberg, where they had enjoyed a taste of freedom and equality for the first time in their lives as black Americans.

Like Heidelberg, Seattle was a small, peaceful, and provincial city back then, but one populated by many different kinds of people, Scandinavians, Italians, American Indians, Chinese, Japanese, and a small but growing number of blacks—1.7 percent of the population in 1950. Many of the newer residents had come to Seattle for work during the war years. To my parents the city certainly seemed, on its face at least, much more tolerant of human differences than the South ever could be because it was so diverse.

My father interviewed at all the hospitals in and around Seattle's First Hill medical district—"Pill Hill," people in Seattle still call it. After passing the Washington state medical and surgical board examinations, he found to his surprise that he was quickly invited to join the surgical staff at Doctor's, the Sisters of Providence, and St. Francis Cabrini hospitals.

The small but growing city—whose population expanded nearly 20 percent from 467,591 in 1950 to 557,087 in 1960—needed good surgeons, and it apparently didn't matter what color the surgeons came in. Or, at least, no one had thought to explicitly exclude nonwhites from the city's medical community, since there were only a handful of nonwhite physicians in the entire state anyway. Of Washington's 2,754 licensed physicians practicing medicine in 1950, just three were listed in census data as "Negro" and ten as "other nonwhite."

My parents stayed at a lovely place, the Sorrento Hotel, high atop Madison Hill near the hospitals overlooking the city, and for both it was a wonderful experience simply to register at the front desk and not have to worry about being turned away because of their race. One night, while my mother and father admired the view of Elliott Bay at sunset from their hotel room window, watching the ferry boats cross back and forth from Bainbridge Island, they realized almost simultaneously that the city possessed practically everything they could ask for.

"Why don't we just stay, John?" my mother remembered asking softly.

Dad took only a moment to reply: Why not?

So it was that in July 1956 my parents decided that Seattle was where we would live. My mother traveled by rail back to St. Louis to pick up my brothers and me from the old house in the Ville, having meantime arranged to have our furniture and household goods, including the beloved china dinnerware she had purchased in Germany, shipped to Seattle from Nashville. Soon we all boarded a westbound Great Northern Pullman to join my father in the Pacific Northwest for good.

My father had arrived in Seattle at about the same time as a Meharry classmate from Louisiana named Philip V. Lavizzo, the father of the girl who would become my first sweetheart fifteen years later. Together that

July, Dad and Dr. Lavizzo became the first black general surgeons in the history of Seattle, and the city, so faraway from everything we had ever known, became our new hometown.

. . .

The Seattle I saw passing outside my mother's car window that night certainly was remarkably different from the city I had known as a boy in the 1950s and 1960s. Back then Seattle called itself the "Queen City of the Pacific Northwest," but in reality it was little more than a sleepy backwater in a far corner of the continent, an afterthought in our national consciousness. For decades Seattle was known for Boeing aircraft and Weyerhaeuser lumber and little else, except its climate, in which rain fell seemingly year-round. It was a happily unsophisticated place that reveled in its provinciality, a town where folks liked to wear lumberjack outfits and hats with floppy ears in the winter, à la Elmer Fudd, and where there was no such thing as a traffic jam or a car horn honked in anger. I still saw Seattle as it used to be. I remembered the summer fishing trips my father and I took to catch salmon off the Pacific coast. And I recalled the minor league baseball games my brothers and I enjoyed as we sat high in the wooden bleachers at Sick's Stadium in Rainier Valley, where, by night, we could watch the stars and moon peek between the clouds, and where, on clear sunny afternoons, Mount Rainier loomed majestically beyond the right field wall like a giant snow-capped sentinel.

Now, however, the city I grew up in called itself the "Emerald City," a place where Oz-like fortunes were indeed being made. Gone were the days of 1969, when Boeing ordered massive layoffs at its manufacturing plants and plunged the city into a terrible recession, prompting the cynical refrain, "Will the last person leaving Seattle please turn out the lights?" Now Seattle had much bigger shoulders of economic might and a population that had more than quadrupled since the days of my boyhood. Distant hillsides once green with virgin firs and pines were gradually being replaced by growing satellite towns like Bellevue with skyscrapers of their own. Multimillion-dollar homes, golf courses, and developments had been carved into these hillsides. The once sleepy backwater I had known as a child was now a city of international renown, one that had seen the birth of new technologies that were fueling the longest sustained period of economic growth America had ever known. Traffic clogged Seattle's streets and freeways now, smog poisoned its air, and sport fishing for coho, king, and silver salmon off the coast was now much more tightly restricted because so many species of the fish were endangered.

One thing hadn't changed. The rain that seemed to fall relentlessly on the pretty city when I was a boy was falling now, and my mother's windshield wipers flipped back and forth in a steady lament as she turned her car onto a quiet street called Lake Washington Boulevard. We arrived at the Leschi Grill after a few minutes, and as we waited in the entryway for the waitress to show us to a table, I put my arm around my mother's shoulder and gave her a quick, warm hug.

The Strangeness of Beauty

LYDIA MINATOYA

Lydia Minatoya (1950–) was raised in Albany, New York. She graduated from Saint Lawrence University and earned a master's degree from George Washington University and a Ph.D. in counseling from the University of Maryland. Minatoya has served as a lecturer at the Maryland program in Tokyo and Okinawa and as an assistant professor at Boston University. She has lived in Seattle for many years, where she is a counselor and faculty member at North Seattle Community College. Her publications include two books and seventeen journal articles on such topics as Japanese and American women, cross-national marriages, and freshman needs assessment. In addition to the many awards she has received for her writing, Minatoya was nominated for the National Book Award in 1999 for her novel The Strangeness of Beauty, *from which the following selection was taken.*

It was Sunday, October 23, 1921. Naomi slept until noon. Akira poked through the kitchen like an amateur, singeing a dish towel as he lit the stove.

Naomi laughed when she saw the scorched rice and watery miso soup he'd prepared. A breakfast already grown cold. She pulled at his sleeve until he sank to the bed. She unwound the eyeglass stems from his ears.

Later, brushing her hair by the window, she saw Mount Rainier. Free from its usual cloud cover, the mountain rose close and startling.

"Rainier-san is out."

Akira glanced past her shoulder. Three-story frame tenements scrabbled toward the crest of Jackson Street. A cluster of leaves, dead and dried, bounced along the buckling sidewalk.

Like a facetious Fujiyama, Rainier was floating over Oki's We Never Close Cafe.

Akira frowned. This was Nihonmachi, Seattle's Japantown. A strange, in-between place where, by day, the streets were filled with American-style industry—with shrieking trains snorting in and out of the King Street Station and delivery carts from Uchida's Uncle Sam Laundry or Kato's Straight-To-Your-Home Ice clattering on cobbled streets. Where truant Japanese American boys in knickers and golf caps flipped milk tops and shot marbles. Yet at dusk Nihonmachi became suffused with Japan—with lantern light, the aromas of soy sauce and Japanese soba noodles wafting from upstairs windows, and the restful sight of neighbors heading home from public baths. Laughing softly, the bathers scuffed in split-toed straw sandals and cotton kimonos across improbably wide American-named streets (Main, Jackson, King) or more intimately scaled numbered avenues (Sixth through Twelfth). Still later, as midnight approached the southern edge of Nihonmachi—the only time and place whites came into our part of town—the mood shifted to things faster and darker: secret-door gambling clubs with knifings at blackjack and mahjong tables; hurried transactions of prostitution.

Thinking of these things, Akira knitted his brow. Though Naomi was happy in Nihonmachi, the idea that he'd brought his bride to so shabby a place always made him feel guilty.

"Look at those scurrying outlaws."

Chuckling, Naomi was pursuing the leaves, watching as they evaded a broom being wielded by Kozawa, the barber.

"I know!" She turned to her husband. "Let's go leaf viewing."

Akira looked at his nineteen-year-old wife, beyond the beauty of her tranquil oval face to the hard work of carrying a child. Naomi's legs were swollen. Her blood pressure was high. Her pregnancy hadn't been easy.

"No," he said, "you're too close to your time."

But she smiled at his stern manner.

"Just to the university," she coaxed. "Soon we'll be too busy."

Akira knotted a tie under the starched high collar of his white shirt. (Indeed, back in Japan the word used to denote a progressive young intellectual was *hakara*, an altered form of the English words "high collar"). He slipped on the vest and jacket to his three-piece gray suit.

Naomi dressed in a dove blue long-skirted suit (to accommodate her pregnancy, the usually fitted jacket fell from a yoke into soft gathers), high black shoes, and a broad-brimmed hat. As Akira walked sideways beside her—lending his arm and solicitously watching Naomi's every quite confident step—they negotiated the narrow stairway down from their second-floor flat.

They boarded a streetcar on the corner of Main Street and Occidental Avenue. Akira dropped two dimes into the glass box at the top of the stairs, watching as the motorman flipped a lever that made the money disappear, listening to the coins' *clinka-clinka* noise as he wound the crank that sorted the change.

The streetcar was already half full with Japanese American passengers out for a Sunday excursion. Most rode as if in Japan: in orderly anonymity, nodding whenever someone they knew boarded but not speaking, respecting one another's need for some distance in a too-crowded society.

After a few minutes, Akira felt Naomi nudge his shoulder.

"Listen to that old couple," she whispered.

It didn't take long to find the pair. The couple—perhaps in their late fifties, dressed in worn go-to-city clothes—were bickering loudly in Japanese.

Yet even after locating them, Akira had trouble following Naomi's instruction. A stray thought popped into his mind—the old fellow needed a partial bridge—and he couldn't track their conversation.

"Aren't they charming?"

Wanting to be a good husband, Akira shook himself back to the moment.

"Stay on the trolley, north to Pike Street," the sturdy wife was exclaiming. "Then take Pike east. That's the best way to the public market."

"No, no!" said the husband. He waved his skinny arms in disgust. "Too much traffic. Get off at Yesler; go north on First, along the waterfront. Then, *zoo-to!*"—the husband had made a zippy sound ending briskly with his tongue just behind his incisors—"you're right there!"

"Your way is fast, all right," grumbled the wife, "but passes all the fishing fleets." She folded her weathered hands in her broad lap and gave a triumphant snort. "Your way *stinks!*"

"What's so charming about them?" Akira whispered in complaint to Naomi. "It's stupid, really. We've already passed both Yesler and Pike; it's clear they've no intention of going to market. And besides, look at their clothes. They're farmers. Probably in from Bainbridge Island. I bet they've been going to the public market twice a week for at least fifteen years!"

"And each time having the same argument." Naomi chuckled.

"They should hear themselves," Akira muttered. "So discordant. It's a disgrace."

"No." Naomi's voice turned firm. "It's no disgrace."

She looked at the couple with tenderness.

"Listen, Akira," she said softly, like a mother sharing life's secrets with a child. "In their argument is the melody of marriage."

Akira paused. Now the couple was squabbling over whether or not the husband should put on his sweater.

"That? *Melody?*"

"Yes," said Naomi. She listened awhile and smiled. "It's a blending, not always smooth, of attachment and independence."

"But in public? They sound so foolish."

"To a couple it's background music, a little scratchy, perhaps, but something they play over and over, like a much loved, well-worn gramophone record."

Akira looked at Naomi with appreciation. Among the earthbound pioneers of Japantown, this type of insight, along with her beauty and high birth in a samurai family, had earned Naomi a reputation as being a bit too ethereal.

Yet he found her radiantly wise.

He gestured toward the old couple.

"Do you think we'll end up like that?" he teased. Warm laughter poured from Naomi's lovely throat.

"Oh, Akira! We already are!"

The trolley turned east, passing big houses facing the lake. At Madison Park, Japanese houseboys—old men with glinting eyeglasses—raked long, sloping, shadowy lawns.

The sky was increasingly overcast. Warm light came and went, streaming like sudden sun showers.

By the time they reached the university, Akira could tell that Naomi was tired. Yet when she saw the leaves she seemed to revive.

She crunched her feet through the splendid carpet. Too big to bend over, she made him pick a bouquet of the brightest colors. She arranged them in a fan and studied them like an exceedingly good hand of cards.

The air smelled of chestnuts roasting.

In a gesture of sharing—similar to times when she drew his hand to her kicking belly—Naomi pushed Akira's cheek toward the grassy quadrangle.

"There." She smiled.

Amid Gothic stone buildings, the first few Japanese American college boys wearing flannel pants and white varsity-style sweaters were joking in accentless English and kicking a football around.

"That's the future," she promised.

But his eyes were too full with Naomi.

The sky had shifted. Sun slanted through branches, anointing her shoulders and hair.

Silent and satisfied, filled with mysteries and blessings, she was as luminous as a Renaissance painting.

That night, well after midnight, Akira awoke with a start.

Naomi was rigid and shuddering. She clutched at the edge of the bed.

"No worry, we have hours to wait," she said with a nervous laugh.

Akira placed a cool towel on her brow and ran down the street to get me.

He knew I came as fast as I could: thrusting my feet in my shoes, grabbing my coat, not caring that he saw me in my night dress. Yet when we arrived, the baby already was crowning.

As he paced the parlor, Akira noticed many things. The scarcity of furniture. A tear in the carpet. The endearing way that the pattern of dust around the spines of books on the bookshelf revealed Naomi's haphazard housekeeping.

Near dawn, when the quiet finally came, Akira noticed his relief. He rested his head on the cool windowpane, then drew back—amazed and laughing, to see the delicate lace of frost. It was so unexpected for Seattle in autumn that he thought it was a heavenly sign. A miracle, just like birth.

It *was* a sign, the early frost.

It meant that his young wife had died.

Yet in this grateful community, Akira has had some trouble.

Take the autumn when Hanae was three and the Seattle Buddhist Church went *matsutake* mushrooming in the lower Cascades.

It was quite an expedition, this annual quest for the elusive matsutake. Into a fine 5 A.M. fall morning would rumble a caravan of open-topped black Model T Fords. Within each car would sit five or six people, ranging in age from infancy to late sixties, wearing their oldest cotton coats—as protection from dirt and gravel over their finest flapper-era American clothes.

The cars' occupants would be perched on blankets—to cushion the jolting ride, to spread on the ground for a picnic, to camp with in the very likely event of a breakdown—and wedged between at least two huge spare tires. For on the mountain roads of Washington State—either dusty and deeply rutted or muddy and slickly treacherous—balloon tires burst as often as bubbles in a glass of champagne.

Each passenger would carry a huge collecting basket representative of our overinflated hopes and an heirloom-quality three-tiered lacquered lunch box artfully filled with individual compartments of sautéed cucumbers, rice balls, pressed fish cakes, and fried chicken *kara age*. (My lunch boxes would contain something more inventive, say, cheddar-cheese-and-mayonnaise sushi.) The lunch boxes would be stacked by courses, tied up with decorative cords, and wrapped in huge silk squares stenciled with each person's family crest. Coming from a land of earthquakes, where insulation equals protection from breakage, the Japanese have made an art of extreme overpackaging.

Yet no matter how jolly the journey, when we arrived in the old-growth forest our mood suddenly changed. As we scattered in our search, thin streams of sun slanted through canopies so high and dense that the light barely brushed the soft forest floor. Among the ancient trees, there was such a sense of sacredness that we all felt subdued and reflective.

Probably for Reverend Mitsui, our spiritual leader, this was the whole point of the excursion. For although the Seattle Buddhist Church always arrived as a clattering caravan, upon disembarking, the beautiful vastness would swallow us completely: separating us, muffling our insignificant voices, enveloping our ridiculously clad bodies. (On the outing when Hanae was three, I—silly twenty-seven-year-old that I was—wore a newly bobbed Dutch-boy hairstyle, a drop-waisted dress, and a pair of strapped *high-heel* shoes! Since then I have allowed my bangs to grow and now wear my hair in a more flattering, side-parted, chin-length cut. In addition, I no longer wear high heels in the forest.)

And when we gathered for lunch in the late morning, we were invariably a more humble, more reverent group.

On the day of three-year-old Hanae's outing, after lunch, as we sprawled on deep fragrant pine needles, Kenji Kubota's boy—Billy, the smart one who had wanted to be a lawyer—offered ways around finer clauses in the Washington State Alien Land Law of 1921.

"Ah, Kenji-san," cooed Mrs. Ota, an angular widow who had her eye on the widower Kenji, "aren't we lucky we have your Billy to explain these things?"

And though his stomach was stuffed with rice balls and his basket brimmed with rare matsutake mushrooms destined to be so wonderfully pungent in broth or steamed with bits of chicken in rice Akira voiced the thought we avoided.

"We'd be luckier not to have these restrictions at all!"

Akira is a good Buddhist but he can't help noticing the material world.

He sees Jackson Street: Yamada's Number One Public Baths, Oki's We Never Close Cafe, Uchida's Uncle Sam Laundry. Despite the proud names, they're sagging frame buildings facing a poorly cobblestoned road. A scientist, he must compare them with the world beyond Japantown: the Neo-Florentine office buildings on Second Avenue, the *Art Décoratif* skyscrapers with marbled lobbies and bronzed elevator doors—that are going up so fast people say Seattle will be the next New York.

Even I can't ignore so much data.

In a place like this, gambling is a kind of men's whooping cough. So I wasn't surprised when Akira took to three-cushion. And like a mother waiting out a child's fever, in the past few years I've watched him go through a kind of progression. *Interest—Entrapment—Obsession.* I sit at home and I label the stages.

There have been some strange symptoms. For a while, Akira was determined to give up high culture. A set of Chippendale chairs, like crazy toadstools, sprang up around our old dining table. Our wooden chopsticks all disappeared, leaving me fumbling with flatware marked *International Sterling.*

"My little girl," Akira would mutter, "will grow up with every advantage."

Epilogue

JOHN TROMBOLD

SEATTLE LITERATURE IS AS DISTINCTIVE and diverse as the city's many neighborhoods and outlying communities. If the modern urban experience is defined, as John Dewey concluded, by people's experience of "the local"—their experience of and identification with local neighborhoods and communities—then the city of Seattle, much like the literature of Seattle, is defined by the sum of its many localities. While *Reading Seattle* focuses on Seattle proper, real and imagined, we want to recognize the important cultural influences that the communities surrounding Seattle exert on the city, and also note that these communities draw much of their cultural sustenance and identities from their relationship with Seattle.

To the south of the city limits, toward Tacoma and Olympia, lie the industrial/suburban communities of Tukwila, Burien, Kent, and Auburn; to the north, stretching toward Everett and Mount Vernon, are the more leafy bedroom communities of Bothell, Lynnwood, and Edmonds; to the west, scattered among the islands, inlets, and peninsulas across the Sound are older Scandinavian fishing villages such as Poulsbo, the naval town of Bremerton, and newer "sunset" (retirement) communities such as Silverdale; and to the east, lying along Lake Washington's eastern shore and creeping up the Cascade foothills, are the core suburban communities of Renton, Bellevue, Redmond, Kirkland, and Issaquah. In the past decade or more, the booming (and sprawling) suburban Eastside has had perhaps the greatest influence on the city. Connected to Seattle by two bridges that span twenty-three-mile-long Lake Washington, the collective Eastside communities now challenge Seattle proper in population and commercial activity and form an important identity of their own.

One particular satellite community, Mercer Island, is both representative of the communities of greater Seattle and something of an anomaly. Known originally as East Seattle, Mercer Island is the epitome of a bedroom community. Located in the middle of Lake Washington, between Bellevue and Seattle, Mercer Island is predominantly residential, and its income earners are almost exclusively commuters. Because of this dependence on the surrounding areas, the construction of the two bridges connecting Mercer Island to the mainland—the shorter East Channel Bridge to Bellevue, in 1924, and the longer, more famous Floating Bridge to Seattle, in 1940—stands as the most important pair of events in Mercer Island history.

Before the two bridges were built, Mercer Island's population collected in the island's northwest corner, near the dock for the ferry to Seattle. Until 1920, the mailing address for all islanders was officially "East Seattle." Today, the Mercer Island Boys' and Girls' Club occupies what was until recently known as the East Seattle School, while the nearby Roanoke Tavern still serves beer in what is reputed to have been a brothel that serviced Depression-era ferry-goers to Seattle.

I grew up on Mercer Island, in a house hidden in one of the many wooded ravines that riddle the island. I went to kindergarten and elementary school at Island Park Elementary, then to junior high at South Mercer Junior High, and finally to Mercer Island High School, the only high school on the island. Growing up on Mercer Island in the late 1960s and 1970s, even with new bridges to Bellevue and Seattle, we looked longingly west to Seattle or east to the mountains for excitement and recreation. The island, with views of Mount Rainier, the Olympic Mountains, and the Cascades, is a secure haven for salmon bakes and the raising of affluent children who ski on snow and water, sail, get bored, and go to Seattle's International District to buy alcohol illegally. There is no Mercer Island mall for hanging out, nor is there even a cemetery for forbidden late-night excursions. Mercer Island was and remains a sheltered place, though only ten minutes' drive from downtown Seattle. Mercer Island adolescents must look for trouble elsewhere, or retreat to boathouses or the boats docked inside them.

Known locally as "Poverty Rock" or "Mercedes Island," and home to more than 20,000 inhabitants, Mercer Island lacks Seattle's Skid Road, gritty piers, and longshoremen as well as much of the ethnic diversity of many of the other communities on Seattle's periphery. The island remains famously homogeneous. A *Seattle Weekly* parodist once invented the Mercer Island character "Tammy Trinkets, President of the Mercer Island Association for the Advancement of Color Coordination," a figure who embodies the contradictions of privilege and social awareness so apparent on the island. A patron of REI and Nordstrom's, Tammy could also be understood to patronize the social cause after which her association is named.

More directly, Karen Russell, daughter of Bill Russell, the legendary NBA player and former coach of the Seattle SuperSonics, underscored the island's ethnic tensions in "Growing Up with Prejudice and Privilege," a 1987 article in *The New York Times*, when she described her experiences growing up black on Mercer Island. Included in her article was a short indictment of island police who stopped and questioned drivers of color, given the rarity of black people on the island—what we now call racial profiling. These days, one of the more common ways of alluding to Mercer Island's social position and racial makeup is to remark that the island has "an excellent school district."

A historical study of Mercer Island, written for the 1976 bicentennial celebration, attests that "because Mercer Island is a unique community filled with leaders and managers at all levels, it became a real challenge to our Mercer Island Bicentennial Committee to find the 'Spirit of '76' at the local level. So when people responded [in the planning for the bicentennial on Mercer Island] . . . it was soon demonstrated that most all Islanders had a deep rooted devotion to our country." There is more to this remark than a simple discussion of Mercer Island's patriotic contribution to bicentennial activities. In the local parlance, these words assert Mercer Island's uniquely aloof and self-protective attributes in respect to the larger world—namely Seattle—while assuring that a nationalistic spirit penetrates even unto the island's "leaders and managers."

Yet the well-educated children of Mercer Island's leaders and managers have not been as easily defined by patriotic exhibitionism as their hardworking, flag-flying parents. As a rule, the island presents the classic problem of new wealth when the strong work ethic and traditional loyalties of the parents prove socially anachronistic to their children's more pleasure-seeking tendencies. A strong spirit of self-reliance among the older generations, a Robinson Crusoe–like island ethos, contrasts with the younger generations' reliance on service-economy amenities. From the parents' point of view, working in the horse stables, cleaning the boats, and caring for the lawn are the best antidotes to laziness and overindulgence.

Reviving the work ethic and the spirit of continual activity, the dot-com boom of the 1990s produced a new generation of couples who bought houses on the island for instant demolition—as did Paul Allen, co-founder of Microsoft, when he returned to his birthplace in grand style by building an enormous house and shocking the more provincial sensibilities of the island's older and already quite comfortable upper middle class. In this social landscape, this community, there lives an amateur naturalist who reveals something of the island's character, even though he has more in common with the island's past and its founding idealism than with its present. Bruce, the son of a surgeon, is in his forties (though he looks much younger) and works at the Mercer Island Recycling Center, which is managed by the island's one school district. Bruce has a spiritual orientation, as did the island's largely Episcopalian first settlers, though as a self-professed Swedenborgian, Bruce lacks a congregation. His is a congregation of one. But he considers his daily walks through the island's protected greenbelt as more than adequate spiritual communion. In effect, Bruce lives the suburban version of a subsistence lifestyle.

Although there have been periods when the polite islanders coming to the recycling center doubted Bruce's social skills, over time he has become something of a social butterfly and is abreast of all the island gossip. The recycling center competes successfully with curbside pickup of recyclable materials because island citizens prefer to support the schools by going to the local center, which has become a social hub in the limited downtown shopping area. What is remarkable about Bruce's relationship with the island is not simply that, with his Protestant and environmental convictions, he recalls its rustic past, but also that his quirks are widely accepted. The island accepts and even sometimes admires this unusual person who refuses to ride in cars and is always willing to engage in a theological discussion while smashing used glass or sorting cardboard. Bruce is averse to publicity, and in this regard as well, he is emblematic of Mercer Island. Yet Bruce is equally a Mercer Island anomaly, since, unlike the rest of the community, he never leaves the island. In his own unique manner, Bruce has lived fully the pastoral dream of the rural local in an increasingly urban setting.

In trying to understand Seattle, an appreciation of the local—even the anomalously local—becomes essential. Similarly, in trying to pull together the best of Seattle prose literature, we have come to see how this literature, like the city itself, is a mosaic of local neighborhood identities. In compiling *Reading Seattle,* we were impressed not only by how much good writing the city has inspired but also by how thoroughly this writing is grounded in the city's many neighborhoods and surrounding communities. However, just as it is impossible to represent every one of these neighborhoods and communities through the selections in *Reading Seattle,* it was also impossible for us to include the many writers we would have liked to.

Raymond Carver, a guiding spirit of Northwest fiction since he began publishing in the 1970s, does not appear in *Reading Seattle* as none of his stories depict Seattle. The same goes for the fiction of Tess Gallagher and that of Stacey Levine. While the work of both of these writers reflects a Seattle sensibility, it does not explicitly render the city.

Furthermore, numerous genre fiction writers are not included here. It would be impossible to include every writer within the legion of Seattle mystery writers whose detectives faithfully pound the city's dark, wet streets. Mystery writers have traditionally fostered a distinctive relationship to their urban setting (from Raymond Chandler's Los Angeles to Chester Himes's New York to Robert B. Parker's Boston), in which the city is often a seductive, menacing, or impervious player, as central to the plot as the crimes the gumshoes seek to solve. This tradition holds true for the many Seattle mystery writers who helped establish the Northwest Noir in the 1970s and 1980s. In recognizing this tradition, we include selections from J. A. Jance, Earl Emerson, and Barbara Wilson. The particu-

larity with which these writers depict Seattle allows readers to share in
the keen understanding of the city that their street-savvy characters have
earned.

Many writers of historical romances set in Seattle, such as Brenda
Wilbee with her *Sweetbriar* series, set during the pioneer years, were also
left out. Our nod to this genre is a selection from one of the most beloved
of all Seattle historical novels, Mary Brinker Post's *Annie Jordan* (1948).
Meanwhile, *Reading Seattle* also omits fantasy and science-fiction novels.
In many of these, such as Elizabeth Ann Scarborough's *The Godmother*
(1994), the city becomes a delightfully envisioned province of magic and
wonderment. Finally, there are some fine juvenile novels set in Seattle.
While these are not represented here, every parent should read them to
his or her child. Two of the most enjoyable, appearing almost a century
apart, are Florence Martin Eastland's *Matt of the Water Front* (1909), about
a boy making his way through the rough-and-tumble world of Seattle's
docks, and Jean Thesman's *The Ornament Tree* (1996), about a girl living
in a boarding house during Seattle's 1919 General Strike.

Overall, a separate anthology is warranted to do justice to all the high-
quality genre fiction set in Seattle. The editor of such a volume might even
include a selection from Mike Grell's *Green Arrow: The Longbow Hunters*
(1987), in which the Green Arrow battles the Seattle Slasher. Many devo-
tees of the graphic novel consider this a landmark work in setting a new
literary and artistic standard for the genre.

As for nonfiction, there are numerous popular and specialized histo-
ries of the city, such as Nard Jones's *Seattle* (1972) and Paul DeBarros's
Jackson Street After Hours (1993), that we regrettably were unable to include.
We also want to call attention to the multiple volumes in Richard C.
Berner's *Seattle in the 20th Century* series, a work whose knowledge and
mastery of detail are a testament to Berner's skills as a veteran archivist.
Among the journalists absent here is David Brewster, founder of the *Seattle Weekly,* who continues to contribute to the literary and civic life of the
city in stewarding the revival of Town Hall, an influential forum for writers and thinkers around town and beyond. The dedicated writers for Seattle's neighborhood and alternative weeklies who help make the city such
a socially informed and engaged place must also be acknowledged. Of

these, Clark Humphrey has been one of the best Seattle chroniclers, both in print and online, for the past two decades.

For readers interested in exploring these writers and the range of exemplary prose that Seattle has inspired, the bibliography lists the works selected for the anthology in addition to other favorites. We hope that *Reading Seattle* will inspire people to read widely and enthusiastically in this outstanding body of literature.

Bibliography

FICTION

Alexie, Sherman. *Indian Killer.* New York: Warner, 1996.

———. *Ten Little Indians.* New York: Grove, 2003.

Anderson, Ada Woodruff. *The Heart of the Red Firs: A Story of the Pacific Northwest.* Boston: Little, Brown, 1908.

Bacho, Peter. *Cebu.* Seattle: University of Washington Press, 1991.

———. *Dark Blue Suit and Other Stories.* Seattle: University of Washington Press, 1997.

Barry, Lynda. *Cruddy.* New York: Scribner, 1999.

Binns, Archie. *The Timber Beast.* New York: Charles Scribner's Sons, 1944.

Briggs, Matt. *Misplaced Alice.* Spokane, Wash.: SpringTown Press, 2002.

———. *The Remains of River Names.* Seattle: Black Heron Press, 2000.

Brown, Rebecca. "A Good Man." *Annie Oakley's Girl.* San Francisco: City Lights Books, 1993.

Burgess, W. A. *Cowards.* New York: St. Martin's, 1997.

Byers, Michael. *The Coast of Good Intentions.* Boston: Houghton Mifflin, 1998.

———. *Long for This World.* Boston: Houghton Mifflin, 2003.

Cady, Jack. *Street.* New York: St. Martins, 1994.

Carver, Raymond. *Where I'm Calling From: New and Selected Stories.* New York: Vintage Contemporary, 1989.

Chabon, Michael. "House Hunting." *Werewolves in Their Youth: Stories.* New York: Random House, 1999.

Champney, Elizabeth W. *The Romance of the Feudal Chateaux.* New York and London: G. P. Putnam's Sons, 1899.

Chin, Frank. *Gunga Din Highway.* Minneapolis: Coffee House Press, 1994.

Clausen, Lowen. *First Avenue.* Seattle: Watershed, 1999.

D'Ambrosio, Charles. *The Point.* New York: Little, Brown, 1995.

Dillard, Annie. *The Living.* New York: HarperCollins, 1992.

Donahue, Peter. *The Cornelius Arms.* Seattle: Missing Spoke Press, 2000.

Eastland, Florence Martin. *Matt of the Water Front.* Cincinnati/New York: Jennings and Graham/Eaton and Mains, 1909.

Emerson, Earl W. *The Rainy City.* New York: Avon, 1985.

Far, Sui Sin. *Mrs. Spring Fragrance and Other Writings.* Amy Ling and Annette White-Parks, eds. Urbana: University of Illinois Press, 1995.

Ford, G. M. *Who in Hell is Wanda Fuca?: A Leo Waterman Mystery.* New York: Walker, 1985.

Fowler, Karen Joy. *Sarah Canary.* New York: Henry Holt, 1991.

Gallagher, Tess. *At the Owl Woman Saloon.* New York: Scribner, 1997.

———. *The Lover of Horses and Other Stories.* New York: Harper & Row, 1986.

Gilpatric, Guy, and Norman Reilly Raine. *The Glencannon Tugboat Annie Affair.* New York: Harper, 1950.

Grell, Mike. *Green Arrow: The Longbow Hunters.* New York: D.C. Comics, 1987.

Guterson, David. *The Country Ahead of Us, the Country Behind: Stories.* New York: Vintage: 1989.

———. *East of the Mountains.* New York: Harcourt Brace, 1999.

Hannah, Barry. "Power and Light." *Captain Maximus: Stories.* New York: Knopf, 1985.

Hart, Alan. *In the Lives of Men.* New York: W. W. Norton, 1937.

———. *The Undaunted.* New York: W. W. Norton, 1936.

Heath, Sarah Ritchie. "The Wager: A Seattle Story." *Overland Monthly* 30:78 (Oct. 1897).

Herbst, Josephine. *The Executioner Waits.* New York: Warner, 1986. (Originally published 1934.)

———. *Pity Is Not Enough.* New York: Warner, 1986. (Originally published 1933.)

———. *Rope of Gold.* New York: Warner, 1986. (Originally published 1939.)

Invisible Seattle: The Novel of Seattle, by Seattle. Seattle: Function Industries Press, 1987.

Jance, J. A. *Lying in Wait.* New York: Morrow, 1994.

Bibliography

Johnson, Charles. *The Sorceror's Apprentice: Tales and Conjurations.* New York: Penguin, 1987.

Johnson, Denis. *Jesus' Son: Stories* by Denis Johnson. New York: Farrar, Straus and Giroux, 1992.

Jones, Nard. *The Case of the Hanging Lady.* New York: Dodd, Mead, 1938.

Jones, Thom. "Cold Snap." *Cold Snap: Stories.* New York: Little, Brown, 1995.

Levine, Stacey. *My Horse and Other Stories.* Los Angeles: Sun & Moon Press, 1993.

Levy, Melvin. *The Last Pioneers.* New York: A. H. King, 1934.

Lindquist, Mark. *Never Mind Nirvana.* New York: Villard, 2000.

Long, David. *The Daughters of Simon Lamoreaux.* New York: Scribner, 2000.

Minatoya, Lydia. *The Strangeness of Beauty.* New York: Simon & Schuster, 1999.

Okada, John. *No-No Boy.* Seattle: University of Washington Press, 1979. (Originally published 1957 by Charles E. Tuttle.)

Olsen, Lance. "Digital Matrix: Barbie: Lust." *Sewing Shut My Eyes.* Normal, Ill.: FC2, 2000.

———. *Tonguing the Zeitgeist.* San Jose, Calif.: Permeable Press, 1994.

Ortega, Joshua. *Frequencies.* Seattle: Omega Point Productions, 1999.

Orton, Thomas. *The Lost Glass Plates of Wilfred Eng.* Washington, D.C.: Counterpoint, 1999.

Paul, Charlotte. *Seattle.* New York: New American Library, 1986.

Post, Mary Brinker. *Annie Jordan: A Novel of Seattle.* Garden City, N.Y.: Doubleday, 1948.

Raban, Jonathan. *Waxwings.* New York: Pantheon Books, 2003.

Robbins, Tom. *Jitterbug Perfume.* New York: Bantam, 1984.

———. *Still Life with Woodpecker.* New York: Bantam, 1980.

Sasaki, Ruth A. "Seattle." *The Loom and Other Stories.* St. Paul, Minn.: Graywolf, 1991.

Scarborough, Elizabeth Ann. *The Godmother.* New York: Ace Books, 1994.

Sherman, Charlotte Watson. "Emerald City: Third & Pike." *Killing Color.* Corvallis, Ore.: Calyx Books, 1992.

Shields, David. "Father's Day." *A Handbook for Drowning: Stories.* New York: HarperPerennial, 1993.

Stadler, Matthew. *Allan Stein.* New York: Grove Press, 2000.

———. *The Sex Offender.* New York: HarperCollins, 1994.

Stevens, James. *Paul Bunyan.* New York: A. A. Knopf, 1925.

Stewart, Jean. *Emerald City Blues.* Huntington Station, N.Y.: Rising Tide, 1996.

Swallow, Jean. *A Woman Determined.* Duluth, Minn.: Spinsters Ink, 1998.

Thesman, Jean. *The Ornament Tree.* Boston: Houghton Mifflin, 1996.

Weihe, Edwin. *Another Life and Other Stories.* Seattle: Pleasure Boat Studio, 2000.

Wilbee, Brenda. *Sweetbriar.* Eugene, Ore.: Harvest House, 1983.

Wilson, Barbara. *Sisters of the Road.* Seattle: Seal Press, 1986.

NONFICTION

Bacho, Peter. *Boxing in Black and White.* New York: Henry Holt, 1999.

Bagley, Clarence B. *A History of Seattle from the Earliest Settlement to the Present Time.* Chicago: S. J. Clarke Publishing, 1916.

Beaton, Welford. *The City That Made Itself: A Literary and Pictorial Record of the Building of Seattle.* Seattle: Terminal Publishing, 1914.

Berner, Richard C. *Seattle in the 20th Century.* Volumes 1–3. Seattle: Charles Press, 1991.

Binns, Archie. *Northwest Gateway: The Story of the Port of Seattle.* Garden City, N.Y.: Doubleday, Doran & Co., 1943.

Brooks, Colette. "Seattle and Vicinity." *Southwest Review* 77:2–3 (1992).

Cayton, Horace R. *Long Old Road.* Seattle: University of Washington Press, 1970. (Originally published 1965.)

Conover, Charles T. *Mirrors of Seattle: Reflecting on Some Aged Men of Fifty.* Seattle: Lowman & Hanford, 1923.

Crowley, Walt. *Rites of Passage: A Memoir of the Sixties in Seattle.* Seattle: University of Washington Press, 1995.

DeBarros, Paul. *Jackson Street After Hours.* Seattle: Sasquatch Books, 1993.

Denny, Emily Inez. *Blazing the Way; or, True Stories, Songs and Sketches of Puget Sound and Other Pioneers.* Seattle: Seattle/King County Historical Society, 1984. (Originally published 1909.)

Eaves, Elisabeth. *Bare: On Women, Dancing, Sex, and Power.* New York: Knopf, 2002.

Egan, Timothy. *The Good Rain: Across Time and Terrain in the Pacific Northwest.* New York: Knopf, 1990.

Guilloud, Stephanie, ed. *Voices from the WTA: An Anthology of Writings from the*

People Who Shut Down the World Trade Organization. Olympia, Wash.: Evergreen State College Bookstore (distributor), 2000.

Guterson, David. "Seattle's Son." *Architectural Digest* 55:12 (1998), 50ff.

Henry, Neil. *Pearl's Secret: A Black Man's Search for His White Family.* Berkeley: University of California Press, 2001.

Hugo, Richard. *The Real West Marginal Way: A Poet's Autobiography.* New York: W. W. Norton, 1986.

Humphrey, Clark. *The Big Book of Misc.: Pseudo-Random Remarks on Popular Culture in Seattle and Beyond, 1986–1999.* Seattle: Misc.Media, 1999.

———. *Loser: The Real Seattle Music Story.* Portland, Ore.: Feral House, 1995.

Jones, Nard. *Seattle.* Garden City, N.Y.: Doubleday, 1972.

MacDonald, Betty. *Anybody Can Do Anything.* Philadelphia: J. B. Lippincott, 1950.

———. *The Egg and I.* New York: Harper, 1973. (Originally published 1945.)

McCarthy, Mary. *How I Grew:* San Diego: Harcourt Brace Jovanovich, 1987.

Moody, Fred. *Seattle and the Demons of Ambition: A Love Story.* New York: St. Martin's Press, 2003.

Morgan, Murray. *Skid Road: An Informal History of Seattle.* Seattle: University of Washington Press, 1982. (Originally published 1951.)

Potts, Ralph Bushnell. *Seattle Heritage.* Seattle: Superior, 1955.

Raban, Jonathan. "America's Most Private City." *Travel Holiday* 174 (Nov. 1991), 60–65.

———. *Hunting Mister Heartbreak: A Discovery of America.* London: Collins Harvill, 1991.

———. "The Unsettling of Seattle." *Architectural Digest* 57:11 (Nov. 2000): 77–90.

Rekdal, Paisley. "Breaking In." *Chattahoochee Review.*

———. *The Night My Mother Met Bruce Lee: Observations on Not Fitting In.* New York: Pantheon, 2000.

Ross, Nancy Wilson. *Farthest Reach: Oregon and Washington.* New York: Knopf, 1941.

Russin, Emily Baillargeon. "Seattle Now: A Letter." *New England Review* 20:2 (1999).

Sale, Roger. *Seattle, Past and Present.* Seattle: University of Washington Press, 1976.

———. *Seeing Seattle.* Seattle: University of Washington Press, 1994.

Sayre, J. Willis. *This City of Ours.* Seattle: J. Willis Sayre, 1936.

Bibliography

Shields, David. *Black Planet: Facing Race during an NBA Season.* New York: Crown, 1999.

Singer, Natalia Rachel. "Blurred Vision: How the Eighties Began in One American Household." *Prairie Schooner* 74:4 (2000).

Sone, Monica. *Nisei Daughter.* Seattle: University of Washington Press, 1991.

Speidel, William C. *Sons of the Profits; or, There's No Business Like Grow Business! The Seattle Story, 1851–1901.* Seattle: Nettle Creek Publishing, 1967.

Watson, Emmett. *Digressions of a Native Son.* Seattle: Pacific Institute, 1982.

———. *My Life in Print.* Seattle: Lesser Seattle, 1993.

———. *Once Upon a Time in Seattle.* Seattle: Lesser Seattle, 1992.

Watt, Roberta Frye. *Four Wagons West: The Story of Seattle.* Chicago: S. J. Clarke Publishing, 1916.